Problem Solving in All Seasons

Grades 3–5

Kim Markworth,
Jenni McCool, and Jennifer Kosiak

NATIONAL COUNCIL OF
TEACHERS OF MATHEMATICS

www.nctm.org/more4u
Access code: PSS14809

Library of Congress Cataloging-in-Publication Data

Names: Markworth, Kim. | McCool, Jenni. | Kosiak, Jennifer, 1972–
Title: Problem solving in all seasons, grades 3 5 / by Kim Markworth, Jenni
   McCool, and Jennifer Kosiak.
Description: Reston, VA : National Council of Teachers of Mathematics, [2016]
   | Includes bibliographical references.
Identifiers: LCCN 2015043127 (print) | LCCN 2015050098 (ebook) | ISBN
   9780873537728 | ISBN 9780873538695 ()
Subjects: LCSH: Mathematics—Study and teaching (Elementary)
Classification: LCC QA135.6 .M3636 2016 (print) | LCC QA135.6 (ebook) | DDC
   372.7--dc23
LC record available at http://lccn.loc.gov/2015043127

The National Council of Teachers of Mathematics is the public voice of mathematics education, supporting teachers to ensure equitable mathematics learning of the highest quality for all students through vision, leadership, professional development, and research.

When forms, problems, and sample documents are included or are made available on NCTM's website, their use is authorized for educational purposes by educators and noncommercial or nonprofit entities that have purchased this book. Except for that use, permission to photocopy or use material electronically from *Problem Solving in All Seasons, Grades 3–5* must be obtained from www.copyright.com, or contact Copyright Clearance Center, Inc. (CCC), 222 Rosewood Drive, Danvers, MA 01923; 978-750-8400. CCC is a not-for-profit organization that provides licenses and registration for a variety of users. Permission does not automatically extend to any items identified as reprinted by permission of other publishers and copyright holders. Such items must be excluded unless separate permissions are obtained. It will be the responsibility of the user to identify such materials and obtain the permissions.

The publications of the National Council of Teachers of Mathematics present a variety of viewpoints. The views expressed or implied in this publication, unless otherwise noted, should not be interpreted as official positions of the Council.

Printed in the United States of America

Contents

PREFACE

This book provides challenging tasks for elementary school students, tasks that can engage them in problem-solving experiences. Children's awareness of seasons and holidays makes the problems in the book authentic and engaging. These tasks can be easily related to other topics and themes that are being studied and discussed in the classroom, providing occasions for cross-disciplinary connections.

The situations in this book provide occasions in which students can engage with content through problem solving. Each problem connects to at least one Common Core content standard at a particular grade level. These problem-solving tasks furnish opportunities for students to explore strategies and make sense of important mathematics. Allowing students time and freedom to engage in this kind of sense making, reasoning, justification, and pattern searching allows them to engage in the processes identified in the Common Core Standards for Mathematical Practice. We see these tasks as invitations for students to learn important mathematical ideas in relevant contexts as they engage in the mathematical practices that are at the heart of the Common Core State Standards for Mathematics (CCSSM; National Governors Association Center for Best Practices and Council of Chief State School Officers [NGA Center and CCSSO] 2010).

WHAT TO EXPECT IN THE FOLLOWING CHAPTERS

The four chapters in this book are organized by season: fall, winter, spring, and summer. Each chapter includes three problem-solving tasks for each grade level; these are arranged in grade-level order from third through fifth grade. The Introduction provides a discussion of problem solving that will set the stage for the seasonal tasks and the implementation guide that is provided for each.

We hope that teachers find some flexibility for differentiation by using problems at different grade levels. If a situation for the students' grade level seems too challenging or too simplistic, alternatives may be found by examining—and potentially adapting—the tasks for other grade levels.

We also hope that teachers take advantage of the possibilities for manipulating the contexts of the problems to better suit their local circumstances. However, we urge caution in manipulating tasks. It is easy to change aspects of a situation in ways that remove the challenge of engaging in relevant and meaningful mathematics. Be sure to maintain the mathematical core of the tasks themselves, preserving students' opportunities to work through the mathematics, even though this may be a struggle.

Each lesson is composed of several components. For each task, blackline masters and other materials are available for downloading and printing on NCTM's More4U website (nctm .org/more4u). The teacher may find that a handout is unnecessary at times; instead, the worksheet may be used as a class display, and students may be encouraged to use alternatives for recording their work.

The discussion of the problem presents the primary content standards and mathematical practices from CCSSM that include the mathematics and processes that students can be expected to employ as they work through the task. The Problem Discussion provides greater detail about the mathematics of the task and ways in which mathematical practices are employed as students solve the problem. Understanding the mathematics is important, and we hope that the problem discussion for each task effectively highlights the mathematical ideas around which each task is structured.

Sections on Strategies and Misconceptions/Student Difficulties identify potential student solution strategies and the challenges and misconceptions that students may encounter as they work through the problem. Following these sections is a detailed description of how teachers might engage students in the task at hand by using the Launch/Explore/Summarize format. In each of these sections, we have highlighted ways to apply the characteristics of the three-phase lesson format in relation to the specific task.

Finally, a section on Differentiation identifies ways in which a task may be expanded or simplified for the variety of learners found in any classroom. Students should be provided with ample time to make sense of and engage in the problems. For students who derive a solution quickly, this section provides suggestions for how their thinking regarding this particular content might be deepened. For students who are unable to engage in *productive struggle* with the task, this section provides suggestions for how the task might be modified without significantly reducing students' opportunity to engage in mathematical reasoning.

What to Expect in the Online Components

The online components for this book include a Microsoft Word version of the problem handouts as well as other materials associated with each problem. The Word version of the handout can be used to change the names of characters in the tasks so that students may make a more personal connection with problem situations. Similarly, changes can be easily made to the contexts of the problems so that they are more relevant to students' local environments and lives.

Thank you for your interest in this book. We hope that it is a valuable resource for you and opens the door to rich and engaging problem solving for your students!

INTRODUCTION

What does it mean to problem solve? People of all ages engage in problem solving. A toddler might investigate how to obtain a toy that is just out of her reach. An adolescent might need to determine how to juggle multiple obligations, responsibilities, and desires effectively. Regardless of the task itself, people who engage in problem solving seek a solution to a challenging and novel task. They may bring a variety of knowledge to the process, investigate several possible solution strategies, and experience various degrees of success with their methods. They may experience failure, struggle, and triumph, all of which contribute to their knowledge base for future problem-solving situations.

PROBLEM SOLVING IN MATHEMATICS

The experiences of failure, struggle, and triumph also apply to problem solving in mathematical contexts. Problem solving in mathematics "means engaging in a task for which the solution method is not known in advance" (NCTM 2000, p. 52). This is an important definition to understand. If one engages in a routine task for which the solution strategy is already known, then one is not participating in authentic problem solving. Instead, the routine task is an exercise, and the person engaging in the task is simply practicing a process or a skill or applying previous knowledge to a context (Eves 1963; Zietz 1999). Authentic problem solving, by contrast, means that the person is engaged in developing new mathematical ideas or applying prior knowledge in new ways.

Although authentic problem solving will almost certainly involve failure, struggle, and success, perhaps the most important of these processes is struggle. It is through active grappling with new concepts that we learn mathematics. Hiebert (2003) emphasizes that classrooms that promote students' understanding "allow mathematics to be problematic for students" (p. 54). As teachers, we are tempted to decrease our students' struggle by removing obstacles or showing them the way. However, it is important to realize that removing students' opportunities to struggle simultaneously reduces their opportunities to learn mathematics with understanding.

The Common Core State Standards for Mathematics (CCSSM; NGA Center and CCCSO 2010) have provided both an opportunity and a challenge for teachers to engage their students in mathematical problem solving. Beyond the clearly defined content standards, the Standards for Mathematical Practice (SMP) are a call for changes to classroom instruction to ensure that students engage in challenging tasks. This engagement means that they will persevere through struggle, justify and explain their reasoning, and participate in critical and mathematically focused discourse that occurs throughout the classroom community. At all levels (K–12), students are expected to—

1. make sense of problems and persevere in solving them;
2. reason abstractly and quantitatively;

3. construct viable arguments and critique the reasoning of others;

4. model with mathematics;

5. use appropriate tools strategically;

6. attend to precision;

7. look for and make use of structure; and

8. look for and express regularity in repeated reasoning. (NGA Center and CCSSO 2010, pp. 6–8).

Authentic problem solving provides opportunities for students to engage in the processes identified in these eight Standards for Mathematical Practice. Problem-solving tasks develop new understanding about particular content, but a student-centered implementation of the task—and some letting go on the part of the teacher—also allows students to develop mathematical processes or habits of mind that are associated with the practice standards. One might think of the content standards as identifying *what* students learn and the mathematical practices as identifying *how* students learn or engage in the content.

Van de Walle (2003) discusses three characteristics of tasks that successfully promote student learning:

1. What is problematic must be the mathematics.

2. Tasks must be accessible to students.

3. Tasks must require justifications and explanations for answers or methods.
   (pp. 68–69)

Tasks that meet these descriptors present opportunities for students to develop new mathematical ideas; that is, the mathematics will be problematic for them, and there will be struggle. If students have already mastered the relevant content standards, these tasks may be fun and engaging activities, but they will not be authentic problem-solving experiences.

Certain lesson formats are more conducive than others to creating problem-solving experiences that promote meaningful mathematics learning. Van de Walle, Karp, and Bay-Williams (2013) advocate a three-phase lesson format. The three phases are as follows:

- *Getting Ready*: Activate prior knowledge, be sure the problem is understood, and establish clear expectations.

- *Students Work*: Let go! Notice students' mathematical thinking, offer appropriate support, and provide worthwhile extensions.

- *Class Discussion*: Promote a mathematical community of learners, listen actively without evaluation, summarize main ideas, and identify future problems. (p. 49)

The Launch/Explore/Summarize terminology used by the Connected Mathematics Project (Lappan et al. 2014) captures the ideas articulated above and effectively illustrates the progression of participating in mathematics: activating prior knowledge, engaging in mathematical thinking about a task, and extracting and summarizing the important mathematical ideas. Each of these phases is discussed in more detail in the following sections.

Launch

The Launch portion of a lesson is the teacher's opportunity to engage students in both the context and the mathematical ideas of a task. It is important to draw students into the circumstances of the task, because doing so allows them to have a personal connection with it and helps them see how mathematics may be used in different ways in their lives or the lives of others. Engaging students in the mathematical ideas of the task is important as well so that students have a general understanding of the problem that they are to solve.

There are multiple ways to engage students in the context of a task. Perhaps the simplest is to ask, "What do you know about ... (e.g., Earth Day, Veterans Day)?" This kind of broad approach will provide a good sense of where the students are in relation to the context of the problem. It may bring misconceptions to the surface, and it may also bring out family traditions that can be shared so that students' understanding and respect for the experiences of others can be developed. Other questions that might be asked include the following:

• Has anyone here ever been...?

• How many of you like to...?

• How many of you celebrate...?

The sharing of students' beliefs and experiences presents the teacher with an opening to add to the conversation, providing more information about the holiday or seasonal event to connect students more closely with the frame of reference.

Depending on your location, your students may have very limited experience with the context of a task. If they have never seen snow before, for example, you may find it challenging to interest them in a situation about sledding or snowfall. Students who have lived their entire lives in an urban setting may not have any prior experiences involving camping or farming. If this is the case, it is still an excellent occasion to expand students' horizons. Perhaps some students have experience with these more unusual occurrences or activities and can share with the rest of the class. Online pictures and videos are excellent sources for context development; we trust that teachers will be able to search quickly and effectively for information about the context and relevant images and videos to support students' contextual understanding.

Beyond providing an opportunity to clarify the context of the task, the Launch is an ideal time to make sure that students understand the problem with which they are about to engage. To do this, students must employ the processes in the first Standard for Mathematical Practice, "Make sense of problems and persevere in solving them." With teacher support, students should establish *what they know* about the problem. This may include knowledge gleaned from the problem itself, such as "Eloise encounters 58 intersections in the maze," or inferences based on the information provided in the problem, such as "Eloise will go straight at all multiples of 3." Students may be inclined to dive right into the problem, performing operations on the numbers provided without thinking much about the problem itself. Asking them, "What do you know about this problem?" and listing their responses on a visual display requires them to think about the problem before diving in.

Students should also be asked to determine *what they want to know*. Their initial focus might be on the answer to the problem. However, students should be encouraged to ask questions that may emerge as they make sense of the problem; getting students to recognize these questions as important gives them a valuable skill in problem solving. Students' identification of these questions helps them realize that the problem solving will not be automatic; they may also be more aware of some mental processes that they use to answer questions while they work toward a solution.

The Launch is also an opportunity for students to develop a tentative plan for solving the problem. This can be tricky to negotiate; students sharing their plans can sometimes limit other students' thinking at the cost of their own problem-solving strategies. Asking students to share their tentative plans with an elbow partner may alleviate this challenge. Voicing their plans may also help students identify places where their understanding of the task is still limited. Therefore, concluding the conversation with, "Who would like to ask a question about this problem?" provides a final occasion to clarify the context or the task before students set out to work.

Finally, it is important that students understand how the Explore portion of the lesson will progress. A variety of classroom materials should be made available for their use (e.g., linking cubes, color counters). Although some students may choose not to use manipulatives, these tools offer an entry point to the problems for those students who are reasoning less abstractly. Students should be assigned to partners or small groups and be clear on the format expected for a final product.

It is important to note that the Launch portion of the task is not the place where the teacher does a similar problem with students or demonstrates how to solve the problem at hand. Doing either of these may drastically reduce the cognitive demand of the task, students' willingness to engage in the challenge, and their chance to learn important mathematics. Engaging students in preliminary processes for problem solving is necessary, both for tackling the task at hand and developing mathematical practices that they can apply to any problem situation. This portion of the lesson should be limited to a meaningful ten minutes that effectively involve students in the context of the problem.

EXPLORE

As students engage in these tasks, the teacher's role is to provide appropriate scaffolding without removing students' opportunities to learn. As a teacher, how can you do this? Ask questions. Listen carefully. Assess a student's understanding of the problem and determine where the more challenging aspects lie. Have students talk about their problem-solving strategies: What has worked and what has not?

The Explore portion of a lesson can be the most challenging for teachers who are not accustomed to teaching mathematics through problem solving. As teachers, our tendency is to want to "help," to make the path easier for our students and reduce their struggle. Although we do not want our students to become so frustrated that they give up on the task, we also need to be cautious about our "helpful" tendencies. Van de Walle's exhortation needs to be taken to heart for this section: "Let go!" (Van de Walle, Karp, and Bay-Williams 2013, p. 49).

Letting go as the students commence working on the task means giving them time to begin tackling the problem. For at least the first several minutes of the Explore portion of a lesson, student groups should be given the space to continue to process the task, share their initial plans, and begin to explore these plans. Collaborative work will provide more ideas for exploration and more insights about how certain mathematical ideas may apply to the task at hand. During this time, the teacher should circulate throughout the room with open ears, simply listening to the immediate challenges and insights. Common threads may surface across groups; however, allowing students the time to discuss without intervention may also provide opportunities for resolution of any misunderstandings or differences.

As students proceed further, brief visits with each of the groups can keep them moving forward. Ask questions like the following:

- Can you tell me why you decided to do this?
- What does this represent?
- What do you think your next step might be?
- What does this number mean in relation to the problem you're solving?

However, when considering this section of the lesson, keep in mind that the teacher's task is to identify and understand students' mathematical thinking in relation to the task as well as their misconceptions and challenges. This is not possible without listening to students' talk—closely and carefully.

Task-specific questions or additional support may be necessary for groups that fail to find access to a task. A note of caution, however: This support should not be provided prematurely. Students learn through struggle, and as long as their struggle is not unproductive frustration, they are probably grappling with important ideas and challenges.

Teachers may feel a similar temptation to rescue students who have gotten a wrong answer or are heading down an incorrect path. If teachers are open and honest about honoring and respecting the learning that occurs through cognitive dissonance or mistakes, students will see their wrong turns or dead-end paths as valuable learning opportunities as well. Allowing students to take wrong turns and arrive at incorrect answers may require a shift in what is honored and emphasized in the mathematics classroom. Processes, strategies, and the longitudinal development of mathematical concepts must be at the core, and mistakes must be valued as learning opportunities by both teachers and students.

Teachers may find it helpful to determine a way to record students' misconceptions, challenges, insights, and strategies throughout the Explore portion of the lesson. In many problem-solving lessons, a particular order for sharing strategies in the Summarize portion of the lesson is appropriate. Knowing this order and being able to attend to the students who have reasoned in particular ways is worthwhile for leading students in a productive discussion of the important mathematical ideas related to each task.

Summarize

The Summarize portion of the lesson is the teacher's opportunity to engage the classroom community of learners in a discussion to bring together essential mathematical ideas. This discussion needs to extend beyond a mere sharing of strategies. Although sharing strategies is important, it is more important that students have an opportunity to discuss the mathematical ideas developed in each task, make connections between strategies, identify generalizations when appropriate to do so, and pose new problems.

Students should be exposed to the strategies that were used throughout the classroom community. There are multiple ways to arrange this exposure. Gallery walks, in which students circulate throughout the classroom to observe others' work, is one effective way to share strategies. It may sometimes be appropriate for students to present their strategies to the whole class. At times, providing time for everyone to share may be important. Generally, however, we suggest that the choices for sharing be based on the mathematical ideas and strategies used by particular groups, with a long-range view to making sure that all students have opportunities to participate in this way. Although students may not have an opportunity in each lesson to present their thinking, they nonetheless ought to be engaged in discussing the strategies that are presented and in making connections between these strategies and their own.

Initially, students may not know how to participate in a community of learners that discusses important mathematical ideas. Although they may focus on non-mathematical ideas at first (e.g., "I like your drawing!"), the teacher can model appropriate probing questions and comments. For example, a teacher might offer comments similar to the following:

- "I'm interested in how you knew that you needed to add these numbers together. Can you please explain that?"

- "I see that you used a lot of the same numbers in your problem-solving strategy, although you had a different way of solving the problem. Why do you think we are seeing the same numbers in these places?"

- "How do you think the first group's use of linking cubes is similar to your drawing?"

- "I'm not sure I understand what this picture represents. Could you please explain that again?"

Students will learn from the teacher's modeling, but explicit attention should also be given to initiating a mathematical discussion. The teacher might ask students to think about the question she just asked and how it helped her clarify her own understanding about the mathematical ideas. The teacher might also consider providing sentence starters to help students structure appropriate and meaningful questions of their own.

It is critical to elicit the mathematical ideas associated with problem-solving tasks and summarize them during the discussion. Anticipating specific questions is helpful, but teachers should also experiment with questions that are particular to the strategies and misconceptions that surface in the classroom. Particular attention can be focused on generalizations that arise from students' thinking. What patterns do they notice? What do they expect would happen with a different set of numbers? What rules can be articulated, either informally or formally?

These generalizations may lead to opportunities for problem posing. Out of many good questions come more questions! Preparation to follow through with students' questions in subsequent problems or to record and post new problems encourages students to think about how these mathematical ideas extend beyond one problem-solving experience. Similarly, if extensions for students have been provided during the Explore phase, students should share the results of these extensions, making deliberate connections to the original task.

In this final discussion, mistakes and misconceptions should be tackled head-on. Teachers may be discomfited by the sharing of incorrect answers, but this should be made to be an acceptable experience for students. This requires a safe community of learners in which students are comfortable with risk, expect mistakes to be made, and see opportunities for learning in these mistakes.

As students engage in more and more problem-solving experiences, they should be encouraged to take on more and more of the classroom discourse. Teachers should guide and facilitate rather than manage and direct. Students should be challenged to ask the questions and make the connections. Increasing the number of student comments occurring between teacher comments increases students' ability to guide the discussion. The teacher needs to know the map, but often the students are capable of choosing the route.

Of course, engaging in mathematical discourse like this takes time, effort, and patience. Students in the upper elementary grades have plenty of ideas but often have difficulty articulating them. However, the only way to improve discourse is *through* discourse, so teachers should use rich tasks to take risks, and—as one preservice teacher described it—"embrace the train wreck" that may occur when following students' trains of thought. These "train wrecks" can lead to profound learning experiences!

FALL

For many students, fall means back to school. There are many other things to celebrate in this season. Tasks in this chapter celebrate fall activities and holidays, from picking apples and harvesting vegetables to Labor Day and Halloween. These contexts provide perfect opportunities for exploring meaningful mathematical concepts in this back-to-school season.

The three third-grade tasks at the beginning of this chapter relate to operations with whole numbers. Multiplication is a common topic for early third-grade study, and the first two tasks tackle this important concept. In the first task, Picking Apples, students explore equal group multiplication and properties of this operation. Labor Day Parade asks students to consider different arrangements of marching band members in arrays, thereby exploring possible factors of composite numbers. The final third-grade task, Election Results, provides a context for students to revisit strategies for addition and subtraction of whole numbers, display results in a scaled picture graph, and interpret these results.

Maize Maze, the first fourth-grade task, provides an opportunity for students to look for patterns in numerical sequences and make connections between these patterns and whole number multiplication and division. The second task makes similar connections between patterns and operations by asking students to determine a number of Halloween trick-or-treaters that would leave a remainder of 1 when grouped by 2, 3, or 4, and no remainder when grouped by 5. Finally, Native American Heritage challenges students to make connections between grade-appropriate geometry concepts and Native American symbols.

The first fifth-grade task requires students to reason about operations with decimals in the context of sharing the harvest from a community garden, also eliciting some proportional reasoning in relation to the number of families being fed. The second task provides a context for students to connect geometric reasoning and fraction concepts as they simulate the flag-folding procedure involved in Veterans Day celebrations. The final problem-solving task in this chapter challenges fifth graders to examine a coordinate grid in relation to the proposed and actual routes of the *Mayflower*'s voyage in the fall of 1620.

MATERIALS FOR EACH TASK, INCLUDING HANDOUTS, ARE AVAILABLE FOR DOWNLOADING AND PRINTING ON NCTM'S WEBSITE AT NCTM.ORG/MORE4U BY ENTERING THE ACCESS CODE ON THE TITLE PAGE OF THIS BOOK.

PICKING APPLES

Orlando, Ronan, Zoe, and Simon went apple picking at a local orchard. Each one of them chose a different kind of apple to pick. Use the information below to find out how many apples each of them collected. Show your work, and use an equation to represent your thinking for each apple picker. Be prepared to explain your reasoning.

	Number of bags	Number of apples in each bag	Total number of apples
Orlando picked Honeycrisp apples.	5	7	
Ronan picked Gala apples.	3	12	
Zoe picked Fuji apples.	6	6	
Simon picked Pacific Rose apples.	7	5	

CCSSM Standards for Mathematical Practice

Practice 1: Make sense of problems and persevere in solving them.

Practice 4: Model with mathematics.

CCSSM Content Standards

3.OA.A.1: Interpret products of whole numbers, e.g., interpret 5 × 7 as the total number of objects in 5 groups of 7 objects each. *For example, describe a context in which a total number of objects can be expressed as 5 × 7.*

Problem Discussion

In Picking Apples, students are asked to model and reason about a situation involving equal groups multiplication (3.OA.A.1). The children in the context have each picked different kinds of apples and in different quantities. They are collecting apples in bags, and for each type of apple, each child's bags have equal numbers of apples. For example, Orlando picks 5 bags of apples with 7 apples in each bag; this is 5 equal groups of 7 apples, or 5 × 7 = 35. Students should be given the opportunity to make sense of this problem by representing it with manipulatives or through a drawing that contains 5 groups of 7 items (e.g., linking cubes, tally marks) (SMP 1). Various strategies may be used, such as counting one by one or skip counting, once students have represented each situation.

Notice that Simon picks a different kind of apple in 7 bags, each with 5 apples. This is modeled by the equation 7 × 5 = 35 (SMP 4). Although the commutative property of multiplication is evident in Orlando and Simon's situations (i.e., 5 × 7 = 7 × 5), the mathematical convention in the United States (and followed by the CCSSM) is that the first factor represents the number of groups, and the second factor represents the number of items in each group. This task provides a context for students to encounter and reason about the commutative property of multiplication and extend their understanding of this property from addition to multiplication.

This problem is also designed to highlight different factors that can lead to the same product. The total of Ronan's Gala apples (3×12) is equal to the number of Fuji apples that Zoe picks (6×6). Zoe's situation is a manipulation of Ronan's: she has the same number of apples but twice as many bags, with half as many apples in each bag. Thus, students have the opportunity to reason about how equivalence may be maintained by manipulating both factors. This idea can also be demonstrated with manipulatives in a way that highlights the conservation of the total number through rearrangement. Students can be asked, "Do you think this might work with other numbers?" and explore different combinations of factors that might have equivalent arrangements.

Students are asked to model each of the apple-picking situations with an equation (SMP 4). If they are unfamiliar with multiplication, they may choose to model the situation by using repeated addition (e.g., Orlando: $7 + 7 + 7 + 7 + 7 = 35$). This is an excellent opportunity to demonstrate how a multiplication equation represents repeated addition in the case of equal groups: 5 groups of 7 is modeled with $5 \times 7 = 35$. If this representation is not evident as students work, attend to it during the Summarize portion of the lesson.

STRATEGIES

- Students may represent each situation by using a manipulative. For example, they may use linking cubes to make 5 groups with 7 cubes in each group.
- Students may create a drawing to represent each situation. For instance, they may draw 5 groups of apples with 7 apples in each group.
- Once students have represented each problem situation, they may count the apples one by one.
- Once students have represented each problem situation, they may skip count by the number of apples in each group (e.g., Orlando: 7, 14, 21, 28, 35). Note that this will be easier for some situations than others.
- Once students have represented each problem situation, they may rearrange the items to make them easier to count (e.g., making groups of 10 apples).
- Students may recognize these situations as equal groups multiplication and use skip counting, derived facts, or recall to determine some answers.
- Students may recognize that Simon's situation is similar to Orlando's and determine that the answer is the same.

MISCONCEPTIONS/STUDENT DIFFICULTIES

- Students may struggle with keeping track of one-by-one counting when items are scattered.

- Students may struggle with certain skip counting sequences (i.e., skip counting by 7, 12, or 6).
- Students may not understand that they have four separate situations to represent and solve.
- Students may struggle to represent each situation appropriately or may not understand how Orlando and Simon's situations are different.
- Students may decide to perform other operations with the numbers provided.

LAUNCH

Begin this task by asking students if they have ever gone apple picking. If this is not an activity that students have engaged in, ask them if they like apples and if they know what kind of apples they particularly enjoy. List some of these varieties in a visual display. Explain that there are many varieties of apples, and these may be enjoyed for different reasons: cooking in a wide array of recipes, storage for later in the year, snacking, and so on.

Discuss the context of the task, that four children have gone apple picking and are collecting different kinds of apples. Ask a student to read the task aloud to the class, and provide a visual display of the table. Have students turn to an elbow partner and say two or three things that they know about the problem. Ask students to share these with the whole class; consider underlining or rewriting parts of the task that they highlight. Next, ask students to discuss with that same elbow partner what it is they are being asked to do with the task and if they have any initial ideas about how to approach the task. In particular, ask them to think about any materials they may need to help them make sense of the problem situations.

Bring the whole class back together to share these thoughts. Emphasize what they are being asked to do in the task (find out how many apples each person collected), and provide any materials that they think will be useful for their work.

EXPLORE

Have students work in groups of three or four on this task. Be sure that students don't "divide and conquer" by assigning each group member a different situation to solve. Instead, have students collaborate to solve each of the four situations presented.

Allow students some time to explore different ways to represent the bags of apples. It is likely that in a group of three students, at least one will have an idea for representing Orlando's apples correctly, either with a drawing or by using manipulatives. Have materials (e.g., linking cubes, drawing paper and pens) ready for students' use, but refrain from suggesting particular representations.

After each group has represented and solved at least one of the situations, ask questions to check for understanding:

- How did you choose to represent Orlando's bags of apples?
- How are you showing 5 bags of apples?
- How are you showing how many apples are in each bag?

- Can you show me how you determined that there are 35 total apples in Orlando's bags? (Take note of the group's counting strategy.) Is there another way you could have figured that out?

- Can you explain how you decided what your equation for this situation looks like?

- If your diagram represents 5 bags with 7 apples in each bag, what do you think Ronan's situation of 3 bags with 12 apples in each bag will look like? (This might be a good question to pose to a student who has not contributed in response to the previous questions.)

Throughout the questioning, make sure that all members of each group understand how the group's representation is related to the problem situation. If a group has solved the problem abstractly (e.g., identifying it as a multiplication problem and skip counting), encourage the students to demonstrate at least one of the situations by using manipulatives or a drawing and connect their reasoning to this representation.

Prior to challenging students to explore some of the ideas in the Differentiation section, ask groups questions such as the following about the commonalities between Orlando's and Simon's, and Zoe's and Ronan's apple-picking situations:

- Do any of the apple pickers have the same number of apples? How is that possible, when they don't have the same number of bags and apples in the bags?

- How can you show me that the order doesn't matter with multiplication?

- How can you rearrange Ronan's apples to get to Zoe's apples?

Finally, tell students that each group will be expected to justify their reasoning in relation to one of the situations provided. On the basis of the different strategies that you observe as students work, assign one situation to each student group and ask them to present their reasoning about it.

SUMMARIZE

Bring the class together to discuss the four apple-picking situations. First, list all the answers for the four situations that the groups would like to defend. For example, one student may suggest that Orlando has picked 35 apples. Without offering judgment, ask the class, "Are there any other answers that anyone would like to defend?" Other questions to ask may include, "I see 35 (and 36) up here twice—are you saying that these people picked the same number of apples?"

Once all possible answers have been listed, ask a group to share and discuss how they represented and solved for Orlando's bags of apples. Encourage other students to ask this group how they represented the number of bags and how they represented the number of apples in each bag. Also be sure to record students' strategies to reinforce understanding of how the group determined the total number of apples. If a group counts one by one, ask the rest of the class, "Did anyone who counted the number of apples differently have a similar representation? What did you do?" or "How might someone determine the number of apples without counting one by one?" Finally, record the equation that this group used to model their thinking, and ask

them and the rest of the class how the equation makes sense with the situation and with their representation.

Ask other groups to defend their answers for the four situations. Consider approaching the situations out of order to highlight mathematical ideas such as the commutative property of multiplication. A revised sequence to consider would be Orlando, Simon, Ronan, Zoe. For each, be sure that the representations and counting strategies are understood and equations are visually represented. If a multiplication equation surfaces through the group presentations (e.g., $5 \times 7 = 35$), discuss how this equation models equal groups (in this case, 5 groups of 7). Then revisit other problem situations and model these appropriately by using a multiplication equation.

Finally, take advantage of any opportunities to discuss students' observations about similarities between Orlando's and Simon's, and Ronan's and Zoe's situations. There is no need to provide instruction about the commutative property of multiplication at this time. Instead, ask students to consider whether or not they think this will always work:

- When you add two or more numbers together, does it matter what order you add them in?
- Do you think this works for multiplication as well?
- How might you test your conjecture?

Conjectures resulting from their observations might be displayed for several weeks or more to revisit as students continue to explore multiplication.

DIFFERENTIATION

- If students struggle to represent the situations, limit the number of situations that they are solving (e.g., limit to Orlando and Simon, or just Orlando).
- If students struggle to represent the situations, consider providing small bags for them to make groups of cubes.
- To extend this task, challenge students to consider the commutative property of multiplication by asking them whether reversing the numbers of bags and apples in each bag always works.
- To extend this task, challenge students to determine what other pairs of factors might be rearranged in a manner similar to Ronan's and Zoe's quantities.
- To extend this task, challenge students by explaining that two other students have also collected a total of 36 apples. However, the number of bags that each of these students has is not the same as Zoe's or Ronan's. How many bags might they have, with how many apples in each bag?
- To extend this task, ask students to consider the following relationship:

    $6 \times 6 = 36$

    $5 \times 7 = 35$

    Notice that the second pair of factors is 1 less and 1 more than the original factors. Challenge students to consider other pairs of equations like this (e.g., 3×3 and 2×4) and determine if it is always the case that the product of the second will be 1 less than the product of the first. Students may also be challenged to consider this question when the initial two factors are different numbers (e.g., 5 × 7 and 4 × 8).

- Challenge students' thinking in this context to include division. For example, ask one or both of the following questions:
  - Zoe picks 45 Red Delicious apples and uses 5 bags. If each bag contains the same number of apples, how many apples does she have in each bag?
  - Ronan picks 21 more Gala apples by putting 7 in each bag. How many more bags of Gala apples has Ronan picked?

Labor Day Parade

Four different towns will bring their fifth-grade bands to march in the Labor Day Parade. Each band needs to determine how to organize the rows of band members so that the same number of members are in each row. The parade officials want to know all the different ways to organize the four marching bands and which band has the most choices to organize into rows of equal size. Use pictures, words, and equations to justify your work.

    Bushnell Marching Band: 24 members

    Wishek Marching Band: 48 members

    Hokah Marching Band: 60 members

    Avon Marching Band: 64 members

CCSSM Standards for Mathematical Practice

Practice 7: Look for and make use of structure.

CCSSM Content Standards

3.OA.A.3: Use multiplication and division within 100 to solve word problems in situations involving equal groups, arrays, and measurement quantities, e.g., by using drawings and equations with a symbol for the unknown number to represent the problem.

Problem Discussion

This task builds on content standard 2.OA.C.4, which calls for students to use addition to find the total number of objects arranged in rectangular arrays and write an equation to express the total as a sum using equal addends. Further, this task will provide students with an opportunity to discuss the meaning of multiplication and division through the context of rows and columns of people in a marching band. As such, this standard focuses on using equal groups and arrays to bridge from repeated addition to multiplicative reasoning. As students draw arrays to represent each marching band (the band names can be changed to reflect local communities), students will use multiplicative language to describe their array. For example, in second grade, students may see 4 rows of 6 people as 6 + 6 + 6 + 6 = 24 people. In this task, however, students will be encouraged to translate this repeated addition reasoning to that of multiplication: 4 groups (rows) of 6 people can be represented by the equation 4 × 6 = 24. By using multiplicative reasoning, students will find all arrays that can be created for each marching band (3.OA.3).

Additionally, this task requires students to represent each array by using an equation involving multiplication. Such equations involve three quantities, which include two factors and one product (product = factor × factor). Through the exploration of this task, students may use one of three array situations. For example, the Unknown Product situation for 3 rows of 8 band members could be represented as 3 × 8 = ? The Unknown Factor situation could be represented in two ways. First, students may think, "If 24 band members are arranged in 3 rows, how many band members will be in each row?" and write the equation 3 × ? = 24. Second, students may think, "If 24 band members are arranged into equal rows of 8 band members, how many rows will there be?" and write the equation ? × 8 = 24. (See Common Core Standards Writing Team [2011] for more information on these and other multiplication and division situations.)

As students create different arrays, a variety of levels of reasoning may be observed. Battista (2012) identifies levels of sophistication for multiplying and dividing whole numbers. At level 1, "students treat numbers as a collection of ones" (p. 7); that is, to find 3 × 8, a student would make 3 rows of 8 objects and count them all. At level 2, "students use skip-counting to iterate composite units" (p. 7); that is, to find 3 × 8, a student would skip count by 3's or 8's to find the product. At level 3, "students use known facts and number properties instead of counting" (p. 7); that is, to find 3 × 8, a student may reason that 2 × 8 = 16, so 3 × 8 is 16 + 8, which equals 24.

This task also offers students a context to explore the structure of multiplication (SMP 7)—in particular, the commutative property. For example, to arrange 24 band members, students can make an array with 3 rows of 8 band members or 8 rows of 3 band members. They may recognize that these two arrays are the same in the mathematical representation but have different meanings in the context of the task. In addition, when students verify that their arrays represent the given number of band members, they may use the distributive property of multiplication over addition. That is, in an array that is 15 rows of 4 band members, they may recognize that 10 rows of 4 are 40 and 5 rows of 4 are 20, resulting in 60 total band members.

STRATEGIES

- Students may randomly determine possible row-and-column combinations for each marching band.
- Students may make an organized list of possible row-and-column combinations for each marching band, beginning with 1 × __ and continuing to 2 × __, and so on.
- When proving that each formation represents the correct number of band members, students may count all members, one at a time.
- When proving that each formation represents the correct number of band members, students may skip count by rows or columns.
- When proving that each formation represents the correct number of band members, students may use a chunking strategy. For example, instead of skip counting 4 rows of 6 as 6 + 6 + 6 + 6, a student may see this as 12 + 12 or see 6 rows of 8 as 40 + 8.
- When proving that each formation represents the correct number of band members, students may use properties of operations or known multiplication facts.

MISCONCEPTIONS/STUDENT DIFFICULTIES

- Students may have difficulty organizing the rows and columns, resulting in an unequal number of band members in each row.
- Students may not be able to find all the possible arrays for each band.

- Students may not see an array with one row as a viable option.
- Students may not be able to explain what the factors in each multiplication equation represent in the context of the problem.
- Students may not realize that, for example, a 2 × 24 and a 24 × 2 formation are different in this context.
- While counting to ensure that all band members are accounted for, students may have difficulty keeping track of each band member if they are using a counting-all strategy.
- While counting to ensure that all band members are accounted for, students may have difficulty skip counting by numbers like 6 or 8.

Launch

Ask students to brainstorm what the word *labor* means to them. They could be encouraged to create a poster to show, for example, "To me, labor means..." and use words or pictures to represent their thoughts. In small groups, have students share their ideas or posters. Next, ask students if they know why we celebrate Labor Day. This discussion could include various information such as the fact that Labor Day—

- honors the American worker and his or her contributions to our nation;
- values the role of work in America;
- was first established and observed in 1882 in New York;
- is celebrated on the first Monday in September;
- informally signifies the end of summer.

Ask students if they have ever been to a Labor Day parade or if their family does anything special for this holiday. Have students share Labor Day experiences. It is likely that a student will mention seeing marching bands in the Labor Day parade. Ask students to describe how the marching bands line up in the parade. Focus on the row-and-column structure of a marching band, in which each row usually has the same number of band members. For example, ask twelve students to create a "marching band" formation in the room. Ask if there are other formations that would have an equal number of band members in each row. Students should create the following arrays: 12 × 1 (12 rows of 1); 1 × 12 (1 row of 12); 2 × 6 (2 rows of 6); 6 × 2 (6 rows of 2); 3 × 4 (3 rows of 4); and 4 × 3 (4 rows of 3).

Hand out and read the task with students. Give students two minutes to work with a partner to discuss what the problem asks them to do and to plan how they will solve the task. Ask students to share their initial ideas about this task with the whole class, highlighting words such as *formation* and their relationship to arrays with an equal number of members in each row. Next, ask pairs of students to conjecture which of the four marching bands will have the greatest number of formations and why. Have pairs of students share their conjectures with the whole class. Students' initial conjectures may include "64 will have the most formations because it is the largest number" or "60 will have the most formations because there are a lot of factor pairs that make 60." Keep a record to readdress their conjectures during the Summarize portion of the activity.

EXPLORE

Have students work in groups of three or four on this task. Allow students to record their pictures, words, and equations to justify their work for finding all the different formations for each marching band. As array drawing proceeds, ask students questions to help them explain their representations:

- How are you using arrays to represent the problem?
- Why did you create an array with 4 rows? How did you decide how many band members will be in each of those 4 rows?
- How do you know that all of the town's band members are represented by this formation (array)? Is there another way to verify this?
- Do you get a different answer if you skip count by columns instead of rows? How do you know?

Additionally, be sure that students are able to connect the numbers in their equations back to the problem situation by asking questions that check for understanding of their symbolic representations:

- I see that you have created an equation by adding 6 together 4 times. Why did you do this? Is there another way to write an equation to represent 4 rows of 6 band members in each row?
- How did you write an equation using your array to represent the total number of band members in the marching band? What do the numbers (factors) mean in the context of the problem?
- Does a 4 × 6 formation have the same number of members as a 6 × 4 formation? How do you know? Are these formations different?
- If you have 24 members and want 4 rows in the formation, how many members of the marching band will be in each row? How can you write an equation to represent this?

As students work to identify the different formations for each of the marching bands, encourage them to verify that they have accounted for all possible formations for each marching band. Questions to check for understanding may include the following:

- What did you notice about the factor pairs for 24? Were they both even, both odd, or one of each?
- What did you notice happens to the number of band members in each row as you increase the number of rows in each formation?
- What would happen if you double (or halve) the number of rows in the marching band formation?
- How do you know you found all formations for each marching band? How could you verify that you found all the formations?

Finally, tell students that each group will be expected to justify its reasoning in relation to one of the marching band formations that it provided.

SUMMARIZE

To focus on the problem-solving process, begin by asking partners to share how they chose to investigate this problem. Ask if other partners solved the problem in a different way. Pick four different groups to share their representations of one of the marching bands. Focus attention on the pictures, words, and equations. Ask questions to check for understanding:

- Does anyone have a formation that is different from those displayed? How is yours different?
- Is a 4 × 6 formation the same as a 6 × 4 formation? Or is it a different formation? How so?
- What does the 2 in your equation (2 × 24 = 48) represent? What about the 24?
- How do you know there are 24 members in this formation (i.e., 6 × 4)? Is there another way to prove this? (Continue asking this question until students no longer have ideas to share. Examples of ways to count the 24 band members may include 6 + 6 + 6 + 6; 4 + 4 + 4 + 4 + 4 + 4; chunking rows or columns, such as 12 + 12 or 8 + 8 + 8; multiplication facts, such as 4 × 6 and 6 × 4.)
- Can any of the bands make a formation that results in a square formation? How do you know?
- What would happen if a town had a prime number of marching band members?

Ask students to share which band had the most formations and to justify their reasoning. Was this what they conjectured at the beginning of the Explore section? If so, is their reasoning still valid? If not, what would their new reasoning be? Students should discuss the fact that 60 has more factor pairs than 64 (i.e., 60 has twelve factors and 64 has seven factors). If time permits, have students explore which whole numbers have an even number of factors and which whole numbers have an odd number of factors. Through concrete examples, students will notice that perfect squares are the only whole numbers with an odd number of factors.

Hokah	Avon
1 × 60	1 × 64
2 × 30	2 × 32
3 × 20	4 × 16
4 × 15	8 × 8
5 × 12	16 × 4
6 × 10	32 × 2
10 × 6	64 × 1
12 × 5	
15 × 4	
20 × 3	
30 × 2	
60 × 1	

Next, ask students to focus on the Bushnell and Wishek marching bands. Ask students if they think doubling the number of band members will result in twice the number of possible formations. Ask students to discuss with their partner what they notice about the number of rows and the number of band members in each row for the two bands. Providing the organized table below may help students see that for a given number of rows in Bushnell's band, the number of members in each row of Wishek's band is doubled. For example, Bushnell's formation of 2 rows of 12 members can be manipulated to make Wishek's formation of 2 rows of 24 members.

Bushnell	Wishek
1 × 24	1 × 48
2 × 12	2 × 24
3 × 8	3 × 16
4 × 6	4 × 12
6 × 4	6 × 8
8 × 3	8 × 6
12 × 2	12 × 4
24 × 1	16 × 3
	24 × 2
	48 × 1

Finally, ask students to form groups of four and decide which formations the parade officials should ask each band to use for the Labor Day parade. Have students justify their choices as they share their thoughts with the class.

DIFFERENTIATION

- To support struggling students, provide manipulatives to make the arrays. A different-colored manipulative could represent each town, and the exact number of manipulatives needed for each town may be provided.
- To support struggling students, provide grid paper to help organize the band members into rows.
- To support struggling students, decrease the number of marching bands.
- To extend this task, ask students to write a letter to the parade officials, describing how each band should be arranged and why each arrangement was chosen.
- To discuss prime numbers, ask students to determine the number of band members that would have the least number of possible arrangements (a prime number would have only two possible arrangements).
- To extend this task, tell students that each band has 12 members in their drum line and that all 12 drum line members need to be in the same row. What are the possible formations that each band can create, given that the drum line members must be in the same row but the size of the other rows can be more or less than 12 as long as each of those rows has the same number of members?

ELECTION RESULTS

Avon Elementary School holds student council elections each year at the beginning of November. Students vote to determine who will be the president of the student council. The student with the most votes becomes the president. On the day of the election, students vote in the morning or the afternoon. The chart below gives information about the students' voting:

	Morning votes	Afternoon votes	Total votes
Connor	68	28	
Peyton	34	10 more votes than Connor had in the afternoon	
Avery	27 more votes than Peyton had in the morning	49 fewer votes than Graydon had in the morning	
Graydon	Twice as many votes as Peyton had in the afternoon		

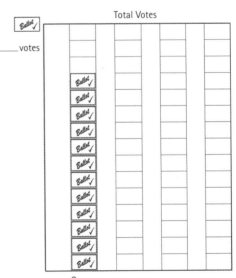

a. If you know Graydon becomes the president, how many votes could he have received in the afternoon? Explain how you found the total number of votes that each officer received.

b. The student council adviser began to display the election results in a picture graph (as shown at the right). Finish the picture graph to display the election results.

CCSSM STANDARDS FOR MATHEMATICAL PRACTICE

Practice 6: Attend to precision.

CCSSM CONTENT STANDARDS

3.MD.B.3: Draw a scaled picture graph and a scaled bar graph to represent a data set with several categories. Solve one- and two-step "how many more" and "how many less" problems using information presented in scaled bar graphs.

3.NBT.A.2: Fluently add and subtract within 1000 using strategies and algorithms based on place value, properties of operations, and/or the relationship between addition and subtraction.

Problem Discussion

Data analysis offers a context for students to solve problems involving the addition, subtraction, multiplication, and division of whole numbers (NCTM 2009a). The Election Results task allows students to apply initial understandings of the four operations to determine the number of votes each student received. The task is further extended as students must determine the scale in the picture graph and use this scale to complete the graph to display each student's total number of votes.

In part (a) of the task, students must determine the total number of votes for each candidate, and they will need to apply a variety of strategies to add and subtract within 1000 (3.NBT.A.2). For example, students may count up, count down, use place value understanding, or use algorithms. Students will need to understand academic language such as *more than*, *fewer than*, and *twice as much* to determine the total number of votes. The story situations represented in the clues build on students' knowledge of addition and subtraction situations—specifically, "add to" and "compare" problem types (2.AO.A.1)—and lay the foundation for multiplicative comparison situations (4.OA.A.1). To determine twice as much, students may use addition and subtraction to find the two equal addends. Students will also need to determine in which order the clues must be used. For example, students will have to determine Graydon's morning votes before they can determine Avery's afternoon vote count. Students will need to explain their choices for the order in which they solved the task and how they solved for each person's total number of votes, based on their understanding of the academic language (SMP 6).

In part (b) of the task, students must examine the adviser's picture graph to determine how many votes each ballot on the graph represents (3.MD.B.3). This graph has 12 boxes, which represent Connor's 96 total votes. This results in each ballot representing 8 votes. Students may use a variety of strategies to determine this number, including guess and check, repeated addition, missing factor approach, and applying the properties of place value and operations. For example, students may decompose 96 into 24 + 24 + 24 + 24 and see that there are 4 sets of (12 × 2), which results in a total of 8 groups of 12. Students will use the commutative property to translate this to represent the situation as 12 groups of 8 votes.

Once students determine how many votes each ballot represents and work to create their picture graph, they must label axes and include a key that clarifies the quantities in the context of the problem (SMP 6). For example, students will need to label the horizontal axis with the names of the students and discuss how the order in which the students are listed on the graph does not change the information that the graph represents. Graydon's afternoon vote total is left for students to determine. This will allow students to consider the reasonableness of their choice and how his total will be displayed on the graph. For instance, students may choose a number that results in the need for more ballots than the grid paper will allow. Students should be allowed to change their choice for Graydon's afternoon votes or extend their graph by taping sheets of paper together. Another interesting discussion that is likely to result from their selection of Graydon's afternoon votes is about a total number of votes that is not divisible by 8, which is the scale that the adviser selected. If this happens, students will need to consider the most appropriate way to represent the "extra" votes or realize that they need to add to or subtract from Graydon's afternoon votes to get a total number of votes that is a multiple of 8. Through class discussions, students will use the picture graph to solve one- and two-step "how many more" and "how many less" problems using information presented in the scaled picture graphs (3.MD.B.3).

STRATEGIES

- To determine the total number of votes for each candidate, students may use place value concepts and properties of operations (e.g., to find the total number of votes for Connor, students may use 60 + 20 + 8 + 8 = 96).

- To determine the total number of votes for each candidate, students may use the standard algorithm to regroup the 16 ones and find a total of 96 votes for Connor.

- To determine Avery's morning and afternoon votes, students may use standard algorithms for addition and subtraction or place value concepts.

- To determine Avery's afternoon votes, students may use the relationship between addition and subtraction by asking, "What do I need to add to 49 to get 76?" Students may represent this using a comparison bar.

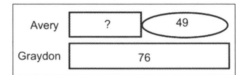

- To determine Avery's afternoon votes, students may subtract 50 from Graydon's morning votes and then add in one more vote (e.g., 76 − 49 = 76 − 50 + 1 = 26 + 1 = 27).

- To determine Graydon's morning votes of "twice as much as 38," students may add 38 + 38, using place value concepts (e.g., 30 + 30 + 8 + 8 = 76) or a standard algorithm.

- To determine Graydon's afternoon votes, students will recognize that Connor currently has the most votes with 96 total votes. Students will then use the relationship between addition and subtraction to determine that Graydon needs at least 21 afternoon votes.

- To determine the scale of the adviser's picture graph, students may use a guess-and-check strategy to guess the number of votes that each ballot represents and use repeated addition to check whether the total is 96 votes for Connor.

- To determine the scale of the adviser's graph, students may decompose 96 into 24 + 24 + 24 + 24 and see that there are 4 sets of 24 (2 × 12), which results in a total of 8 groups of 12 by use of the associative property (e.g., 4 × 24 = 4 × (2 × 12) = (4 × 2) × 12. Students will use the commutative property to translate this to represent the situation as 12 groups of 8 votes.

- To determine how many ballots are needed to represent the other three candidates, students may repeatedly subtract 8 by using manipulatives or counting-down strategies until all votes are accounted for.

- To determine how many ballots are needed to represent the other three candidates, students may use multiplication or division strategies, including missing factor approach (e.g., 8 × ___ = 88), decomposing and applying properties of operations (e.g.,

88 = 80 + 8; 80 is 10 groups of 8, and one more group of 8 results in 11 groups of 8), or known facts.

MISCONCEPTIONS/STUDENT DIFFICULTIES

- Students may have difficulty with terminology such as *twice as much*.
- Students may make a mistake on a number of ballots that affects later vote counts. For example, incorrectly finding Peyton's afternoon vote count will result in errors in Avery's and Graydon's vote counts.
- Students may have difficulty finding the scale that the adviser used to create the picture graph.
- Students may have difficulty determining how to graph Graydon's total number of votes if their total is not divisible by 8.

LAUNCH

To begin this task, ask students to share what they know about local, state, and national elections. Responses may include the following:

- The person with the most votes wins the election.
- Ballots are used to record votes.
- A person must be a citizen to vote.
- A person must be 18 years old to vote.
- The United States has political parties.
- Candidates campaign when they run in elections.

As students share their responses, be sure to elaborate on important aspects of elections. For example, in the United States, Election Day for the president of the United Sates occurs every four years on the Tuesday after the first Monday in November. In Canada, federal elections take place every four years on the third Monday in October. Federal elections for prime minister occur every five years (though if a term does not last this long, an election can be called sooner). Next, list the election dates and the recent U.S. presidents on the board as in the chart below (a similar table can be generated for Canadian prime ministers; however, the patterns that students notice are likely to be different). Ask students if they notice a pattern in the dates. Students should recognize that each year is 4 more than the previous election year. A corresponding pattern students may recognize is that the U.S. presidential election years are multiples of 4.

Year	1996	2000	2004	2008	2012
President	Bill Clinton	George W. Bush	George W. Bush	Barack Obama	Barack Obama

Next, ask students if they have ever heard of a student council. Ask them what offices students may hold on the student council. These offices may include president, vice president, secretary, and treasurer. Ask students to describe what duties each of these offices may entail.

EXPLORE

Hand out and read through part (a) of the task with students. Ask students what it means for Graydon to win the election. Students should discuss the fact that Graydon will have the most votes of the four candidates. Ask students to work with a partner and use the clues to determine the number of votes that each student received in the morning and afternoon as well as the total number of votes. Ask questions to check for understanding:

- How did you find the total of number of votes that Connor received? Is there another way to determine this total?
- How did you determine 10 (or 27) more votes? Can you show me another way to find 10 (or 27) more votes?
- How did you determine 49 fewer votes? Can you use a different strategy to check your result?
- What does it mean that Graydon has twice as many votes as Peyton?
- How did you decide how many votes Graydon needed in the afternoon to have the most votes?

Have students verify their results with another group to ensure that all students have the correct answers.

	Morning votes	Afternoon votes	Total votes
Connor	68	28	96
Peyton	34	38	72
Avery	61	27	88
Graydon	76		

Hand out and read though part (b) of the task. Ask students what information is provided in the picture graph. This short discussion should focus on the notion that each ballot does not represent one vote for Connor. Next, have students work with their partners to determine the scale of the picture graph and complete the graph for the remaining candidates. Posing these questions may help to check for understanding:

- How do you know that one ballot in the picture graph does not represent one vote?
- Could the ballot represent 4 votes? How do you know?
- How many votes does each of your ballots in your picture graph represent? How do you know?
- How did you determine the number of ballots you will need in your picture graph to represent the total number of votes for Peyton and Avery? Is there a way to check this result?
- How does your picture graph show that Graydon received the most votes?

As students work on creating the picture graph, they may recognize that they do not have enough space on the graph to include the required number of ballots. This will occur if they selected an afternoon total that would make Graydon's total votes more than 120 (15 ballots representing 8 votes each). In this case, they may want to add extra space to the top of their graphs by taping sheets together. Additionally, students may determine that Graydon's total number of votes is not evenly divisible by 8. Students can be encouraged to find the closest multiple of 8 to their current total and adjust Graydon's afternoon vote count accordingly. For example, if Graydon's total number of votes is 107, students can skip count by 8 to see that 96 + 8 = 104, which is a multiple of 8, and subtract 3 from Graydon's afternoon total, or see that 96 + 8 + 8 = 112 and add 5 to Graydon's afternoon total. Students can also be encouraged to determine what fraction of a ballot could be used to represent Graydon's total and create a partial ballot. For example, if Graydon has 100 total votes, they may recognize that is half-way between 96 and 104 and state that they need 4/8, or 1/2, of a ballot.

SUMMARIZE

Display the adviser's picture that represents Connor's total number of votes. Select students to share how they determined the number of votes that each ballot represented. Sequence these strategies in order of sophistication, beginning with those who used a guess-and-check strategy, then those who looked for groups of 12, and finally those who used number facts. Ask students to share how they labeled the axes and why providing a key is important. Ask different groups of students to share strategies for how they found Connor's total number of votes from the clues. Strategies may include the use of manipulatives, place value concepts, properties of operations, and standard algorithms for addition and subtraction.

Next, ask students to share strategies for how they found Peyton's and Avery's (one at a time) total number of votes and how they determined how to represent this number on the picture graph. Strategies may include the use of manipulatives, place value concepts, properties of operations, and standard algorithms for addition and subtraction. Some students may use multiplication and division ideas of doubling and halving to combine or break apart a number into two equal addends. Strategies such as repeated addition, repeated subtraction, and skip counting may be used to determine how many ballots are needed to denote each person's total number of votes.

Ask students next to trade their picture graph with another group and verify that the group represented Graydon's total number of votes accurately by comparing their calculations based on the picture graph with the numbers in the table. Students are likely to have decided on different totals for Graydon's number of votes. To discuss the rationale behind the chosen number of afternoon votes for Graydon, ask students to share their choice and reasoning. Also ask students whether they changed their original choice for Graydon's afternoon votes once they were required to graph the totals. Those who changed their choice should be asked to explain why they chose this new number of afternoon votes. Students may share ideas similar to those found in the Explore section above.

Display two picture graphs, each of which has a different order of candidates (they may also differ in the number of votes that Graydon received). Ask students whether the order of the bars for Connor, Peyton, and Avery matter. Students should recognize that the order does not change the information in the picture graph. Next, focus on one picture graph. Ask

students one- and two-step "how many more" and "how many less" questions based on this picture graph. These questions can include the following:

- How many fewer votes did Peyton receive than Avery? How do you know? Did anyone solve it differently?
- How many total students voted in the student council election? How do you know? Did anyone solve it differently?

DIFFERENTIATION

- To support struggling students, change Graydon's morning clue of "Twice as many votes as Peyton had in the afternoon" to "38 more votes than Peyton had in the afternoon."
- To support struggling students, provide concrete manipulatives to determine each officer's total number of votes.
- To support struggling students, fill in missing components on the adviser's picture graph, such as the title, the axes, or the key that represents the scale of 8 votes per ballot.
- To extend this task, have students create a different picture graph with a scale of their choice. Initiate a discussion about how the scale affects the display or what scale they prefer. For example, a scale of 2 votes per ballot would be less efficient; however, a scale factor of 5 would result in partial ballots.
- To extend this task, ask students during the Launch portion of the lesson what are the earliest and latest possible days in November that Election Day can occur. Note that since Election Day occurs on the first Tuesday after the first Monday in November, the earliest date is November 2, and the latest date is November 8.

Maize Maze

Eloise is going on a family trip to a corn maze. Her friend tells her that she can get through the maze successfully if she uses a pattern. At the first junction, she should make a right turn. At the second junction, she should make a left turn. At the third junction, she should go straight, and she should repeat this pattern of right, left, and then straight until she gets out of the maze. Eloise uses this pattern in the corn maze and finds that she comes to 58 junctions in the maze. Does Eloise go right, left, or straight at the 58th junction? Make a poster that shows two different ways to solve this problem.

CCSSM Standards for Mathematical Practice

Practice 2: Reason abstractly and quantitatively.

Practice 8: Look for and express regularity in repeated reasoning.

CCSSM Content Standards

4.OA.A.3: Solve multi-step word problems posed with whole numbers and having whole-number answers using the four operations, including problems in which remainders must be interpreted. Represent these problems using equations with a letter standing for the unknown quantity. Assess the reasonableness of answers using mental computation and estimation strategies including rounding.

4.OA.C.5: Generate a number or shape pattern that follows a given rule. Identify apparent features of the pattern that were not explicit in the rule itself. *For example, given the rule "Add 3" and the starting number 1, generate terms in the resulting sequence and observe that the terms appear to alternate between odd and even numbers. Explain informally why the numbers will continue to alternate in this way.*

Problem Discussion

This problem applies a repeating pattern to a contextual situation: Eloise is expected to determine the 58th term in an ABC repeating pattern sequence. A repeating pattern is a cyclical repetition of an identifiable core. In this case, the pattern core is the series of moves that Eloise must make when she encounters junctions in a corn maze: right, left, or straight ahead. This problem may be solved by simply acting out or recording the 58 junctions. For example, students could use RLS to represent the core of the pattern and extend this pattern until they have determined the 58th junction:

RLS RLS RLS RLS RLS RLS RLS RLS RLS RLS RLS RLS RLS RLS RLS RLS RLS RLS RLS R

In the sequence above, the core of the pattern has been repeated 19 times, resulting in 57 terms. The 58th term is the first term in the next iteration of the core: go right. Students may use a variety of symbols or manipulatives to represent the problem, including using ABC instead of RLS, arrows, or linking cubes, among other choices.

Although this problem may be solved in a concrete way, the prompt, "Find two different ways to solve this problem," asks students to extend beyond this, potentially to more abstract and quantitative methods (SMP 2). There are multiple ways that students may do this, including multiplication, division involving interpreting remainders (4.OA.A.3), and examining an arithmetic sequence (4.OA.C.5).

This task's connections to multiplication involve skip counting and finding multiples of 3 that are near the targeted term in the sequence. Students might skip count by 3 through 57 and identify this as the last in the core sequence, *straight ahead*. The term immediately following must then be the first in the core sequence, *right*. Similarly, students might identify a close multiple of 3 (e.g., 3 × 15 = 45, 3 × 19 = 57, or 3 × 20 = 60) or a combination of multiples of 3 (e.g., 3 × 10 + 3 × 9 = 57) and then use this multiple of 3 to work forward or backward to the targeted term. For example, if a student realizes that 60 is a multiple of 3 and thus means *straight ahead*, she can work backward to 59 *left* and 58 *right*.

This task also allows students an opportunity to make sense of a remainder in this context. Computing 58 ÷ 3 yields an answer of 19 with a remainder of 1 (19 R 1). The 19 in the quotient corresponds to the number of iterations of the pattern core, which ultimately can be disregarded in solving the problem. The 1 from the quotient, however, indicates the number of terms past the last full iteration of the sequence, making the final move a right turn.

Finally, this task provides an opportunity to think about arithmetic sequences in context, as well as an opportunity to identify patterns in reasoning and commonalities between terms (SMP 8). Students might be asked, "At which junctions does Eloise go right (left, straight)? What do these numbers have in common?" In the case of the right turns (term numbers 1, 4, 7, 10, 13...), they are all 1 more than multiples of 3 (or 2 less than multiples of 3). Turning left and going straight ahead have similar arithmetic sequences increasing by 3 (the number of terms in the core sequence) but starting at different quantities. Left turns will always take place when the term number has a remainder of 2 when divided by 3, and going straight ahead will always occur at term numbers that are multiples of 3. Thus, the students may find some regularity or repetition in their reasoning, enabling them to generalize an informal rule about when specific turns will take place.

STRATEGIES

- Students may build and extend the pattern through the 58th term by using manipulatives, such as linking cubes.
- Students may symbolically represent and extend the pattern through the 58th term (e.g., RLS..., ABC...).
- Students may use a two-column table to identify the correspondence of terms to the directional moves (left, right, or straight ahead) that are made.
- Students may skip count by 3's to determine the 57th term and extend the pattern to the 58th term.
- Students may identify multiples of 3 that are close to the 58th term and either work backward or forward through the pattern sequence to determine the targeted term.

- Students may divide (58 ÷ 3) and use the remainder to determine how far into the next pattern sequence the 58th term is.
- Students may, when prompted, generate arithmetic sequences to determine terms that are right turns (1, 4, 7, 10…), left turns (2, 5, 8, 11…), and straight ahead (3, 6, 9, 12…).

MISCONCEPTIONS/STUDENT DIFFICULTIES

- If students have limited experience with repeating patterns, they may struggle to extend the pattern sequence.
- Students may not recognize how skip counting by 3's is connected with the pattern sequence.
- Students may find it challenging to skip count by 3's beyond familiar multiples.
- Students may identify multiples of 3 that are close to the targeted term but not understand how to use this multiple to find other near terms.
- If using division, students may not understand how the quotient and remainder (19 and 1) connect with finding the 58th term.
- Students may struggle to skip count by 3's when starting with a quantity that is not a multiple of 3.

LAUNCH

Begin the lesson by asking students if any of them have ever been to a corn maze. Students may have limited experience with either growing corn or corn mazes, so sharing images from the Internet may be useful to help them develop understanding of the context. If students have experience with corn mazes, have them share these with the class. Otherwise, have students share experiences with other mazes that they have encountered themselves (e.g., at museums, in gardens, in puzzle books). If these are also limited, students may discuss video games that have maze-like contexts. Display a maze (either referred to by a student or an online image), and discuss three terms related to mazes: *start*, *junction*, and *end*. Ask students to identify the start and end of the displayed maze. Then discuss the term *junction* as it relates to mazes: a place where the user needs to make a decision about the route. Junctions may also be called *forks*, *decision points*, or *nodes*.

As needed, read the problem aloud to the students. Review the directions left, right, and straight. If possible, demonstrate these options on the display of a maze. Ask the students what is meant by the pattern of turns taken in the maze. Have students discuss with a neighbor what is meant by a pattern and what this means for the turns that Eloise takes in the corn maze. Ask two or three students to share their ideas about what it means for this pattern to continue. Students may say, "It means Eloise is going to have to make those turns over and over," or "She is going to go right, left, straight, right, left, straight, and so on, until she is out of the maze." Pose the following questions about repeating patterns to help them clarify their understandings:

- What is the part that repeats?
- What turn should come after a right turn? Left? Straight? How do you know?

Consider writing students' responses on a visual display.

Finally, ask students to articulate what they are trying to solve in this problem. Have students discuss what it means to have two ways of solving a problem. Ask students to think about possible approaches to solving the problem and discuss their ideas with a neighbor.

EXPLORE

Assign students to groups of three to work on this task. It may be helpful to create groups with a combination of students who tend to think concretely and students who tend to think abstractly. The presence of more abstract thinkers may facilitate the group's use of multiplication or division to solve the problem by a second, less concrete method.

As students work on this task, circulate throughout the room, taking note of the groups' strategies. Ask questions to check for their understanding of the task and the strategies they are using:

- How are you using the manipulatives to help you solve the problem?
- Can you explain how these symbols on your paper relate to the problem?
- How do you know that Eloise will make a right turn at the 58th junction?
- I see that you are skip counting by 3, or identifying multiples of 3. What is important about those numbered junctions?
- How are you using a multiple of 3 to find out what Eloise should do at the 58th junction?
- Why did you decide to divide 58 by 3?
- How does the 19 in your quotient relate to the problem? How does the remainder 1 relate to the problem?

Students may consider extending the pattern through the 58th term by using two different representations (e.g., using 58 linking cubes and writing RLS through the 58th term) as two different ways of solving the problem. Encourage students to see these as similar, and challenge them to consider how skip counting, multiplication, or division might apply to this scenario.

If students have successfully identified two ways of solving the problem, one of which is a more abstract method, challenge them with one of the following questions:

- Can you list all the junctions where Eloise should make a right turn? What do you notice about these numbers? (Adapt this question for left turns or straight-ahead moves.)
- Is there a way that you can determine the move for any numbered junction? What if the junction number is too big to build, like junction 1143?

These questions may provide the impetus for students to explore the generalizations of the junction numbers and their relationships to multiples of 3.

Finally, ask students to prepare a poster illustrating their two different methods for solving this problem.

SUMMARIZE

Allow students ten minutes to engage in a gallery walk through the classroom to observe other groups' strategies for solving the problem. Provide each group with a set of sticky notes, and encourage them to provide feedback on the sticky notes for the work that they see. Specific prompts may encourage students to focus their comments and questions on the mathematical aspects of the posters:

- What strategies do you see that are similar to the way that you solved the problem?
- What questions do you have about a group's method for solving the problem?
- What do you like about how these students showed their mathematical thinking?
- What similarities do you see between your strategy and that of another group?

After students have seen and commented on other groups' posters, allow two or three minutes for students to return to their own posters and reflect on the feedback they received.

Engage in a class discussion that summarizes the different ways to solve the problem. Discuss the methods in the following order:

1. Using manipulatives, symbols, or a table to extend the pattern through the 58th term
2. Skip counting by 3 to find a multiple of 3 that is close to the targeted term number
3. Finding multiples of 3 that are close to the targeted term number and counting forward or backward to the 58th term
4. Using division to find that there are 19 iterations of the pattern with 1 remaining junction

Ask questions to connect the strategies explicitly with one another. For example, if students used skip counting by 3, ask, "Where do you see these multiples of 3 in the other group's work with linking cubes?" If students used division, ask, "What does the 19 in the quotient mean, and where do we see that number in the linking cubes and the multiplication strategy?" and "Why is that 1 so important? Where do we see the 1 in the multiplication strategy?"

If students have been challenged to generalize about the junction numbers where specific turns take place, have them share their findings. If this was not a part of the Explore section, consider sending groups back to work, having some groups work on right turns, other groups work on left turns, and one or two groups work on straight-ahead moves. (Part of the Summarize section may have already generated a generalization for the straight ahead junctions as multiples of 3. If so, this may be skipped.) Reconvene the class for another class discussion that identifies the arithmetic sequences for each of the moves and discusses ways to describe the sequences effectively.

DIFFERENTIATION

- The targeted term may be lowered for students. A note of caution: Lowering the number may facilitate students' use of more concrete strategies (extending the pattern by using manipulatives or symbols), instead of encouraging abstract strategies.

- If students have used skip counting or multiplication to solve the problem, challenge them to solve the problem by using division. If students have used division to solve the problem, challenge them to connect their solution strategy to multiplication or skip counting.

- Challenge students to identify the sequence of junction numbers that correspond with a particular move at a junction: right, left, or straight ahead. Ask them to generalize a rule for the type of move (e.g., right turns are 1 more than a multiple of 3).

- Challenge students to figure out how they could determine what type of move any junction number would signal. (For students who have learned the divisibility test for 3, there is an interesting potential connection here as well.)

- Ask students to write their own problem that involves a different number of elements in the core of their repeating patterns. Have them share their problems with classmates.

TRICK OR TREAT?

Evan is going trick-or-treating with a large group of his friends. He notices several things:

- When they go to a door in groups of 2, there is always 1 trick-or-treater left to go alone.
- When they go to a door in groups of 3, there is always 1 trick-or-treater left to go alone.
- When they go to a door in groups of 4, there is always 1 trick-or-treater left to go alone.
- When they go to a door in groups of 5, everyone is included in a group.

How many trick-or-treaters could be in Evan's group? Create a poster that demonstrates and explains how you solved this problem.

CCSSM STANDARDS FOR MATHEMATICAL PRACTICE

Practice 1: Make sense of problems and persevere in solving them.

Practice 3: Construct viable arguments and critique the reasoning of others.

CCSSM CONTENT STANDARDS

4.NBT.B.6: Find whole-number quotients and remainders with up to four-digit dividends and one-digit divisors, using strategies based on place value, the properties of operations, and/or the relationship between multiplication and division. Illustrate and explain the calculation by using equations, rectangular arrays, and/or area models.

4.OA.B.4: Find all factor pairs for a whole number in the range 1–100. Recognize that a whole number is a multiple of each of its factors. Determine whether a given whole number in the range 1–100 is a multiple of a given one-digit number. Determine whether a given whole number in the range 1–100 is prime or composite.

4.OA.C.5: Generate a number or shape pattern that follows a given rule. Identify apparent features of the pattern that were not explicit in the rule itself. *For example, given the rule "Add 3" and the starting number 1, generate terms in the resulting sequence and observe that the terms appear to alternate between odd and even numbers. Explain informally why the numbers will continue to alternate in this way.*

PROBLEM DISCUSSION

This task is an excellent opportunity for students to engage in making sense of problems (SMP 1). Students need to develop an understanding that the number of trick-or-treaters in the whole group will have a remainder of 1 when divided by 2, 3, and 4. However, when the number of trick-or-treaters in the whole group is divided by 5, there are none left over (4.NBT.B.6). This remainder (or lack of remainder in the case of division by 5) needs to be connected contextually to the problem as students make sense of the situation.

This is a measurement division situation (or repeated subtraction), in which the given number of trick-or-treaters in a group is peeled away from the larger group to determine the number of groups, rather than being distributed into a given number of groups to determine the size of each group (partitive division; fair sharing) (3.OA.A.2). Thus, the remainder is the trick-or-treater who is left when the maximum number of groups has been formed of a specific size.

Once students have made sense of the problem, they can use many different strategies to solve it, presenting an opportunity for them to defend their own strategy and critique others (SMP 3). These multiple strategies also provide an opportunity to make connections among multiplication, division, factors, multiples, divisibility tests, number patterns, remainders, and subtraction (4.NBT.B.6, 4.OA.B.5, and 4.OA.C.6). Although most students may come up with 25 trick-or-treaters as the answer, the problem has multiple answers. Students who are ready for a challenge may be asked to find other solutions; adding 60 (the least common multiple of 2, 3, 4, and 5) to a solution will generate another correct solution. Correct solutions therefore include 25, 85, 145, 205…, although 25 may be the most viable solution in the context of the problem.

STRATEGIES

- Students may use trial and error with multiples of 5 to identify a multiple of 5 for which the number that is 1 less is a multiple of 2, 3, and 4. For example, the student may see whether the number 14 (1 less than 15) is divisible by 2, 3, and 4. When this does not work, he may proceed to the next multiple of 5.

- Students may use logic to determine that the solution must have a 5 in the ones place. This conclusion results from logical deduction:
    ○ The solution must be a multiple of 5, so it has a 0 or 5 in the ones place.
    ○ Any number with a 0 in the ones place is a multiple of 2, so it cannot be the solution.
    ○ Therefore, the solution must have a 5 in the ones place.
  Students may then use trial and error with multiples of 5 with a 5 in the ones place.

- Students may make lists of multiples for 2, 3, 4, and 5. Then they will check the lists for a number that is common to them for 2, 3, and 4 but also has a number that is one greater on the list of the multiples of 5.

- Students may identify the least common multiple (12) of 2, 3, and 4 (although they might not use this terminology). They may then check values that are 1 greater than the LCM and its multiples (12, 24, 36… ; 13, 25, 37…) to see whether the value is divisible by 5.

- Students may make lists of numbers that are 1 greater than multiples of 2, 3, and 4. For example, numbers that are 1 greater than multiples of 4 are 1, 5, 9, 13…. (Note how this strategy aligns with content standard 4.OA.C.6.) Then the students may check these lists for a common value and check to see whether this value is a multiple of 5.

- Students may use divisibility tests (e.g., if the sum of the digits of a number is a multiple of 3, then that number is also divisible by 3) in connection with the strategies above to determine whether numbers are multiples of 2, 3, 4, or 5.

Misconceptions/Student Difficulties

- Students may not recognize the significance of there being 1 trick-or-treater left over when the trick-or-treating friends are grouped by 2's, 3's, and 4's.
- Students may identify a multiple of 5 that satisfies limited criteria. For example, 15 would work for 1 trick-or-treater left over when the trick-or-treating friends are grouped in 2's, but it does not satisfy the criteria for 3's and 4's.
- Students may identify a value that works for 1 trick-or-treater left over when the trick-or-treating friends are grouped by 2's, 3's, and 4's, but is not a multiple of 5 (e.g., 13).
- Students may assume that any multiple of 2 is also a multiple of 4.
- Students may overgeneralize divisibility tests. For example, they may apply the test for divisibility by 3 to divisibility with other numbers, such as 4.

Launch

Begin this task by asking students how many of them are considering going trick-or-treating on Halloween. Ask them if they will be going with a group of friends, with family members, or by themselves. If students have trick-or-treated in groups before, ask them if any groups ever split into smaller groups, and when this might be a good idea.

Display the problem statement of Trick or Treat? to the class. Have a student read the brief introduction aloud. Then, call on different students to read aloud the four criteria of the problem and the question. Ask students to turn to one another and discuss what they know about the problem. Have students share their ideas. If they mention something that is explicitly stated in the problem, underline that portion of the problem. If they mention something that is an inference from the problem, (e.g., the number of trick or treaters is a multiple of 5; 1 more than a multiple of 3; not a multiple of 4), make sure that these are recorded for students to see.

Next, ask students to turn to a different neighbor and discuss *what they want to know*. Have students share their thoughts, highlighting particular questions that are not the final answer. For example, a student might indicate that a question they would like to answer is, "What are multiples of 5?" This question is not the final answer, but it may be a question that they need to answer along the way to finding their final solution, depending on the method they choose.

Finally, have students think to themselves about one last question: "What is your plan?" Do not have them share their thoughts in response to this question until they are in their respective working groups.

Explore

Assign students to small groups to work on this task. First, ask students to share their ideas for a plan, one at a time, without interruptions. Then direct them to discuss which of these plans they would like to pursue. Remind them that they may decide to switch plans as they work, especially if their initial plan is not fruitful.

Allow groups several minutes to work together before asking questions. Circulate throughout the room, and listen to all initial ideas about solving the task. As students continue their work or try different solution strategies, ask questions that check for understanding:

- What do these grouping explanations mean to you?
- What does it mean to you when it says that 1 trick-or-treater is left to go alone?
- What do you know about the solution?
- Why are you considering multiples of 5?
- How you do you know that you're looking for an odd number?
- How did you decide that value would not work?
- How do you know that the solution has to have a 5 in the ones place?
- Can you show me why you think 25 is the answer?

If students have come up with an incorrect solution, ask them to explain their reasoning. If they do not realize their misconception as they explain, ask them to demonstrate how their solution works, using linking cubes or another manipulative. Read each criterion aloud as they demonstrate, as needed.

Provide poster paper and markers so that students can create posters that illustrate and explain their solution strategies. Explain to the class that they will be doing a gallery walk, so the posters should clearly justify their reasoning for students who may have used a different solution strategy.

SUMMARIZE

Allow ten minutes for students to circulate throughout the classroom to look at posters. When students come back together as a group, ask them to turn and talk with a neighbor about any number patterns that were important to either their own solution strategy or other groups' solution strategies.

Call on students to share number patterns that were important. As students share a particular number pattern, write this pattern on the board (e.g., 1, 5, 9, 13…) and examine what is important about the pattern. For example, with the number pattern listed above, each of these values will leave a remainder of 1 when divided by 4. Be sure to ask students to connect the number pattern to the problem itself, explaining how the numbers are important to the criteria of the task. Other patterns that might be included in this discussion follow:

- 1, 3, 5, 7, 9…
- 1, 4, 7, 10, 13…
- 5, 10, 15, 20, 25…
- 2, 4, 6, 8, 10, 12…
- 3, 6, 9, 12, 15…
- 4, 8, 12, 16…
- 12, 24, 36, 48…

Next to each number pattern itself, record the meaning of the pattern in relation to the context of the problem if this will be helpful for students. Finally, ask students how the number patterns were used to solve the problem. Emphasize connections between the number patterns as students discuss their strategies. For example, how is the number 12 important in the final three patterns? As the patterns are presented, ask students to share how these patterns connect with their strategies, if applicable, thereby reviewing the strategies that groups used.

To conclude, discuss the following two Standards for Mathematical Practice: "Make sense of problems and persevere in solving them" (SMP 1) and "Construct viable arguments and critique the reasoning of others" (SMP 3). Ask students questions to explore how they demonstrated SMP 1 in their work on this task:

- What was helpful to you as you tried to make sense of this problem?
- What was tricky about understanding this problem?
- How did you or your group demonstrate perseverance in this problem?

In addition, ask students what challenges they faced as they used the skills called for in SMP 3:

- What did you have to keep in mind as you put together your poster?
- What did you find helpful or confusing about others' posters?
- How might you do your poster differently next time?

DIFFERENTIATION

- For students who struggle to make sense of the remainder of 1 for this situation, allow them to find a value with an unspecified remainder when divided by 2, 3, and 4. That is, the number of trick-or-treating friends will have *some* trick-or-treaters left over when groups of 2, 3, or 4 are made. Solutions for this modification are 5, 25, 35, 55, 65….
- Challenge students to find other solutions. Also ask them if they can find a pattern in the solutions (they are 60 apart), how many solutions there are (an infinite number of solutions—although not contextually), and how this pattern relates to the numbers in the problem (adding the least common multiple of 2, 3, 4, and 5).
- Challenge students to write a similar problem of their own.

NATIVE AMERICAN HERITAGE

Native Americans used symbols for a variety of purposes. They used them to give directions to hunting locations, represent important rituals, and identify specific clans. These symbols varied from tribe to tribe and appeared on a variety of objects used by a tribe. Below are some symbols used by Native Americans of different regions of the United States.

a. Sort the symbols into categories based on the types of angles in the symbol.

b. Sort the shapes on the basis of the presence or absence of perpendicular and parallel lines.

c. Sort the shapes on the basis of the number of lines of symmetry.

CCSSM Standards for Mathematical Practice

Practice 6: Attend to precision.

CCSSM Content Standards

4.G.A.1: Draw points, lines, line segments, rays, angles (right, acute, obtuse), and perpendicular and parallel lines. Identify these in two-dimensional figures.

4.G.A.2: Classify two-dimensional figures based on the presence or absence of parallel or perpendicular lines, or the presence or absence of angles of a specified size. Recognize right triangles as a category, and identify right triangles.

4.G.A.3: Recognize a line of symmetry for a two-dimensional figure as a line across the figure such that the figure can be folded along the line into matching parts. Identify figures exhibiting line symmetry and draw lines of symmetry.

Problem Discussion

This task requires students to analyze, compare, and describe two-dimensional shapes on the basis of angle and line properties as well as line symmetry. Students are first asked to sort Native American symbols into categories based on the types of angles (4.G.A.1) that they have. The number of categories for this part of the task could range from four (i.e., right, acute, obtuse, none) to eight or more (i.e., right, acute, obtuse, none, acute and obtuse, acute and right, obtuse and right, all three types of angles). Next, students sort the symbols on the basis of the presence or absence of parallel and perpendicular lines (4.G.A.2). Again, the number of categories could vary, depending on how students choose to categorize the symbols. The third part of this task asks students to focus on line symmetry (4.G.A.3). Students may simply sort the symbols into two categories based on the notion of "symmetrical" or "not symmetrical," or they could use more than two categories and focus on the number of lines of symmetry that a symbol exhibits.

In the Summarize section of this task, students are encouraged to use precise language as well as attend to precision when identifying each attribute of a symbol (SMP 6). For example, some symbols have slightly curved lines. Students should be asked to determine whether these slight curves form an angle. Through rich classroom discussions of the attributes of the symbols, students will begin "to move from describing shapes using their own informal geometric vocabulary to using the formal mathematical vocabulary for characteristics and properties of shapes" (NCTM 2009a, p. 49). In addition, students will be asked to create their own personal symbol that uses the mathematical vocabulary in this task (e.g., *acute angle, parallel line, perpendicular line, line of symmetry*). Using these terms and concepts to construct examples will help "students form richer concept images connected with verbal definitions" (Common Core Standards Writing Team 2013, p. 15).

Strategies

- Students may use Venn diagrams (templates are available at More4U) to help sort and organize the symbols.
- Students will sort on the basis of the presence or absence of each type of angle.
- Students will sort on the basis of the number of each type of angle and will place a symbol into a category based on which type of angle is most prevalent.
- Students will sort on the basis of the presence or absence of each type of line property.
- Students will sort on the basis of the number of each type of line (perpendicular or parallel) and place a symbol into a category based on which type of line (perpendicular or parallel) is most prevalent.
- Students will sort on the basis of the presence or absence of a line of symmetry.
- Students will sort on the basis of the number of lines of symmetry.

Misconceptions/Student Difficulties

- Students may not attend to precision. For example, they may see slightly curved lines as acceptable, resulting in a curved "vertex" of an angle.
- Students may struggle to sort symbols that have more than one type of angle or type of line property.

- Students may find one line of symmetry and not look for other lines of symmetry.
- Students may think a rectangle has lines of symmetry along the diagonals.

Launch

Ask students if they know when Native American Heritage Day is celebrated. If no one offers the correct day, share with them that in 2008 President George W. Bush signed a law designating the Friday after Thanksgiving as Native American Heritage Day. Also share that this day is intended to encourage all Americans to learn more about the history and contributions of Native Americans. Other facts that could be shared are listed below:[1]

- Approximately 60 percent of the current foods we use were first cultivated thousands of years ago by Native Americans.
- Native American villages were often located near waterways and trails. Some of these sites became modern cities, such as St. Louis, Chicago, Kansas City, Pittsburgh, and Detroit. In addition, about half of our states have Native American names.
- More than 24,000 Native Americans served in World War II. Perhaps the best known of these were the Navajo code talkers, volunteers who used the Navajo language to encrypt tactical messages. This code was never broken.

Explain to students that Native Americans used many symbols to communicate with one another. A variety of activities can make use of these symbols. For example, students can be assigned a symbol and asked to think about its meaning and why Native Americans may have chosen it to represent the particular object or idea. If possible, students should be given time to use the Internet to investigate their symbol. They may be surprised to find that the symbol represents more than just the physical object. For example, the bear track symbolizes not only the bear but also characteristics associated with a bear, such as power, courage, and unpredictability. Information available at many websites regarding the interpretation of Native American symbols can help students understand the deeper meaning behind each symbol. Next, ask students to describe their Native American symbol to a partner, using geometric vocabulary such as *acute*, *obtuse*, *right*, *perpendicular*, *parallel*, *symmetric* and *line of symmetry*. Create a class list of terms that were used during these discussions.

Explore: Sorting by angles

Hand out the task and the Venn diagram templates. Allow students to cut out the symbols so they can sort them into categories. Ask students to complete part (a) of the task by sorting the symbols into categories based on the types of angles in the symbol. Once students have finished, ask them to share their categories with a partner. During this time, partners should verify that each shape fits the category identified. Ask the following questions to check for understanding:

- How do you know this angle is acute, right, or obtuse?

[1]Adapted from curricular material from the Montana Office of Public Instruction (http://opi.mt.gov/pdf/IndianEd/Resources/IdeaBook.pdf) and the Minnesota Department of Education (http://education.state.mn.us/MDE/EdExc/StanCurri/Curri/).

- Are there other types of angles in this shape?
- How did you decide on your categories?

SUMMARIZE: SORTING BY ANGLES

To summarize, ask students to share some of the categories they created for part (a). As students share their categories, ask them to discuss how they decided if an angle was acute, right, or obtuse. Students should be encouraged to share an example of a symbol that meets each category. The rest of the class should be asked to find a different symbol that would meet these criteria and show a partner to verify.

EXPLORE: SORTING BY TYPES OF LINE SEGMENTS

Ask students to complete part (b) of the task and sort the shapes based on the presence or absence of perpendicular and parallel line segments. Once students have finished, ask them to share their categories with a partner. During this time, partners should verify that each shape fits the category identified. Ask the following questions to check for understanding:

- How did you decide on your categories?
- How do you know that these line segments are parallel (or perpendicular)?
- Do any shapes have both parallel and perpendicular line segments? How did you sort those?

SUMMARIZE: SORTING BY TYPES OF LINE SEGMENTS

Next, ask students to share categories for part (b). Again, students should give an example of a symbol that fits each category. The rest of the class should be asked to find a different symbol that would meet the criteria and show a partner to verify. This discussion could connect the overlap between the right angle category (or categories) from part (a) with those symbols that have perpendicular line segments. This discussion could also focus on common shapes such as rectangles. Symbols composed of a rectangle will have perpendicular line segments, right angles, and parallel line segments. Students can then be asked what other quadrilaterals have these attributes in order to focus on comparing and classifying shapes (e.g., all squares have perpendicular line segments, right angles, and parallel line segments, so all squares are rectangles).

EXPLORE: SORTING BY LINES OF SYMMETRY

Ask students to complete part (c) of the task and sort the shapes on the basis of the number of lines of symmetry. Once students have finished, ask them to share their categories with a partner. During this time, partners should verify that each shape fits the category identified. Ask the following questions to check for understanding:

- How do you know that this shape has a line of symmetry? Can you show me the line of symmetry?
- Do any shapes have more than one line of symmetry? How do you know?

Summarize: Sorting by lines of symmetry

Ask students to share categories for part (c). Again, students should give an example of a symbol that fits each category. The rest of the class should be asked to find a different symbol that would meet the criteria and show a partner to verify. During this discussion, have students focus on the definition of a line of symmetry as a line across a two-dimensional figure "such that the figure can be folded along the line into matching parts" (4.G.A.3) or a line that divides a two-dimensional figure into two halves that are mirror images of each other.

To conclude this task, students should create a symbol to represent something important in their life that illustrates at least two of the vocabulary terms from the sorting task (e.g., types of angles, parallel or perpendicular line segments, line of symmetry). They should then describe their symbol and the meaning behind it, using these mathematical terms. Students should also be encouraged to write a definition in their own words for each of the mathematical terms they used in creating their symbol. These definitions can be shared with the whole class.

Differentiation

- To support struggling students, encourage the use of tracing paper to help in determining whether an angle is acute, right, or obtuse.
- To support struggling students, encourage the use of tracing paper or a reflective surface to verify whether a symbol has a line of symmetry.
- To extend this task, ask students to create symbols with specific attributes, such as "two right angles and two lines of symmetry."
- To extend this task, ask students to describe their symbol to a friend as the friend tries to draw the symbol on the basis of the description.
- To extend this task, ask students to sort the symbols into two groups: polygons and not polygons.
- To extend this task, ask students to look at the symbols in terms of rotational symmetry.
- To extend this task, ask students to use a protractor to measure the angles in their own or other Native American symbols.

Community Garden

The local community garden has just finished the final harvest of the season. The participants will be delivering vegetables to three different charities that will distribute them to families in need. Each charity delivers vegetables to a different number of families. Using the information below, help the community garden determine how many pounds of each vegetable to deliver to each of the charities.

Charity A feeds 13 families.

Charity B feeds 17 families.

Charity C feeds 24 families.

Vegetable	Pounds
Carrots	152.34
Peas	43.53
Green Beans	62.07
Peppers	127.26
Squash	98.9

CCSSM Standards for Mathematical Practice

Practice 4: Model with mathematics.

CCSSM Content Standards

5.NBT.B.5: Fluently multiply multi-digit whole numbers using the standard algorithm.

5.NBT.B.6: Find whole-number quotients of whole numbers with up to four-digit dividends and two-digit divisors, using strategies based on place value, the properties of operations, and/or the relationship between multiplication and division. Illustrate and explain the calculation by using equations, rectangular arrays, and/or area models.

5.NBT.B.7: Add, subtract, multiply, and divide decimals to hundredths, using concrete models or drawings and strategies based on place value, properties of operations, and/or the relationship between addition and subtraction; relate the strategy to a written method and explain the reasoning used.

5.NF.B.6: Solve real world problems involving multiplication of fractions and mixed numbers, e.g., by using visual fraction models or equations to represent the problem.

Problem Discussion

This task provides students with an opportunity to apply their mathematical understanding to model a real-world situation. In alignment with SMP 4, "Model with mathematics," students will "identify important quantities in a practical situation" by "making assumptions and approximations to simplify a complicated situation" (NGA Center and CCSSO 2010, p. 7). For example, students must consider how many people are served by each charity. This will require assumptions about the number of people in each family. Students may also realize that an exact answer is not necessary in this context and use approximations by rounding to the nearest whole pound of each vegetable. Students may also use concrete manipulatives to represent each pound of a given vegetable, drawings, or equations to model this situation (SMP 4). For example, using rounding and a visual model (see below), a student may find the number of carrots needed for charity A by reasoning, "Charity A feeds 13 families, which is about 1/4 of the families because the charities feed 54 families all together, and 13/54 is close to 0.25. So I need to find 1/4 of 152. I did this by dividing an area of 152 into four equal parts, so one part is 152 divided by 4, or 38 pounds of carrots to charity A."

$$152$$

| 38 | 38 | 38 | 38 |

$$152 \div 4 = 38$$

This task also builds on the strategies that students use for calculating quotients of whole numbers (4.NBT.B.6), such as place value strategies, properties of operations, drawings, and estimation. The task requires students to apply this knowledge to perform the four operations with decimals to the hundredths (5.NBT.B.7). However, because this task is a modeling task, students may choose to solve it by using strategies that do not require the use of operations on decimals. For example, students may choose to solve the task by rounding each decimal to the nearest whole number and applying operations with whole numbers (5.NBT.B.5 and 5.NBT.B.6). Students may also choose to determine what fraction of the vegetables each charity should receive, thereby applying operations on fractions to solve the task (5.NF.B.6). As a result, the Summarize section of the task requires students to present their problem-solving processes and focus on the reasonableness of their answers (SMP 4). This section also draws students' attention to the relationship between multiplication and division of whole numbers as well as decimals.

STRATEGIES

- Students may distribute the same number of pounds of each vegetable to each of the three charities.

- Students may use a trial-and-error method to determine how many pounds of vegetables each charity should receive and check the reasonableness of each of their answers. For example, a student may guess that charity A should get 3 pounds of carrots and charity B should get 3.5 pounds, and then see how many pounds are left over for charity C (5.NBT.B.7).

- Students may make assumptions about how many people are in each family and then use the number of people (or a rounded value of the number of people) rather than the number of families. For example, if they assume that each family has 4 people, charity A would feed 4 × 13, or 52 people. They may use 50 or 52 in their calculations (5.NBT.B.5 and 5.NBT.B.6).

- Students may round the number of pounds of each vegetable to the nearest whole number and use operations with whole numbers to find the answer (5.NBT.B.5 and 5.NBT.B.6).

- Students may find a unit rate (pounds of vegetables per one family) and then use multiplication to find the number of pounds for each charity (5.NBT.B.5 and 5.NBT.B.6).
- Students may determine what fraction of the vegetables each charity will receive. For example, they may say that charity A should receive 13/54 of the vegetables, which is roughly 1/4 (5.NF.B.6).
- Students may determine the amount that each charity will receive as a decimal representation and use that number to multiply decimals. For example, they may find that charity A should receive 13/54, or approximately 0.24 of the pounds of each vegetable. Therefore, 0.24 × 152.34 results in approximately 36.56 pounds of carrots for charity A (5.NBT.B.7).

MISCONCEPTIONS/STUDENT DIFFICULTIES

- Students may have difficulty organizing their solution process because of the open nature of the task.
- Students may not realize that they can use rounding to simplify the calculations.
- Students may perform the incorrect operation, such as multiplying the number of families by the total number of pounds.
- Students may have difficulty making assumptions, such as the number of people in each family or whether or not the vegetables need to be distributed equally among the three charities.

LAUNCH

Ask students to work with a partner or small group to brainstorm about the types of foods that are grown in a garden. Next, ask students to share their experiences with gardening. If students are unfamiliar with community gardens, explain to them that some towns or cities designate a plot of land in which volunteers plant and harvest goods that are distributed to the greater community. Often this food is delivered to local charities for distribution to people or families in need.

To elicit prior knowledge related to decimal operations, provide students with the following data from a recent harvest at a community garden:

159.3 pounds of beans

158.7 pounds of melons

140.5 pounds of squash

128.8 pounds of tomatoes

Ask students first to estimate the total number of pounds of food harvested. Did all students have the same estimate? Next, ask students to find the exact total number of pounds, using addition strategies for decimals. Have students compare their estimate with the actual amount. How close were they? How did estimation help students check the reasonableness of their actual answer? In the context of this situation, would an estimate be a valid answer?

Students may share that their estimate was very close to the actual amount, and therefore, in this situation, an estimate is valid. They may also see that the difference between their estimate and the actual answer was a few tenths of a pound, which is very little weight, and thus they may see that the estimate was an efficient process to use to obtain a reasonable answer.

Explore

Hand out the task to pairs of students. Give students a few minutes to read the task and formulate a plan to solve it. Because of the openness of this task, students will need to make assumptions based on the context. These assumptions may include the following:

- The number of people in each family may vary; thus the pounds per family may be different. Students could deal with this in a variety of ways, including the following:
  - Assume the size of a typical family and multiply by the number of families that each charity serves to find the total number of people served by each charity
  - Vary the size of the families in each charity's region and find the total number of people that each charity serves
- Rounding to the nearest whole number of pounds is an efficient strategy.

After students have devised their plan, have them implement it. Ask questions to check for understanding:

- Tell me about those numbers. How did you determine how many pounds of carrots charity A should receive? Why did you perform that operation? What assumptions did you make?
- If charity A served more families, would the pounds of carrots allotted for these families be smaller or larger than the pounds of carrots allotted for the families served by the other charities? Why?
- Do you think all the other groups will get the same answer that you did? Why or why not?
- Show me the equations that you used to model this situation. What do those numbers represent? How did you know you needed to perform those operations?
- How many pounds of carrots will each family served by charity A, B, and C receive?
- Why do you think your answer is reasonable?
- How many total pounds of vegetables will each charity receive?

After students have implemented their plan, tell them that they will need to be prepared to present it, including their assumptions and calculations.

Summarize

Select pairs to share their assumptions and findings. These pairs can be selected in order of sophistication of their strategies, starting with those who used whole number operations, then moving to those who used operations with fractions, and finally selecting those who used operations with decimals. As students share their assumptions, ask the class whether everyone made similar assumptions. You may want to have students share their drawings, strategies, and equations. Focus attention on the reasonableness of the answers, how the assumptions played a role in the final answer, and the differences in the answers found.

Ask questions to check for understanding:

- Based on your assumptions, why do you think your answer is reasonable?
- Did anyone use similar assumptions but end up with different answers? Why? Are both answers reasonable?
- Referring to your equation, how can you explain what the numbers in it represent?
- This group rounded to the nearest whole number, and that group used decimals. How do their answers compare? Do you think both answers are reasonable? Why?

The Summarize section of the lesson should connect the strategies used by each pair instead of focusing on a single correct answer. Students should be encouraged to grapple with how their assumptions and their calculations affect the precision of the answers.

DIFFERENTIATION

- To support struggling students, have students round the number of pounds to the nearest whole number before beginning the task.
- To support struggling students, provide manipulatives for students to use to distribute pounds to the three charities.
- To extend this task, ask students to write a letter to the community garden organizers to explain how many pounds of each vegetable each charity should receive. This letter should include the assumptions that students made in order to find their answer.
- To extend this task, ask students to consider how many pounds of each vegetables families of different sizes should receive.
- To extend this task, ask students to determine how much it would cost to purchase the same number of pounds of each vegetable at a local grocery store. Students could then consider how much money was spent by the community garden to plant and harvest the same amount of food.

FOLDING THE FLAG

At the end of a Veterans Day ceremony honoring all those who served in the armed forces of the United States, the U.S. flag was folded into a triangle resembling a tricornered hat worn by colonial soldiers. Use the flag-folding directions below to determine what fraction of the area of the whole flag is represented by the folded triangle. (Diagrams for steps 1–5 in the flag-folding process appear in the Problem Discussion.)

   Step 1. Fold the lower striped section of the flag lengthwise over the blue field of stars.
   Step 2. Fold the folded edge up to the open edge.
   Step 3. Create a triangle by folding the bottom right corner to the open edge.
   Step 4. Fold the triangle over to create a new triangle.
   Step 5. Continue the triangular folding until the entire length of the flag is folded. When the flag is completely folded, only a triangular blue field of stars will be visible.

CCSSM Standards for Mathematical Practice

Practice 7: Look for and make use of structure.

Practice 8: Look for and express regularity in repeated reasoning.

CCSSM Content Standards

5.NF.B.4a: Interpret the product $(a/b) \times q$ as a parts of a partition of q into b equal parts; equivalently, as the result of a sequence of operations $a \times q \div b$. *For example, use a visual fraction model to show* $(2/3) \times 4 = 8/3$, *and create a story context for this equation. Do the same with* $(2/3) \times (4/5) = 8/15$. *(In general,* $(a/b) \times (c/d) = ac/bd$.*)*

Problem Discussion

The official standard ratio of the hoist (width) to fly (length) of the U.S. flag is 10 to 19, as outlined in Executive Order 10798, issued in 1959. For other purposes, there are several other common hoist-to-fly ratios, including 2 to 3, 3 to 5, and 5 to 8. In this activity, students will model the customary flag-folding ceremony, using a 4-inch by 6-inch flag replica that has a 2 to 3 hoist-to-fly ratio to find the fractional part of the area of the U.S. flag after it has been properly folded into a triangle. This task extends students' reasoning about area concepts related to 4.MD.A.3, which calls for applying area and perimeter formulas to rectangles using whole number quantities. Students will also apply initial concepts of multiplying a whole number by a fraction (5.NF.B.4a) as they consider the length of one side of the resulting folded isosceles right triangle as $1/4$ of the width of the original rectangular flag, as shown in steps 1 and 2 (below and at the top of the next page):

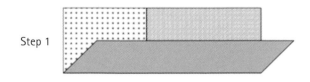

Step 1

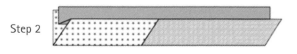

Step 2

As the flag is folded, students will draw the new figure on dot paper and record the new dimensions of the folded flag. After step 1, the hoist (width) of the flag will be cut in half, from 4 inches to 2 inches. In step 2, the hoist is cut in half again from 2 inches to 1 inch. At this point, students may notice that going from 4 inches to 1 inch could have been accomplished in a single step by taking $1/4$ of the original width of 4 inches, and they may relate this to multiplying a whole number by $1/2$ and then taking $1/2$ again (5.NF.B.4a). In either case, students will be able to interpret the product $1/4 \times 4$ as "1 part of a partition of 4 inches into 4 equal parts." Using the flag as a visual fraction model, students can also verify that the product of $1/4 \times 4$ is equivalent to the operation of $1 \times 4 \div 4 = 1$. Students can also use the visual fraction model to verify that the product $1/2 \times (1/2 \times 4)$ is equivalent to $1/4 \times 4$ by using the associative property of multiplication.

When completing steps 3 and 4, students will use their flag model to "prove" that during the folding procedure they created an isosceles right triangle by noting that two of these triangles can be joined at the hypotenuse to make a square. To "prove" that the triangle is an isosceles triangle, students must reason that folding the bottom right corner of the resulting rectangle up to the open side of the rectangle (step 3) creates a right triangle. To justify that the triangle is a right triangle, students must use geometric reasoning relating the attributes of squares and rectangles (5.G.B.3). For example, each time the rectangular flag is folded, a new rectangle is formed (steps 1 and 2 above). Therefore, during step 3, students will notice that there is a right angle at the bottom right corner of the 1-inch by 6-inch rectangle, and once this is folded to form the first triangle (step 3), a right angle is produced. Additionally, this fold also forces the adjacent sides that form the right angle of the triangle to be congruent. That is, in step 3, vertex A is a right angle, and the side lengths AB and AC are congruent.

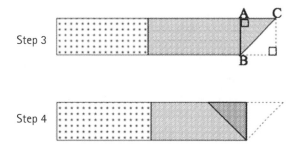

Step 3

Step 4

If students unfold their triangles after step 4, they will see a small rectangle formed by two isosceles right triangles (in bold below).

Students will then be able to reason that this small (bold) rectangle is indeed a square by using attributes of rectangles and squares (5.G.B.3). For example, students may note that this small rectangle is formed by two isosceles right triangles. Hence, all four sides of the rectangle are congruent, making the rectangle a square.

As students continue to fold the flag (step 5), they will notice that the right isosceles triangle is repeated in each fold. All the triangles are the same size and shape as the first right triangle, which was created during step 3. (Because of the thickness of the paper, a small amount of paper may be left over, and it can simply be tucked behind the isosceles right triangle. This often occurs during official flag folding ceremonies since the dimensions of official flags do not always result in precise triangles. Using thin paper, such as wax paper, allows the creases to be visible and reduces the thickness of the resulting triangles.)

Step 5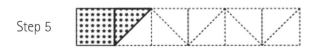

During the Summarize section, students can use the structure (SMP 7) of unfolded flags that they previously recorded to determine that a total of 48 right triangles completely tile the flag, making the final right triangle $1/48$ of the total area of the flag. They may also reason that the 1-inch by 6-inch rectangle formed in step 2 was folded into 12 right triangles or 6 small squares, and since there are four 1-inch by 6-inch rectangles that compose the whole flag, the whole rectangle of the flag has a total of 12 × 4 = 48 right triangles, or 6 × 4 = 24 small squares, in the whole rectangle. These counting strategies also make the final right triangle $1/48$ of the total area of the flag.

Students may also look at the structure of their folded flag (SMP 7) to find the area of the resulting right triangle—not by using the formula for the area of a right triangle (6.G.A.1) but by recognizing that the area is half the area of the 1-inch by 1-inch square created in steps 3 and 4. Students will then verify that the area of one right triangle would result in a total flag area of 24 square units (SMP 3). For example, after decomposing the rectangle into 4 rows of 12 triangles, each having an area of $1/2$ square units, students will notice that this is the same as 4 rows of 6 square units, resulting in an area of 24 square units, making the area of one small square $1/24$ of the total area of the flag. Students can then reason that the area of one right triangle, which is half of the area of one small square, is $1/2 × 1/24 = 1/48$ square units. To extend the idea of units of area measure, students can be encouraged to consider tiling a region with a different two-dimensional unit (Clements and Sarama 2009). For example, students may notice that there are 12 triangles in each of the four 1-inch by 6-inch rectangles, which results in 48 triangles, each having an area of $1/2$ square inches. Therefore, the area of the whole flag is 48 × $1/2$, or 24 square inches.

In the Summarize section, students will be asked to use repeated reasoning to make generalizations about the area of the triangle resulting from folding flags of various dimensions (e.g., 3 by 5, 6 by 10, 8 by 12). For example, when folding a 6-foot by 10-foot flag, the resulting isosceles right triangle formed in step 3 will have legs of length $1^1/2$ feet ($1/4$ of 6 feet can be found by taking half of 6 and then half of 3). Students can generalize this pattern and recognize that for a flag of any dimensions, the resulting right isosceles triangle will have legs whose length are one-fourth of the shorter length of the flag (SMP 8).

STRATEGIES

- Students may open up their flag after each fold to determine how the size of one rectangle compares with the original rectangle (steps 1 and 2).
- Students may stop folding after step 4 because they notice that the pattern of isosceles right triangles will repeat, and instead they may draw in the triangles or simply record those folds on the dot paper.
- Students may choose to use the dot paper to record their folds and measurements instead of folding the paper.
- Students may notice that there are 12 triangles in the 1 × 6 rectangle, recognize that 4 of these small rectangles fit into the entire 4 × 6 flag, and compute 4 × 12 to determine that there are 48 triangles in the entire flag.
- Students may use the unit squares formed after step 4 to determine that there are 24 unit squares in the flag, and each triangle is half the area of a square, so there are 48 triangles in the flag.
- Students may use the resulting isosceles right triangles, each with an area of $1/2$ square units, to verify that the area of the whole flag is 24 square units by finding $48 × 1/2$ (48 triangles, each with an area of $1/2$ square units) or $1/2 × 48$ (the area of the rectangle is $1/2$ of 48 square units).

MISCONCEPTIONS/STUDENT DIFFICULTIES

- Students may not be precise and purposeful when folding, and this will result in unequal rectangles and triangles.
- Students may have difficulty recording their folds on the dot paper.
- When recording their triangle folds, students may neglect to record the vertical folds that occur after each diagonal fold.
- Students may focus only on the 1 × 4 small rectangle and determine that the triangle represents $1/12$ of the area of the entire flag.
- Students may struggle to find the length of a side of the triangle.
- Students may not recognize that the area of one triangle is half the area of one of the squares made in steps 4 and 5.

LAUNCH

Begin the lesson by asking students if they know why Veterans Day is celebrated in the United States. Veterans Day honors those who have served or are currently serving in the U.S. armed forces. This federal holiday is observed on November 11, which marks the anniversary of the signing of the armistice that ended combat in World War I. Explain to students that in a local Veterans Day celebration, a stadium is divided into six equal-sized sections of seats, arranged in the shape of a hexagon. Five of the sections are for the five branches of the U.S. military (Army, Marine Corps, Navy, Air Force, and Coast Guard), and one section is reserved for people who support veterans but may not have served in one of these five branches of the military. In the center of the stadium, a large U.S. flag is on display.

Have students work with a partner to determine the center of such a stadium. Distribute a regular hexagon (a template is available at More4U) to each pair of students, and explain that one partner will fold the hexagon to find its center while the other will record the folds on paper. Ask students to follow the steps below and respond to the questions shown.

1. Fold the hexagon to make a trapezoid. Record this new shape on your paper. How do you know it's a trapezoid? What fraction of the hexagon is the trapezoid?

2. Fold the trapezoid two times to make a triangle. Record each fold using dashed lines. Without unfolding—

   ○ What fraction of the trapezoid is one triangle? How do you know?
   ○ What fraction of the hexagon is one triangle? How do you know?

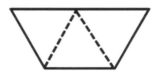

Next, explain to students that there is typically a flag-folding ceremony at Veterans Day celebrations. Ask students to share what they know about this ceremony or whether they know how to fold a U.S. flag properly. A flag-folding video from the Internet may be shown to help students see the steps involved and the precision required to fold a flag appropriately. The ceremony requires that the rectangular flag be folded thirteen times (the same as the number of stripes in the flag representing the thirteen original colonies), resulting in a right triangle that represents the tricornered hat worn by colonial soldiers. Tell students that depending on the dimensions of the flag, some extra fabric may need to be tucked away to produce a single triangle. Explain that the standard dimensions of the U.S. flag forms a hoist (width) to fly (length) ratio of 10 to 19. To help students in understand this ratio language, you might display a rectangular flag with a hoist dimension of 10 inches and a fly dimension of 19 inches in the classroom. Also highlight the fact that different dimensions are used for the U.S. flag, and one common size has a hoist-to-fly ratio of 4 to 6 (or 2 to 3). Tell students that they will be working with this common ratio to represent the U.S. flag.

EXPLORE

Give partners the handout, including the 4-inch by 6-inch flag to cut out, along with one or two sheets of one-inch dot paper. Have students work together to fold the flag according to the outlined procedure, recording their steps on the dot paper. If students are unfamiliar with dot paper, have them work together to create a representation of the 4-inch by 6-inch flag (see below). If students struggle to understand the directions, the whole class can be led through each step to ensure that all students fold correctly and record their folds on the dot paper. Explain to students that precise, tight folds are important to reduce error but even so, eliminating it entirely is almost impossible. Thus, their drawings on dot paper will serve to represent ideal, precise folds. Have students work with their partners to label lengths of each shape on the dot paper (see the example below). Next, have students determine what fraction of the flag's area that the area of the final triangle represents. As students work, ask questions to check for understanding:

- What shape is the flag now that you have folded it once? Twice? How do you know?
- What is the area of the flag after you have folded it once? Twice? How do you know?
- What kind of triangle is this? How do you know? Is there a more specific way to name that triangle?
- What shape is this shape (indicate one of the squares)? How do you know?
- What is the length of one side of the triangle? How do you know?
- What is this angle measure (indicate the right angle)? How do you know?
- How many of these unit squares are in the entire flag? How many of the triangles are in the entire flag? How do you know?

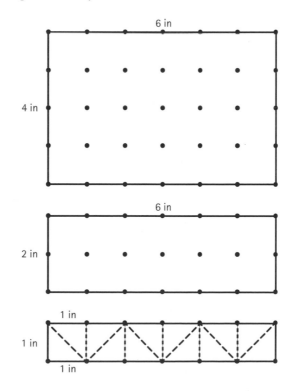

Summarize

To summarize, ask students to share their diagrams with another group. During this time, students should discuss how they found the fraction of the flag's area represented by the right triangle. Bring students back together and ask them to share their answers. Select a pair who counted 24 square units to verify that the triangle represented $1/48$ of the area of the whole flag. Next, select a pair who counted 48 triangles to verify that the triangle was $1/48$ of the area of the whole flag. If students used only one or neither of these verification strategies, ask students to consider the merits of each omitted strategy. For example, ask, "Could we count the squares (or triangles) to find what fraction of the flag's area is represented by the triangle?" As students share their strategies, ask questions to check for understanding:

- What shape was the flag after you folded it once? Twice? How do you know?
- What fraction of the flag's area was represented after you have folded it once? Twice? How do you know?
- What kind of triangle was created by the fold in step 3? How do you know? Is there a more specific way to name that triangle?
- What is the length of one side of the triangle? How do you know?
- What shape resulted from steps 3 and 4 (point to one of the squares)? How do you know?

Differentiation

- To support students who struggle to make precise folds, assist them in the folding process or provide paper that is easy to fold, such as wax paper.
- To support students who struggle to make precise folds, allow them to use the diagrams from the Launch or Explore section.
- To support students who struggle to determine the leg lengths of the isosceles right triangle, ask them the dimensions of the rectangle after each fold.
- To support students who struggle to determine the leg lengths of the isosceles right triangle, have them open up their flag and iterate their partner's triangle along the short edge to see that four triangles would fit along this side, resulting in the triangle having a leg length of 1 inch.
- To extend the task, students can research what each fold of an official flag-folding ceremony represents.
- To extend the task, students can use the same strategies to determine the fractional part of the area that the folded right triangle represents in a standard U.S. flag with a hoist-to-fly ratio of 10 to 19.

SETTING SAIL

On September 6, 1620, the *Mayflower* set sail to America. The ship set out from Plymouth, England, to Virginia but landed on the tip of what is now known as Cape Cod, Massachusetts, on November 11, 1620. Use the coordinates and the grid below to create a map of both the intended route and the actual route of the *Mayflower* and determine which route was longer.

Intended Route: (16, 5), (0, 0)

Actual Route: (16, 5), (14, 4), (9, 3), (7, 4), (5, 4), (2, 2)

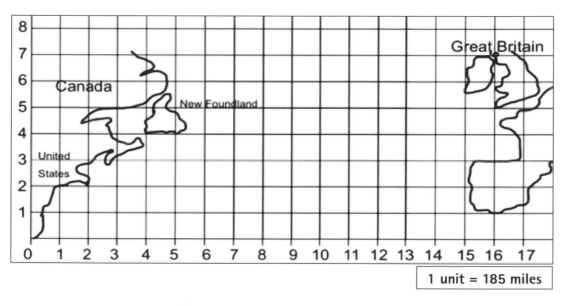

1 unit = 185 miles

CCSSM STANDARDS FOR MATHEMATICAL PRACTICE

Practice 5: Use appropriate tools strategically.

Practice 6: Attend to precision.

CCSSM CONTENT STANDARDS

5.G.A.1: Use a pair of perpendicular number lines, called axes, to define a coordinate system, with the junction of the lines (the origin) arranged to coincide with the 0 on each line and a given point in the plane located by using an ordered pair of numbers, called its coordinates. Understand that the first number indicates how far to travel from the origin in the direction of one axis, and the second number indicates how far to travel in the direction of the second axis, with the convention that the names of the two axes and the coordinates correspond (e.g., *x*-axis and *x*-coordinate, *y*-axis and *y*-coordinate).

5.G.A.2: Represent real world and mathematical problems by graphing points in the first quadrant of the coordinate plane, and interpret coordinate values of points in the context of the situation.

Problem Discussion

This task requires students to graph points on a coordinate plane to estimate the total distance of two routes from England to America. Extending their work from grade 4, where they represented quantities on a number line by using a given measurement scale (4.MD.A.2), students will now investigate the meaning of both the *x*-coordinate and the *y*-coordinate (5.G.A.1) in the context of the voyage of the *Mayflower*. Students will use the given coordinates of two routes—the intended route and the actual route—to create a map, and they will use a given measurement scale to compare the estimated length of both routes (5.G.A.2). As students locate the ordered pairs and share their maps with others, they will need to attend to the vocabulary related to the coordinate plane, including *x-axis, x-coordinate, y-axis,* and *y-coordinate* (SMP 6).

"To construct a full understanding of Cartesian coordinate systems, merely having students locate points is not enough; students must also analyze distances between points and how those distances can be determined from coordinates" (Battista 2007, p. 890). This task gives students the opportunity to grapple with how to determine the distance between points and, ultimately, the length of each route. The intended route is a single straight line. The actual route will require students to measure and combine a number of segments measured in units corresponding to 185 miles each. Students may choose to round these measurements to the nearest whole, half, quarter, or eighth of a unit. Further, to determine the diagonal distances, students may need to create their own rulers, with units that are the same length as one of the units on the map. This decision will allow for a discussion about precision in measurement (SMP 6, SMP 5).

To find the length of the intended route, students will need to attend to precision by specifying the units of measurement to find the straight-line distance between the points (16, 5) and (0, 0) to the nearest whole unit or fractional unit. On the map, this length is between 16.5 and 17 units, resulting in a distance of approximately 3,052.5 miles to 3,145 miles. To find the length of the actual route, students may use their rulers to measure the five line segments that connect the ordered pairs to the nearest whole or fractional unit. Starting from (16, 5) to (14, 4) on the map, and continuing through the segments that mark the route, these lengths are approximately 2.25 units, 5 units, 2.25 units, 2 units, and 3.5 units, respectively, for a total distance of 15 units, or approximately 2,775 miles. During the Summarize activities, it will be important to highlight the fact that the distance between (7, 4) and (5, 4) is exactly 2 units, but the diagonal distance between the points (9, 3) and (7, 4) is slightly longer than 2 units, since the length unit is not the same as the diagonal length. Likewise, the distance between the points (14, 4) and (9, 3) is slightly longer than 5 units. Questions that could be discussed may include "How will rounding to the nearest half unit rather than quarter unit affect the length that you find for the route?" and "Is the distance between the opposite corners of one square unit the same as one unit?"

Strategies

- Students will count the lines to plot points, such as 7 lines over and 4 lines up when plotting the coordinate point (7, 4), without recognizing the numbers labeled on each axis.

- Students will use previously plotted points to plot nearby points more efficiently.
- Students will use the numbers labeled on each axis to locate a given point. For example, to plot the point (7, 4), a student will visually find the intersection of the vertical line labeled "7" and the horizontal line labeled "4."
- Students will use the point (7, 4) to locate the point (5, 4) by moving 2 units to the left of (7, 4).
- Students will round to the nearest whole, half, or quarter inch when measuring the lengths of the routes.
- Students may use a ruler to measure from point (16, 5) to point (2, 2) to find an estimate of the actual route.
- Students may create their own ruler (or use a standard ruler to determine approximately how many centimeters or inches long a unit is) to measure each segment of the actual route and sum these distances to find the total distance of the actual route.
- Students may determine how many units long each journey is by creating their own ruler (or use a standard ruler to determine approximately how many centimeters or inches long a unit is) and multiply that number by 185 to find the length of each route in miles.

MISCONCEPTIONS/STUDENT DIFFICULTIES

- Students may reverse the x- and y-coordinates in an ordered pair. For example, they may move up first instead of to the right first.
- Students may not recognize that coordinate points are given in reference to the origin, or (0, 0).
- Students may miscount the lines by counting the starting line (x- or y-axis) instead of focusing on the interval between the lines. For example, to plot the point (5, 4) students may count the y-axis as 1 and land on an x-coordinate of 4 instead of 5.
- Students may not begin at the origin each time that they plot a new point.
- Students may not realize that the diagonal distance between two points is not the same length as the sum of the vertical and horizontal distances between two points.
- Students may not understand that the diagonal of one square unit is not equivalent to 1 unit.
- Students may not know how to use a ruler accurately.

LAUNCH

Ask students if they know when the *Mayflower* set sail for America. Have students share information about this ship. Some interesting facts may include the following:

- The ship carried 102 passengers and about 25 crew members.
- The ship had three masts.
- The ship was approximately 110 feet long and 25 feet wide.
- The ship was often used as a cargo ship rather than a passenger ship.

Next, explain to students that they will be given a map of the *Mayflower*'s voyage. Ask students to share what they know about the important features of a map. Students may mention a variety of features, including—

- colors;
- cities, towns, states, counties;
- roads or highways;
- rivers, lakes, oceans;
- a key, indicating the measurement scale.

If students do not mention the key on the map, elicit this information by asking them how to find the actual distance between two cities on a map.

EXPLORE

Distribute the task to students. Provide tools, such as tracing paper and rulers. Read through the task with students and ask them to identify the general location of Plymouth, England, and the meaning of *origin* in the context of this problem. Ask students to identify the key for the map. Have students talk with a partner about the meaning of the key (1 unit = 185 miles). Students should share their understanding of the key with the entire class.

Have students work individually to plot the coordinates for the intended and actual routes. Ask questions to check for understanding about the coordinate plane:

- Which coordinate indicates how many units to the right you need to move?
- Where is the origin? What are the coordinates of the origin?
- How did you find where to place the point (5, 4)? What do these coordinates mean in relationship to the origin?
- What is another way that you could identify the location of the coordinates (7, 4)? Focus on using the origin and another point on the graph, such as (5, 4) or (9, 3).
- How many units apart are the points (7, 4) and (5, 4)? Is that the same as the number of units from (9, 3) to (7, 4)? How do you know?

Next, have students work with a partner to check their ordered pairs for the two *Mayflower* routes. Partners should also share strategies for how they located the points on the coordinate grid.

Finally, have students work individually to find the distance of each route by using the map key. Ask questions to check for understanding related to measurement concepts:

- How did you find the distance between these two points?
- How will rounding to the nearest half unit rather than quarter unit affect the length of the route?
- How did you find the distance in miles? Is there another strategy that you could use to find this distance?

SUMMARIZE

Begin by focusing on the strategies for plotting the ordered pairs to create the map. Ask students to share their strategies for locating points on the coordinate grid. If possible, display the coordinate grid, and allow students to demonstrate how they plotted points. Ask whether someone used a different method for locating the ordered pairs. For example, a student may plot (7, 4) by going to the right 7 units and up 4 units from the origin or use the previously plotted point (9, 3) and move two units to the left and one unit up from there. Other students may just look at the number labels on the axes and find the junction of the vertical line labeled "7" and the horizontal line labeled "4."

Ask students to share with their partners how they measured the distance between points. This will allow students to compare different units of measurement and to verify the appropriate use of their method. For example, students may have created their own ruler, partitioned into units that are the same size as in the map key, or they may have used a standard ruler to approximate the length of one unit on the map. Other students may attend to precision by further partitioning their ruler into half or quarter units. Once both partners agree with each other's process, ask students to compare their total distances for each route. Students could also be asked to record their lengths on the board to show the range of solutions. Ask pairs to discuss why their answers for a particular route are not exactly the same. If they are the same, ask students to discuss why this may have occurred.

Next, ask a few students to share their strategies for finding the lengths of the two routes. Ensure that students identify the size of the unit used to measure the distance between points. Rounding to the nearest quarter unit will be more precise than rounding to the nearest whole unit. Ask students questions to focus on the precision of their answers. For example, "Which gives a more precise length, measuring to the nearest whole unit or measuring to the nearest quarter unit? Why?"

To conclude the task, ask students to reflect on the strategies that they used and those that were shared by their peers. Have students record how they would change their solution process on the basis of this reflection and why. If they would not change any processes, have them explain why not.

DIFFERENTIATION

- To support struggling students, have students work with a partner to solve the task.
- To support struggling students, give them just two points (beginning and ending points) for each route.
- To support struggling students, provide a ruler partitioned into the same units as the map scale.
- To support struggling students, have them round their measurements to the nearest unit.
- To extend this task, ask students to work with a partner to determine how many days the *Mayflower* voyage lasted. Using this information, students could determine how many miles the *Mayflower* traveled each day if it traveled the same number of miles every day.

- To extend this task, use the known measurements of the *Mayflower* deck (approximately 80 feet by 20 feet), and ask students to estimate how many students would fit on the deck of the *Mayflower*.

WINTER

For many students, winter is a time for cold temperatures and snow. However, winter is also a season for diverse celebrations, from New Year's to Valentine's Day to Mardi Gras. The tasks in this chapter engage students in multiple mathematical domains through these contexts.

Snow fights and winter festivals serve as contexts for two of the third-grade tasks, Snowballs and Winter Fest. Snowballs asks students to divide snowballs equally among three forts and then consider factors of a number for sharing the snowballs equally among the children at each fort. In Winter Fest, students calculate time spent by two boys in festival activities. Between these two tasks with outdoor settings is Boxing Chocolates, a task in a Valentine's Day context that invites third graders to explore relationships between area and perimeter.

The first fourth-grade task provides an opportunity for students to model multiplication and division in the context of donating pairs of gloves for others to wear in cold weather. Two holiday-related tasks are then offered for fourth graders. One is linked to New Year's resolutions and asks students to reason about the size of fractional parts of a year. Saint Patrick's Day supplies the backdrop for the other task as students determine angle measures that would complete a circle.

The fifth-grade tasks begin with a task that requires students to find the difference between two mixed numbers that have different denominators and represent measurements of accumulated snow. The second task engages students in addition and subtraction of fractions in the context of a Mardi Gras parade. The third task challenges fifth graders to calculate volume and make conversions between measurements in a snow removal setting.

MATERIALS FOR EACH TASK, INCLUDING HANDOUTS, ARE AVAILABLE FOR DOWNLOADING AND PRINTING ON NCTM'S WEBSITE AT NCTM.ORG/MORE4U BY ENTERING THE ACCESS CODE ON THE TITLE PAGE OF THIS BOOK.

SNOWBALLS

A group of children made 120 snowballs to share equally among their 3 snow forts. Each fort has a different number of children. If each child at a fort must have the same number of snowballs as every other child at that fort, how many children and snowballs can be at each fort? Use pictures and equations to show your thinking.

CCSSM STANDARDS FOR MATHEMATICAL PRACTICE

Practice 7: Look for and make use of structure.

Practice 8: Look for and express regularity in repeated reasoning.

CCSSM CONTENT STANDARDS

3.OA.A.3: Use multiplication and division within 100 to solve word problems in situations involving equal groups, arrays, and measurement quantities, e.g., by using drawings and equations with a symbol for the unknown number to represent the problem.

PROBLEM DISCUSSION

This task requires students first to share 120 snowballs equally among three snow forts. Once this is done, students will need to determine how many children can be at each fort so that each child at each fort has the same number of snowballs but all the forts have different numbers of children. Students can use a variety of multiplication and division strategies to determine that each fort will have 40 snowballs. These strategies may include drawings, skip counting, basic facts, properties of whole numbers, equations, arrays, area models, and so on (3.OA.A.3). For example, students may use a tape diagram or area model (as shown below) to partition the 120 snowballs into three equal-sized piles, recognizing that 40 snowballs would be in each of those piles.

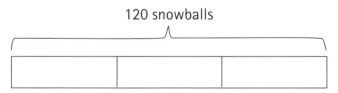

Using concrete manipulatives such as blocks or counters, students may create an array consisting of 12 rows of 10 and recognize that this array can be partitioned into three equal-sized parts, with each consisting of 4 rows of 10, resulting in 40 snowballs for each fort (as shown on the next page).

Once students have determined that each fort will have 40 snowballs, they will need to recognize that the number of children at each fort must be a factor of 40 in order for each child to have the same number of snowballs. To solve this part of the task, students should again be encouraged to use a variety of strategies or visual representations. For example, a student may guess the number of children at a fort and then use a drawing or manipulatives to distribute the 40 snowballs equally among these children to determine whether each child has the same number of snowballs. Students may also identify two factors whose product equals 40, such as 8 and 5, and use this fact to conclude that one fort could have 8 children, each with 5 snowballs, or 5 children, each with 8 snowballs.

As students share their representations and solution strategies during the Summarize section, they will be encouraged to find all possible combinations of the number of children at each fort and the total number of snowballs that each child will have. The table below shows all the possibilities for sharing the 40 snowballs at one fort among different numbers of children.

Number of children in a fort	Number of snowballs per child
1	40
2	20
4	10
5	8
8	5
10	4
20	2
40	1

STRATEGIES

- To divide 120 by 3, students may use a guess-and-check strategy by choosing a number of snowballs and subtracting that number three times to see if the result is zero.
- To divide 120 by 3, students may skip count by 3's until they reach 120.
- To divide 120 by 3, students may use a sharing interpretation and distribute snowballs to each fort, either one by one or in groups, such as groups of 10 snowballs.
- To divide 120 by 3, students may use an area model or array model to partition the 120 snowballs into three equal-sized piles (see the area and array models above).
- To divide 120 by 3, students may use the distributive property, reasoning, for example, 90 + 30 = 120, and 90 ÷ 3 = 30 and 30/3 = 10, so each fort needs 40 snowballs.
- To determine the number of children in each fort, students may use a guess-and-check strategy—for example, choosing 3 children and then determining whether 40 snowballs can be shared equally among 3 children.

- To determine the number of children in each fort, students may use multiplicative reasoning to identify factors that multiply to 40. For example, students may realize that $40 = 5 \times 8$ and use those factors to determine that one fort could have 5 children with 8 snowballs each.

- To determine the number of children in each fort, students may use properties of whole numbers, such as the commutative property. For example, they may reason that if 5 children, each with 8 snowballs, is a solution, then 8 children, each with 5 snowballs, will also be a possibility.

- To determine the number of children in each fort, students may use properties of whole numbers, such as the associative property. For example, they may reason that $40 = 5 \times 8 = 5 \times (4 \times 2) = (5 \times 4) \times 2 = 20 \times 2$, so 20 children, each with 2 snowballs, would be a viable solution.

Misconceptions/Student Difficulties

- Students may struggle to divide 120 by 3.
- Students may have difficulty understanding that each of the three forts has a different number of children. Likewise, they may have difficulty understanding that the children at each of the three forts have different numbers of snowballs.
- Students may have difficulty finding all the factor pairs of 40.
- Students may have difficulty organizing their work and keeping track of what the numbers represent in the context of the task.

Launch

Ask students if they have ever made snowballs or snow forts. If they have, ask them to describe how they made their snowballs and snow forts. Tell students that today they will be solving a task involving snowballs and snow forts. Pose the following question: "Twenty-four snowballs need to be shared equally among four children. How many snowballs does each child get?" Ask students to work with a partner to draw a picture and create an equation to solve this problem. Have students share their drawings and equations with the class. Possible equations may include $24 \div 4 =$ ___ , $4 \times$ ___ $= 24$, $4 + 4 + 4 + 4 + 4 + 4 = 24$, and so forth. For each of the equations, ask students to explain what each number represents in the context of the problem and how their drawing supports their equation. Students may draw four piles or columns and distribute the 24 snowballs one or more at a time until all 24 have been shared equally to represent $24 \div 4 =$ ___ . Students may represent $4 \times$ ___ $= 24$ with 4 groups of 6 snowballs. Finally, if students create the equation $4 + 4 + 4 + 4 + 4 + 4 = 24$, a discussion about what each 4 means in the context of the problem should include reasoning such as the following: "One 4 would represent giving one snowball to each of the 4 children until there are no snowballs left. We can do this 6 times, so each child has 6 snowballs."

Explore

Hand out the task and read it to students. Tell them that they will first work with a partner to determine how many snowballs each fort has. Reread the first sentence and ask students to share what they know about the problem and what they need to determine to solve it.

 66 Problem Solving in All Seasons

Provide manipulatives for students to use to solve this task. As students work with a partner to determine how many snowballs each fort has, ask questions to check for understanding:

- How many forts are there? How many snowballs are there all together?
- Could each fort have 10 snowballs? Would there be any snowballs left over? How do you know?
- What do the numbers in your equation represent?

If students finish this part of the task early, ask them to use a different equation or strategy to prove their solution. Before moving on to the next part of the task, allow students to share their equations and solution strategies with the class. Possibilities are identified in the Strategies list.

Next, reread the second part of the task and ask students to share what they know about the problem and what they are trying to find. Use this time to clarify that each fort has 40 snowballs but does not have the same number of children. As students work with a partner to determine how many children can be in each fort, encourage them to draw pictures and use equations to represent their thinking. Ask questions to check for understanding:

- How many children do you think could be at the first fort? Would each of them get the same number of snowballs? How do you know? Can you draw a picture to show this?
- Could one of the forts have 3 children? How do you know?
- What do the numbers in your equation represent?
- How are the numbers in your equation represented in your drawing?

If students finish this part of the task early, ask them whether they can find other numbers of children that could be at one of the forts.

SUMMARIZE

Ask partners to work with another group to discuss their solutions. After a few minutes, bring the groups together to share their equations and drawings with the whole class. Begin by asking one group to share the number of children in one of their forts. Ask how many snowballs each child has in this fort and how they determined this solution. Did any other groups have this solution for one of their forts? If so, ask whether they used a different equation or drawing to determine the number of snowballs that each child has. Repeat this process until all solutions have been shared (see the table in the Problem Discussion).

To conclude, ask students to write about which fort they would most like to be in and why. Also, ask them to write about which fort they would least like to be in and why.

DIFFERENTIATION

- To support struggling students, reduce the number of snowballs to 60.
- To support struggling students, change the second part of the task to have the same number of children in each fort.

• To extend this task, ask students to investigate how doubling or tripling the number of total snowballs affects the number of solutions.

Boxing Chocolates

The Chocoholic Chocolate Company wants to create three different boxes of chocolates for Valentine's Day with 20, 32, and 36 chocolates in a box. The chocolates will be arranged in a rectangle, and the space needed for each chocolate is one square inch. The company would like to order ribbon to go all the way around the sides of each box, and the managers are wondering whether they can order the same length of ribbon for all three boxes. Is this possible? Explain why or why not. Use a diagram to support your reasoning.

CCSSM Standards for Mathematical Practice

Practice 1: Make sense of problems and persevere in solving them.

Practice 3: Construct viable arguments and critique the reasoning of others.

CCSSM Content Standards

3.MD.D.8: Solve real world and mathematical problems involving perimeters of polygons, including finding the perimeter given the side lengths, finding an unknown side length, and exhibiting rectangles with the same perimeter and different areas or with the same area and different perimeters.

Problem Discussion

Boxing Chocolates is a task that asks problem solvers to think simultaneously about the ideas of area and perimeter of rectangles. Mathematically, the idea is to find rectangles with different dimensions and areas (boxes holding different quantities of chocolates) but with the same perimeter (requiring the same amount of ribbon to go around the sides of the box) (3.MD.D.8). This task's approach may be somewhat different from traditional tasks involving area and perimeter variation, so students will need to make sense of the context and what the task is asking them to do (SMP 1). Students will also need to persevere until they have proven that there are arrangements that will create boxes with the same perimeter, and doing so may involve exhausting the possibilities for area arrangements for each quantity (SMP 1).

Multiple rectangular arrangements are possible for each of the quantities of chocolates in this task. The dimensions of these arrangements correspond to the factor pairs for the numbers. The table on the next page identifies the arrangements for a box of 20 chocolates and provides a visual representation of each arrangement and its resulting perimeter (length of ribbon needed). Note that each of these dimensions could be reversed, demonstrating the commutative property of multiplication.

Boxes of 20 chocolates (area = 20 square inches)		
Dimensions	Visual representation	Perimeter
1 × 20		42 inches
2 × 10		24 inches
4 × 5		18 inches

The tables below identify the possible dimensions for the other two quantities of chocolates, without visual representations.

Boxes of 36 chocolates (area = 36 square inches)	
Dimensions	Perimeter
1 × 36	74 inches
2 × 18	40 inches
3 × 12	30 inches
4 × 9	26 inches
6 × 6	24 inches

Boxes of 32 chocolates (area = 32 square inches)	
Dimensions	Perimeter
1 × 32	66 inches
2 × 16	36 inches
4 × 8	24 inches

The three tables demonstrate a single shared perimeter of 24 inches. Thus, if the 20 chocolates are arranged in a 2 × 10 array, the 32 chocolates are arranged in a 4 × 8 array, and the 36 chocolates are arranged in a 6 × 6 array, all the boxes will have the same perimeter: 24 inches.

Students will need to demonstrate their reasoning and justify their arrangements of chocolates in boxes that all have the same perimeter (SMP 3). They may need to make sense of other students' reasoning and critique others' solutions that may not align with their own solution or solution strategy (SMP 3). To do so, students will need to think about perimeter and area flexibly and accurately.

STRATEGIES

- Students may use 20, 32, and 36 square tiles to create rectangular arrangements. Then they will count or calculate the perimeter for each arrangement.
- Students may find factors of 20, 32, and 36 to find rectangular arrangements for each quantity. Students may then use the factor pairs to determine the perimeter for each arrangement.
- Students may identify a possible perimeter for one box of chocolates and check to see whether this perimeter will work for each of the other quantities of chocolates.
- Students may identify all factor pairs for each quantity of chocolates and determine which pairs of factors result in the same sum (half of the perimeter).

MISCONCEPTIONS/STUDENT DIFFICULTIES

- Students may confuse the concepts of area and perimeter and attempt to identify arrangements of chocolates that result in perimeters of 20, 32, and 36 inches.
- Students may attempt to arrange the required number of square tiles (e.g., 20 tiles) as a rectangular border, as illustrated below.

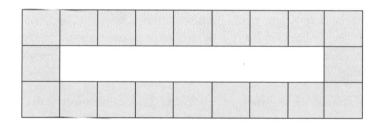

- Students may identify the factor pairs for each quantity of chocolates but decide that these will not result in the same perimeters, since none of the factor pairs are common across chocolate quantities.
- Students may fail to identify all factor pairs for the required number of chocolates and thus miss one of the possibilities that would result in a common perimeter.

LAUNCH

Begin this task by asking students what they know about gifts that are commonly given for Valentine's Day. Students may mention flowers, jewelry, cards, chocolates, and so on. Ask students what kinds of chocolates they have seen in grocery stores or other shops, marketed specifically for Valentine's Day. How do they know that these chocolates are for Valentine's Day? What makes them stand out as special for the holiday? A brief history of heart-shaped chocolate boxes may be shared at this time; this information is easily found online.

Explain to students that they will be working on a task that involves concepts that they have worked on in third grade: area and perimeter. Display the task for the students, and ask them to read it to themselves silently. Then have them reflect with a partner or in a small group: What do they know from the problem? What do they want to know?

Bring the class back together; have students share with the whole group what they have just discussed. Display in a list things that they know from reading the problem. In a separate list, identify any questions they might have. If some of these are questions that the whole class would benefit from discussing (perhaps because they indicate misconceptions or confusion), resolve these issues as a class before moving to the Explore portion of the lesson.

EXPLORE

Ask students to work in groups of two or three on this task. Provide each group with 75–100 square tiles, string, rulers, and any other tools that they request for their work. Allow the groups several minutes to explore different ideas related to the task before intervening. Their initial exploration may involve some incorrect reasoning, such as confusion between area and perimeter. Allow this faulty reasoning to play out for a bit to allow the groups to resolve the difficulties on their own if possible.

If groups struggle to get started on this task, first ask them to revisit what they know about the problem. When students refer to a required quantity of chocolates, ask them if they might be able to show you an arrangement with square tiles. Suggest that they record the rectangle's dimensions. Ask, "How many inches of ribbon would be needed to go around a box like this? How do you know?" Have students refer to the square tile arrangement as they explain this measurement to you, and encourage them also to record this measure alongside the dimensions of the rectangle.

As students work, circulate throughout the room, and ask questions to check for understanding:

- How do you know that these dimensions could make a rectangular arrangement of chocolates with 20 (or 32 or 36) chocolates?
- How did you determine the amount of ribbon that would be needed to decorate this box?
- How do the dimensions of the box relate to the total number of chocolates?
- How do the dimensions of the box relate to the amount of ribbon needed to decorate the box?
- How do you know if you have identified all possible arrangements of 20 (or 32 or 36) chocolates?
- How do the dimensions of each of the boxes relate to the 24 inches of ribbon? Do you think there is another quantity of chocolates that could be boxed with the same amount of ribbon?

Note that the final question extends students' thinking beyond the answer to this task. Be prepared with this and other questions (see Differentiation) that might push student thinking in meaningful ways.

Allow students five to ten minutes to wrap up their work and prepare a justification for their conclusion. Remind them that they should have a diagram to support their reasoning.

SUMMARIZE

Begin the final part of the task by asking students to vote on whether or not they think it is possible to arrange all three quantities of chocolates in ways that would allow the company to use the same length of ribbon to decorate all the boxes. Some students may think it is not possible, thereby creating an opportunity for all students to defend their arguments and critique the reasoning of others (SMP 3). Remind all students to be respectful of other groups as they engage in this discussion.

Ask a group whose members are convinced that it is not possible to order the same length of ribbon for all three boxes to present their reasoning to the rest of the class. Before other groups argue against this reasoning (most likely by pointing out a missed arrangement of chocolates), have other groups in the same camp share any additional mathematical observations that they made. If necessary, have the class clarify area and perimeter and how these concepts relate to the task at hand. (Even if the Launch portion of the lesson did this, students may have lingering confusion or continue to mix up the terms.)

After the groups have rested their case in defense of the impossibility of same-length ribbons, ask a group from the other camp to try to convince them otherwise. Again, once the students in this group have presented their reasoning, ask other groups to contribute additional mathematical observations from their work, or strategies that they used to solve this problem. Encourage students to question each other respectfully as they examine other groups' reasoning and encounter alternative strategies. Allow this conversation to continue until the groups who did not find a viable solution are convinced that one exists.

Finally, highlight some of the mathematical ideas that were evident in this task. Some questions that might bring out these ideas include the following:

- How does the number of chocolates relate to area?
- How does the amount of ribbon needed relate to perimeter?
- Is it possible to arrange the same number of square units in different ways so that they have different perimeters? How is this task an example of that?
- Is it possible for rectangles to have the same perimeter but different areas? How is this task an example of that?

Also, it may be fruitful to have students reflect on how they engaged in the practices in SMP 1 and SMP 3 throughout this task. If doing so is appropriate, commend students on their engagement in argument and respectful critique.

DIFFERENTIATION

- If students are overwhelmed by three quantities of chocolate, change the problem to arrangements of 32 and 36 chocolates.

- If students confuse area and perimeter, include a review of these concepts during the Launch portion of the lesson or in a math review prior to the task.

- If students struggle to conceptualize the problem, examine a rectangular box of chocolates during the Launch portion of the lesson. How many chocolates does it hold, and how do they know (multiplying the dimensions of the array)? What length of ribbon would be needed to go around the box?

- Challenge students to identify other quantities of chocolates that could be sold in rectangular boxes that would use ribbon of the same length.

- Challenge students to identify the least amount of ribbon needed for each quantity of chocolates.

- Challenge students to identify other quantities of chocolates that could be arranged in a square box.

- Challenge students to arrange a required number of chocolates (e.g., 36 chocolates) as well as they can in a heart shape. Have them estimate the perimeter. Ask, "Is the area 36 square inches?"

WINTER FEST

Cade and Eli went to Winter Fest, and each completed three activities. Below are the times they spent at each activity. Cade and Eli want to know who spent more time doing activities at the festival. Use pictures to help explain your reasoning.

Cade

12:26 – 1:02	Ice skating
1:04 – 1:32	Sledding
1:36 – 2:18	Snowman building

Eli

2:49 – 3:37	Sledding
3:38 – 4:04	Snowman building
4:26 – 4:43	Ice skating

CCSSM STANDARDS FOR MATHEMATICAL PRACTICE

Practice 5: Use appropriate tools strategically.

CCSSM CONTENT STANDARDS

3.MD.A.1: Tell and write time to the nearest minute and measure time intervals in minutes. Solve word problems involving addition and subtraction of time intervals in minutes, e.g., by representing the problem on a number line diagram.

PROBLEM DISCUSSION

In this task, students will explore strategies for determining elapsed time to the nearest minute. The task builds on reasoning that second-grade students are expected to use to identify and write times to the nearest five minutes (2.MD.C.7). In this task, students will need to compare the total amount of time that two boys, Cade and Eli, spent participating in three activities, rather than how much total time the two boys spent at Winter Fest. For example, although Eli was at Winter Fest for a longer time than Cade (one hour and 54 minutes, compared with Cade's one hour and 52 minutes), he spent less time doing the activities (one hour and 31 minutes, compared with Cade's one hour and 46 minutes). Students may use a variety of strategies, such as counting up to the next time interval, mental addition strategies, or a number line (3.MD.A.1). They will use these strategies to determine how many minutes are between two given times, such as 1:04 and 1:32 (e.g., 6 minutes to 1:10, then 20 minutes to 1:30, and then 2 more minutes to 1:32) or how many minutes until the next whole hour, such as 3:38 to 4:04 (e.g., 22 minutes to 4:00 and then 4 more minutes to 4:04). Additionally, students must reason about a period of time that includes noon, which is often difficult (Van de Walle, Karpe, and Bay-Williams 2013).

A number line diagram can serve as a general tool for solving problems involving addition and subtraction of time intervals. Students' use of this tool to reason about intervals of time should be encouraged, since they are often familiar with this concrete representation from their work with whole number addition and subtraction (SMP 5). As students use this tool, they will choose the length of "jumps" that make sense to them. On the next page are two examples of number line diagrams that students may use to represent the interval of time between 3:38 and 4:04.

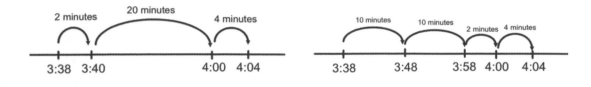

STRATEGIES

- Students may find the elapsed time for the three events by using a counting-up strategy and add these minutes to find the total time that each boy spent in activities.
- Students may use a diagram such as a number line to keep track of the minutes and hours between time intervals. (The diagrams above provide examples.)
- Students may find the elapsed time from the beginning of the first event to the end of the last event and then take away the small amount of time between events.

MISCONCEPTIONS/STUDENT DIFFICULTIES

- Students may have difficulty keeping track of the number of minutes as they count up.
- Students may apply addition and subtraction strategies for whole numbers but fail to consider how these strategies must be adjusted to account for the 60 minutes in one hour.
- Students may have difficulty making the transition from minutes to hours and minutes.
- Students may not realize that the time elapsed from the beginning of the first event to the end of the last event is different from the total amount of time spent participating in the three events.
- Students may not realize that the next whole hour after Cade's start time of 12:26 is 1:00.

LAUNCH

To introduce this task, ask students to describe activities that people do when it snows. Students should be encouraged to share their ideas with the whole class. Select one activity, such as sledding, and ask them to talk to a partner about how long they would like to spend sledding. Have students share their times on the board. Some students may write their time in minutes (e.g., 35 minutes, 120 minutes), and other students may give their time in hours (e.g., $1\frac{1}{2}$ hours, 2 hours). If no students give a number of minutes greater than 60, place 90 minutes in the list, and ask students to determine what this time would be in hours and minutes. Have students share how they completed this conversion. Next, tell the students that two friends participated in three Winter Fest activities, and their task is to determine which boy spent the most time doing the activities.

EXPLORE

Hand out the task and select a student to read it to the class. Ask students to talk to a partner to determine whether the times given are A.M. or P.M. and how they know. As students work individually on this task, ask questions to check for understanding:

- How long was Cade ice skating? Was it more than an hour or less than an hour? How do you know?
- Did Eli spend more time sledding or building a snowman? How do you know?
- How did your picture help you determine the amount of time Cade participated in activities?
- How many hours and minutes does each boy participate in activities?
- Which boy was at Winter Fest longer? How much longer? How do you know?

If students do not create a picture to show their thinking, encourage them to do so. Take note of students' use of diagrams and other strategies to solve this task. Specifically, note the different ways in which students use a number line diagram to solve this task.

SUMMARIZE

To move the lesson to completion, ask students to work with a partner to share their strategies and solutions. Then select groups to share their strategies and solutions with the whole class. Highlight multiple strategies for finding the elapsed time for a single event and the combined events, as well as strategies that produced the total time at Winter Fest and subtracted the amount of time between activities. If no one used the subtraction strategy, encourage the students to work with a partner to use this strategy to verify their initial results. Connect these strategies to number line diagrams as shown in the Problem Discussion. Ask questions to check for understanding:

- How many minutes did each boy spend participating in each of the activities?
- Who spent more time sledding (or building a snowman or ice skating)? How many more minutes? How do you know?
- How many total hours and minutes did each boy spend participating in all three activities? Which boy spent more time participating in all three activities? How do you know?

To conclude this task, ask students to think of another Winter Fest event and record a time interval that Cade could have spent at this event. Have students explain how a number line diagram can help them find the elapsed time for this event.

DIFFERENTIATION

- To support struggling students, provide them with number lines already marked with the beginning and ending times for each event.
- To support struggling students, provide times to the nearest five minutes.

- To extend this task, give the start time and elapsed time for certain events or the end time and elapsed time for certain events and ask for the start or end time. For example, ask, "If Eli was at the Winter Fest for one hour and 46 minutes and left at 2:13, when did he arrive?"

- To extend this task, ask students to plan activities for Winter Fest at their school and indicate the elapsed time for each of their events. Students could be given a set amount of time for the festival, such as 2 1/2 hours.

Donating Gloves

The fourth-grade classes at Washington Elementary School are collecting pairs of gloves to donate to a local charity. Mr. Allen's class collected three times as many pairs of gloves as Ms. Williams's class. Ms. McHugh's class collected twice as many pairs of gloves as Ms. Williams's class. If the three classes collected a total of 360 pairs of gloves, how many pairs of gloves did each class collect? Use pictures and equations to support your answer.

CCSSM Standards for Mathematical Practice

Practice 4: Model with mathematics.

Practice 7: Look for and make use of structure.

CCSSM Content Standards

4.OA.A.1: Interpret a multiplication equation as a comparison, e.g., interpret $35 = 5 \times 7$ as a statement that 35 is 5 times as many as 7 and 7 times as many as 5. Represent verbal statements of multiplicative comparisons as multiplication equations.

4.OA.A.2: Multiply or divide to solve word problems involving multiplicative comparison, e.g., by using drawings and equations with a symbol for the unknown number to represent the problem, distinguishing multiplicative comparison from additive comparison.

Problem Discussion

In this task, students will solve a problem involving multiplication as comparison. This builds on grade 3 standards that require students to view the product of 6×4 as 6 equal groups of 4 or with an array or area model with 6 rows and 4 columns (3.OA.A.1 and 3.OA.A.3). In a multiplicative comparison situation, the relationship between the quantities is based on "how many times as much" one quantity is compared with the other quantity. This "scalar interpretation of multiplication is an important application for students to encounter and begin to understand, as it can build depth of understanding when learning multiplication by a fraction" (NCTM 2009b; p. 20).

To solve this task, students should be encouraged to use drawings, equations, or tables to represent each quantity and understand that "three times as many" represents a relationship involving multiplication rather than addition (4.OA.A.2). For example, Ms. Williams's class collected 60 pairs of gloves, and Mr. Allen's class collected 180 pairs of gloves—three times as many as Ms. Williams's class. In this example, students can translate this verbal statement into $3 \times 60 = 180$ (4.OA.A.1) and use a representation such as a tape diagram (as shown on the lower half of the next page) to model the situation (SMP 4). By investigating different representations, students will explore the structure in this task. For example, the total number of pairs of gloves collected must be a multiple of 6 (SMP 7). This can be seen in the table on the next page. Other patterns that may arise in the Summarize section of the lesson include the following:

- Mr. Allen's class's collection of pairs of gloves must be divisible by 3 (i.e., must be a multiple of 3).
- Ms. McHugh's class's collection of pairs of gloves must be divisible by 2.
- If you increase the number of pairs of gloves collected by Ms. Williams's class by 1 pair of gloves, you increase the total number of pairs of gloves collected by the three classes by 6.
- If you double the number of pairs of gloves that Ms. Williams's class collected, you will double the number of pairs of gloves collected by Ms. McHugh's and Mr. Allen's classes, as well as the total number of pairs of gloves collected in all three classes.

Number of pairs of gloves collected in Ms. Williams's class	Number of pairs of gloves collected in Ms. McHugh's class	Number of pairs of gloves collected in Mr. Allen's class	Total number of pairs of gloves collected in all three classes
1	2	3	6
2	4	6	12
3	6	9	18
⋮	⋮	⋮	⋮
6	12	18	36
⋮	⋮	⋮	⋮
60	120	180	360

Students may also see this structure by creating a visual representation of the task by using a strip or tape diagram, as shown below. For example, they may represent the number of pairs of gloves collected by Ms. Williams's class with one rectangle and then realize that the number of pairs collected by Ms. McHugh's class is twice as many, or two rectangles, and the number of pairs collected by Mr. Allen's class is three times as many, or three rectangles. Students may recognize that there are six equal-sized rectangles, representing the 360 pairs of gloves. This results in each rectangle representing 360 divided by 6, or 60 pairs of gloves.

STRATEGIES

- Students may use a guess-and-check strategy by guessing the total number of pairs of gloves for any of the classes.
- Students may use a guess-and-check strategy by noticing the need to guess the number of pairs of gloves collected by Ms. Williams's class.

- Students may use a guess-and-check strategy by noticing the need to guess the number of pairs of gloves collected by Ms. Williams's class and using multiplicative comparisons to modify their guess. For example, if a student guesses 20 pairs of gloves for Ms. Williams's class, they will notice that Mr. Allen's class will collect 60 pairs of gloves, and Ms. McHugh's class will collect 40 pairs of gloves, for a total of 120 pairs of gloves. Students may then notice that they need three times as many total pairs of gloves and use $20 \times 3 = 60$ as their next guess for the number of pairs of gloves collected by Ms. Williams's class.

- Students may use a picture to model the situation. For example, they may draw 10 pairs of gloves for Ms. Williams's class and show the 30 pairs for Mr. Allen's class and the 20 pairs for Ms. McHugh's class. Next, they may iterate this picture six times to get a total of 360 pairs of gloves.

- Students may create a table of values to represent the relationships among the numbers of pairs of gloves collected in each of the classrooms.

- Students may create a table of values to represent the relationships among the numbers of pairs of gloves collected in each of the classrooms and notice the structure of the table. For example, students may recognize that if they increase the pairs of gloves collected by Ms. Williams's class by 1 pair, the total number of pairs of gloves for all three classes increases by 6.

- Students may create a tape/strip diagram to represent the relationships between the numbers of pairs gloves collected in each of the classrooms.

MISCONCEPTIONS/STUDENT DIFFICULTIES

- Students may not recognize "three times as many" as a multiplication statement.
- Students may have difficulty multiplying a two-digit whole number by a one-digit whole number.
- Students may not realize that the number of pairs of gloves collected by Mr. Allen's class must be a multiple of 3. Likewise, the number of pairs of gloves collected by Ms. McHugh's class must be a multiple of 2.

LAUNCH

Ask students if they have ever collected items for charity, and if so, what items they collected. They may share items such as the following:

- Canned food
- Clothes
- Coats, hats, and gloves
- Money

To assist students with the academic language that the task demands that they understand, show them the picture on the next page, and ask them to write three statements (verbal or numerical) to describe it.

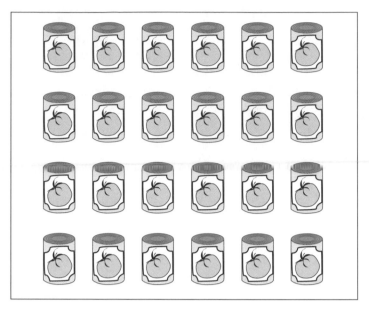

Below are examples of statements students may write:

- 4 × 6 = 24
- 6 × 4 = 24
- There are four groups of 6.
- There are six groups of 4.
- 6 + 6 + 6 + 6 = 24
- 4 + 4 + 4 + 4 + 4 + 4 = 24

Next, have students work with a partner to complete the two sentence frames below and explain how each sentence is represented by the picture:

24 is _____ times as many as _____.
24 is _____ times as many as _____.

Students should share their sentences and explanations with the class.

EXPLORE

Explain to students that they will be investigating the number of pairs of gloves that three different fourth-grade classes have collected to donate to charity. Distribute the task to students and ask a student read it to the class. Have students work with a partner to solve the task. Students who struggle to make drawings to represent the situation should be encouraged to organize their thinking in a table.

As students work to create their visual models, ask questions to check for understanding:

- Which class collected the most pairs of gloves? How do you know?
- Which class collected the fewest pairs of gloves? How do you know?
- Can you show me a drawing to represent the number of pairs of gloves collected by Mr. Allen's and Ms. Williams's class?
- If Ms. Williams's class collected 4 pairs of gloves, how many pairs would Mr. Allen's class need to collect to have 3 times as many? Can you show me a drawing to represent this? What equation would represent this?
- If Ms. Williams's class collected 4 pairs of gloves, how many pairs would Ms. McHugh's class need to collect to have twice as many? Can you show me a drawing to represent this? What equation would represent this?
- If Ms. Williams's class collected 4 pairs of gloves, how many pairs of gloves were collected in all by the three classes? How do your drawings help you show this? What equation would represent the total number of pairs of gloves?

Tell students that they will be sharing their strategies with one another and should take a few minutes to organize and redraw their representations if needed.

SUMMARIZE

To begin the final portion of the lesson, ask students to work with another student pair to find one or two strategies that are different from their own and record these strategies. Strategies may include guess and check, a table of values, a tape diagram, and drawings. Next, to facilitate a discussion related to the structure of this multiplicative comparison problem, ask students who used a guess-and-check strategy to share which class they focused on initially and how many pairs of gloves they guessed for that class. As they share this information, include it in a table as well as a drawing to show the links among the three strategies. Do this for a few initial guesses, asking the students to share their rationale for each guess. For example, if a student guessed 20 pairs of gloves for Ms. Williams's class, the students will notice that this number results in only 120 pairs of gloves in all, so they may use this information for a new guess for Ms. Williams's class that will result in a greater total number of pairs of gloves. If another group indicated that Ms. Williams's class collected 6 pairs of gloves, help students fill in the corresponding tape diagram as shown below. Ask questions to check for understanding:

- How did you determine how many pairs of gloves Mr. Allen's and Ms. McHugh's classes collected? How can we represent these values in a tape diagram?
- How can we use the table and the tape diagram to determine how many pairs of gloves were collected by all three classes?
- Do we need to increase the number of pairs of gloves Ms. Williams's class collected? How should we do that? Why?

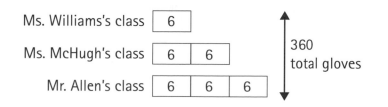

To conclude this task, ask students to use one of the strategies or visual representations discussed to complete an exit ticket that asks students to determine how many pairs of gloves each class collected if the total number of pairs was 420.

DIFFERENTIATION

- To support struggling students, rewrite the task to include only one multiplicative statement. The following is an example:

  The fourth-grade classes at Washington Elementary School are collecting pairs of gloves to donate to a local charity. Mr. Allen's class collected 3 times as many pairs of gloves as Ms. Williams's class. If the two classes collected a total of 360 pairs of gloves, how many pairs of gloves did each class collect? Use pictures and equations to support your answer.

- To support struggling students, change the total number of pairs of gloves collected by all three classes to a smaller multiple of 6, such as 60.

- To support struggling students, provide a tape or strip diagram, such as the one below, which students can fill in to solve the task.

Ms. Williams's class   [   ]

Ms. McHugh's class   [|]

Mr. Allen's class   [| |]

- To extend this task, ask students to create their own multiplicative comparison task using a context of their choice.

- To open up this task, tell the students that the three classes collected more than 300 pairs of gloves and ask how many each class could have collected.

- To extend this task, change the multiplicative statements to involve fractional quantities, as in the following example:

  The fourth-grade classes at Washington Elementary School are collecting pairs of gloves to donate to a local charity. Mr. Allen's class collected three times as many pairs of gloves as Ms. Williams's class. Ms. Williams's class collected half as many pairs of gloves as Ms. McHugh's class. If the three classes collected 360 total pairs of gloves, how many pairs of gloves did each class collect? Use pictures and equations to support your answer.

- To extend this task, the class can have a glove drive (or canned food drive) and keep track of the number of pairs of gloves collected by different classrooms. Students could then record comparative (addition or multiplication) statements related to the number of items that each class collected.

LAST YEAR'S RESOLUTIONS

Simone is having a New Year's Eve party. When her friends arrive, she asks them to recall one resolution that they made a year ago and determine what fraction of the year they kept that resolution. Then Simone asks her friends to talk in pairs to compare their fractions and decide which of the two of them kept a resolution longer. For each conversation between Simone's friends, decide which friend kept a resolution longer, and explain how you know. Justify your reasoning with a fraction model.

Conversation 1

Simone kept her resolution for $2/3$ of the year.	Justin kept his resolution for $3/12$ of the year.

Conversation 2

Akilah kept her resolution for $7/8$ of the year.	Danny kept his resolution for $6/6$ of the year.

Conversation 3

Hayden kept his resolution for $1/24$ of the year.	Adam kept his resolution for $1/8$ of the year.

Conversation 4

Heather kept her resolution for $3/4$ of the year.	Taylor kept her resolution for $5/6$ of the year.

Conversation 5

Taylor kept her resolution for $5/6$ of the year.	Polo kept his resolution for $5/12$ of the year.

Conversation 6

Piper kept her resolution for $11/24$ of the year.	Miguel kept his resolution for $7/12$ of the year.

Conversation 7

Polo kept his resolution for $5/12$ of the year.	Penelope kept her resolution for $11/24$ of the year.

Conversation 8

Devonte kept his resolution for $4/6$ of the year.	Miguel kept his resolution for $7/12$ of the year.

CCSSM STANDARDS FOR MATHEMATICAL PRACTICE

MP1: Make sense of problems and persevere in solving them.

MP5: Use appropriate tools strategically.

CCSSM CONTENT STANDARDS

4.NF.A.2: Compare two fractions with different numerators and different denominators, e.g., by creating common denominators or numerators, or by comparing to a benchmark fraction such as $1/2$. Recognize that comparisons are valid only when the two fractions refer to the same whole. Record the results of comparisons with symbols >, =, or <, and justify the conclusions, e.g., by using a visual fraction model.

Problem Discussion

Solving this task provides students with an opportunity to compare fractions in multiple ways. The context of the task—New Year's resolutions—and its application of fractions (fractional parts of a year) may be unusual for students, providing an opportunity for them to make sense of an unusual problem and consider how the given fractions relate to the context of the problem (SMP 1). The pairs of fractions provided in the problem are deliberately chosen to elicit various ways of thinking about comparison of fractions, making it necessary for students to persevere when strategies don't carry over to new comparisons (MP1).

Van de Walle, Karp, and Bay-Williams (2013, pp. 310–11) identify three ways to compare fractions conceptually, aside from comparing fractions with common denominators:

- Common numerator
- More than/less than a benchmark number (4.NF.A.2)
- Distance from a benchmark number (4.NF.A.2)

This task supplies several pairs of fractions for comparison, allowing students to engage in the three strategies identified above. In addition, it requires students to justify their reasoning by using a visual fraction model. Students will need to choose a concrete or visual model that demonstrates their thinking, be sure that their fraction models refer to the same whole for their comparisons, and use this tool to communicate and justify their reasoning (SMP 5).

In reasoning about common numerators, the number of parts in each fraction (the numerators) is the same. The difference between the two fractions lies in the size of the parts (the denominators). The same number of smaller parts will result in a fraction that is smaller than one with larger parts. Although comparison with common numerators is not an expectation of the content standard related to this problem, we have included two examples of this reasoning for students who may be unfamiliar with it (3.NF.A.3d).

Conversation	Fraction comparison	Potential reasoning – Common numerators
3	$1/24 < 1/8$	Since a twenty-fourth of a year is a shorter period of time than an eighth of a year, $1/8$ is greater than $1/24$.
5	$5/6 > 5/12$	Since sixths of a year are longer periods of time than twelfths of a year, five of these longer periods will be greater than five of the shorter periods.

Three fraction comparisons in this task lend themselves to reasoning about the size of a fraction in relation to a benchmark number, such as $1/2$ or 1 (4.NF.A.2). In these cases, one fraction may be larger than the benchmark and the other smaller. Students can then use transitivity implicitly to reason about the size of the two given fractions.

Conversation	Fraction comparison	Potential reasoning – More than/ less than a benchmark number
1	$2/3 > 3/12$	Since $2/3$ is greater than $1/2$, and $3/12$ is less than $1/2$, $2/3 > 3/12$. (Students may reason about the comparison to one-half by thinking about how many parts would be counted with a fraction equivalent to one-half. For example, with twelve parts making up the whole, six of those parts would need to be counted to make an equivalent fraction to $1/2$. Three is less than six, so $3/12 < 1/2$.)
6	$11/24 < 7/12$	Since $11/24$ is less than $1/2$ ($1/2 = 12/24$), and $7/12$ is greater than $1/2$ ($1/2 = 6/12$), then $11/24 < 7/12$.
2	$7/8 < 6/6$	Seven-eighths is less than one whole, and six-sixths is equivalent to one whole. Therefore, $7/8 < 6/6$.

Finally, three fraction comparisons in this task promote reasoning about the distance from the fractions to a benchmark number, such as $1/2$ or 1, as shown at the top of the next page (4.NF.A.2). This reasoning may occur when both fractions are less than or greater than the benchmark number. In thinking about the comparative distance from the benchmark, students can decide which one is the larger fraction.

Students may choose from a variety of fraction models to make the comparisons in these conversations (SMP 5). They may choose fraction circles or other area models, representations on the number line (as demonstrated on the next page for conversation 4), or even set models (e.g., using 5 red linking cubes and 7 blue linking cubes to represent $5/12$ of a year). The CCSSM content standards emphasize a number line model for fractions, so encouraging students to represent at least one conversation with this model may be warranted.

Using some of these models—or simply reasoning about these fraction pairs—may also elicit the strategy of finding equivalent fractions with a common numerator or denominator (also 4.NF.A.2). Watch for this strategy to surface; it may be more common when one numerator or denominator is a factor of the other. If the strategy does surface, attend to it in the Summarize portion of the lesson.

Conversation	Fraction comparison	Potential reasoning – Distance from a benchmark number
4	$3/4 < 5/6$	Both of these fractions are less than the benchmark number, 1. Three-fourths is $1/4$ less than 1, while $5/6$ is $1/6$ less than 1. Consider how this might be represented on an open number line: Since $3/4$ is the greater distance away from 1, it is the smaller fraction. Thus, $3/4 < 5/6$.
7	$5/12 < 11/24$	Since $11/24$ is $1/24$ less than one-half, and $5/12$ is $1/12$ less than one-half, the larger fraction can be determined by identifying the fraction that is the smaller distance from one-half. Since $1/24$ is less than $1/12$, $11/24$ is the larger fraction.
8	$4/6 > 7/12$	Both of these fractions are greater than one-half, so the larger fraction is the fraction that is the greater distance from one-half. Since $1/6$ is greater than $1/12$, $4/6 > 7/12$.

STRATEGIES

- Students may represent the fractions by using a familiar area model (e.g., fraction circles) and compare the fractions by comparing the size of each representation.
- Students may identify or estimate the location of each fraction on a number line by using benchmark numbers of $1/2$ and 1.
- Students may use a set model to represent each fraction, taking care that each fraction refers to the same whole. For example, they may use 12 linking cubes as the whole and represent $4/6$ as 8 red cubes and 4 blue cubes, and represent $7/12$ as 7 red cubes and 5 blue cubes. Note how this representation aligns with comparison of fractions by finding common denominators.
- Students may compare fractions with common numerators by reasoning about the size of the parts.
- Students may compare fractions by identifying that one is larger or smaller than a benchmark number and the other is not.
- Students may reason about each fraction's distance from a benchmark number, using this value and the distance to determine which fraction is larger.
- Students may identify equivalent fractions with common numerators or common denominators and compare these equivalent fractions.

- Students may convert each fraction to a length of time (e.g., $7/12$ of a year is 7 months) and compare the lengths of time.

Misconceptions/Student Difficulties

- Students may compare fractions by reasoning about the size of the numerators and assume that the larger numerator indicates the larger fraction.
- Students may compare fractions by reasoning about the size of the denominators and assume that the larger denominator indicates the larger fraction.
- Students may compare the fractions by reasoning about the size of the numerators and denominators and experience conflict when the comparison is not consistent.
- Students may assume fractions are equivalent when the numerators and the denominators are the same value apart (i.e., $3/4$ and $5/6$).
- Students may attempt to make equivalent fractions but do so incorrectly. For example, students may add the same value to the numerator and denominator to make an equivalent fraction.
- Students may represent the fractions as parts of different wholes, making their comparison of the two fractions inaccurate.

Launch

Ask students if any of them have ever heard of New Year's resolutions. Discuss what they know about resolutions, and share any personal experiences with resolutions (or family members' resolutions). Highlight the fact that many people who commit to a resolution do not keep it for very long. Some interesting research is available online on the historical predecessors of New Year's resolutions and the percentage of people who keep their resolutions. This information may offer some captivating tidbits for this discussion.

It may be helpful to students to have an example of a resolution, such as exercising at least three times a week. Ask students what it would mean if someone said that she had kept this resolution for half of the year. Have students discuss the implications of this fraction. For one-half of the year, this person exercised at least three times each week, and then halfway through the year, she stopped exercising at least three times a week. Students may recognize that this means the person with this resolution stopped exercising at least three times a week at the end of June.

Display the Last Year's Resolutions task for all the students to read silently to themselves. Ask students to summarize what they know about Simone's party. What does Simone ask her friends to do when they arrive at her party? Then what does Simone ask her friends to do in pairs? Explain to the students that they will be getting eight "conversations" between pairs of Simone's friends, and for each conversation they will need to determine which friend kept a resolution longer. Reiterate that they will need to provide a visual fraction model to support their reasoning. Point out the various fraction models that are available for use throughout the classroom (e.g., linking cubes, fraction circles, fraction rectangles, whiteboards for number lines, etc.). Tell them that the choice of tool is theirs to make, but they will benefit from trying different models to support their thinking as they compare the fractions in different conversations.

Explore

Assign students to eight different groups in the classroom. Give each group a different conversation to analyze. Have multiple copies of each conversation available; students will move on to a new conversation when they have completed one. Ideally, students should find solutions for three conversations, one for each of the following fraction comparison strategies:

1. Common numerators: conversations 3 and 5
2. More than/less than a benchmark number: conversations 1, 2, and 6
3. Distance from a benchmark number: conversations 4, 7, and 8

This will allow students to progress at different rates through the conversations. It is more important for students to make comparisons in a few conversations with a depth of understanding than it is for them to make all of the comparisons.

As students work in their groups to compare a particular pair of fractions, circulate throughout the classroom, taking note of the conversations that each group is working on and their comparison strategies. Ask questions to check for understanding:

• How do you know that this fraction is the larger one?
• How does your visual fraction model show your thinking?
• How was a benchmark number important to your problem solving?
• How did you know that this fraction was equivalent to that length of time?
• Why did you decide to find an equivalent fraction?

After groups have explained their reasoning for the fraction comparison that they have been given, also ask whether their strategy could be generalized: "Do you think you could do that on any problem?" This question will help students think about the conditions under which their particular strategy is useful.

After a group has justified and recorded their thinking thoroughly, provide another conversation to analyze. Choose a conversation from another strategy grouping, ultimately providing each group of students with the opportunity to complete at least one comparison from each group. Encourage students to choose a different fraction model to support their thinking. Continue to check for understanding with each group. Record the comparisons that each group has completed and the strategies used for each.

With five to ten minutes remaining in the Explore section, assign each group a different conversation's comparison to present to the class. If possible, for each comparison choose a group that has used the strategy that the fraction pairing was intending to elicit. Also attend to the different visual fraction models that have been used and attempt to have a variety of models presented. Have each group make a whiteboard or poster display of their problem and their solution and be prepared to share.

Summarize

Ask students to present their solutions and share their strategies for comparing the fractions in the following order of conversations: 3, 5, 1, 6, 2, 4, 7, and 8. Ordering the conversations and comparisons in this way will allow the elicited strategies to be presented together, so that the mathematical discussion can summarize the strategies.

After the first two presentations (and questions from the class), ask the class to summarize what they know about how they can compare two fractions that have the same numerator. Record a class conjecture. Have students generate two fractions that might be compared in this way, and discuss how they could apply their conjecture to this problem.

After the next three presentations and questions from the class, ask the class again to summarize what they know about how they can compare two fractions when one is greater than or less than a benchmark number and the other is not. Again record a conjecture, and ask students to generate two fractions that might be compared in this way.

After the final three presentations and questions from the class, summarize the class's thinking for the final strategy in a similar way. Ask students to reflect on the visual fraction models that students used to justify their thinking throughout comparisons in the eight conversations. As a class, discuss the benefits and challenges associated with the models. For example, with a set model, having the fractions represent the same whole might be challenging, and with an area model (e.g., fraction circles), the tool doesn't align well with the context. If students have not used a number line, demonstrate how this representation might be used with a particular problem. Conversation 4 is a good candidate for this discussion.

Finally, if students have converted one fraction to an equivalent fraction with a common numerator or a common denominator, have them discuss this strategy by revisiting one of the comparisons that has already been presented. Ask the class if this would always work, and if so, why. Record this strategy as a final option for comparing fractions.

DIFFERENTIATION

- For students who have difficulty making sense of the context and the fractions in it, ask them during the Launch to discuss and compare the fractions $3/12$ and $4/12$. Ask, "How do these fractions relate to the context? What does it mean for the part of the year that each person kept his or her resolution? Which fraction is larger, and how do you know?"

- For students who struggle, ask them to complete a comparison in one of the common numerator conversations first and then a comparison in a more than/less than a benchmark number conversation.

- Consider providing copies of a full-year calendar in a 4-month by 3-month array. Students may choose to use this as a visual fraction model for this context.

- Challenge students to put all of the fractions in order from least to greatest.

- Challenge students to place all the fractions on a number line.

- Challenge students to select one of the conversations and add a person whose fraction falls between the smaller and the larger fractions. What could this person's fraction be?

MORE-LEAF CLOVERS?

The clover leaf below has an angle that measures 90 degrees. This clover leaf could be used four times to make a four-leaf clover, without any gaps or overlaps of the leaves.

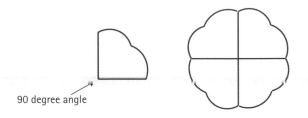

90 degree angle

Which of the other clover leaves provided (clover leaves A–H) could be repeated several times without gaps or overlaps to make a complete clover? How many leaves would each of these clovers have? Explain your reasoning, and connect it with the size of the clover leaf's angle.

Clover leaf A	Clover leaf B	Clover leaf C	Clover leaf D

Clover leaf E	Clover leaf F	Clover leaf G	Clover leaf H

CCSSM STANDARDS FOR MATHEMATICAL PRACTICE

Practice 6: Attend to precision.

Practice 8: Look for and express regularity in repeated reasoning.

CCSSM CONTENT STANDARDS

4.MD.C.6: Measure angles in whole-number degrees using a protractor. Sketch angles of specified measure.

4.MD.C.7: Recognize angle measure as additive. When an angle is decomposed into non-overlapping parts, the angle measure of the whole is the sum of the angle measures of the parts. Solve addition and subtraction problems to find unknown angles on a diagram in real world and mathematical problems, e.g., by using an equation with a symbol for the unknown angle measure.

Problem Discussion

What angle sizes would allow for more than four leaves in a clover if these angles were iterated around a central point? This task asks students to identify the angle sizes of unusual clover leaves (4.MD.C.6) and determine whether or not these angles could be composed to make a many-leaf clover without any gaps or overlaps. In the process, students will recognize angle measure as additive (4.MD.C.7).

This task also provides an opportunity for students to make mathematical connections to factors and multiples as they consider whether a quantity like the measure of the angle at the center of each clover leaf is a factor of 360, or whether 360 would be in a list of multiples of this quantity. Students may think about this concept as either factors of 360 or multiples of other quantities, providing additional opportunities to make connections between factors and multiples and to clarify this language (SMP 6).

Five of the clover leaves provided will iterate to create a complete more-leaf clover without any gaps or overlaps. These clover leaves have angles with measures that are factors of 360. In this context, the other paired factor will indicate the number of leaves that would be needed to complete the clover. For example, clover leaf B measures 45 degrees. Since 8 × 45 = 360, these clover leaves will make an 8-leaf clover.

Clover leaf	Size of angle in degrees	Does it make a more-leaf clover?	Number of leaves × size of angle = 360
A	50	No	
B	45	Yes	8 × 45 = 360
C	60	Yes	6 × 60 = 360
D	40	Yes	9 × 40 = 360
E	70	No	
F	15	Yes	24 × 15 = 360
G	80	No	
H	120	3-leaf clover!	3 × 120 = 360

The five clover leaves that will create full clovers without gaps or overlaps in this problem do not exhaust the possibilities for sizes of clover leaves with this property. Switching the factors creates a different clover. Consider, for example, the factor pair of 8 and 45: 8 leaves with 45-degree angles or 45 leaves with 8-degree angles would each create a complete clover. If this problem is limited to whole numbers of degrees, any factor of 360 could be considered.

Students may not have the time to explore all eight of the clover leaves provided. However, they should be given the opportunity to explore several so that they can notice repeated reasoning and recognize how the angle measures relate to the creation of a complete clover (SMP 8). Although many students may attempt to solve the task by iterating the clover leaves without gaps and overlaps to see what works, working through this process with several clover leaves will provide more opportunities for them to make the connection between the size of the angle and the 360-degree turn that they are trying to complete.

STRATEGIES

- Students may copy or trace each clover leaf multiple times to determine whether a complete clover can be made without gaps or overlaps.
- Students may cut out each clover leaf and use it to create a complete clover by iterating the angle unit.
- Students may measure each clover leaf's angle and write multiples of the angle measure to determine whether 360 is a multiple of the angle measure.
- Students may measure each clover leaf's angle and divide 360 by this measure. If the quotient is a whole number, they will identify this value as the number of clover leaves it will take to make the complete clover. If the quotient is not a whole number, they will decide that this clover leaf cannot make a complete clover without gaps or overlaps.

MISCONCEPTIONS/STUDENT DIFFICULTIES

- Students may have difficulties measuring the angles with a protractor.
- Some variation may occur in students' angle measurements (45 degrees versus 46 degrees), which could change their answers for each clover leaf.
- Students may attempt to combine clover leaves with different angle measures to make a complete clover.
- Students may come to incorrect conclusions if they make mistakes in copying, tracing, or iterating the angle.
- Students may make computational errors in determining multiples.
- Students may make computational errors with division.
- Students may consider the possibility of completing a clover with a portion of a clover leaf.

LAUNCH

Begin this task by asking students how many of them have ever found a four-leaf clover. Discuss the traditionl idea that finding a four-leaf clover will bring good luck. Connections may be made to Saint Patrick's Day, although the three-leafed shamrock, unlike the four-leaf clover, has important religious connections to this holiday. List questions that students generate about four-leaf clovers or Saint Patrick's Day; these may provide online research extensions for students who complete the mathematical task.

Display a visual of the More-Leaf Clovers? task. Allow some time for students to read the task to themselves. Ask one student to demonstrate using a protractor to measure the angle size of the individual leaf of the four-leaf clover. As this student works, highlight skills that students may continue to struggle with; these challenges may depend in part on the protractors that are available in the classroom. Then ask students, "How many degrees do the angles of these four clover leaves measure all together?" Students may have varying background information related to circles and 360 degrees, so allow several minutes for students to share their knowledge about how 360 degrees relates to the complete clover on display.

Finally, provide a visual display of the eight clover leaves, A–H, for investigation, and ask students to explain to a neighbor what the task is asking them to do. Listen for misconceptions, and allow some opportunity for students to ask clarifying questions about the task. Maintain the cognitive demand of the task by clarifying the context but not suggesting strategies for solving the problem.

EXPLORE

Assign students to eight different groups in the classroom. Supply all eight clover leaves to each group, but explain that the students do not need to work on them in order. Some groups may be tempted to "divide and conquer": instead of working as a group, each student in the group will take a different clover leaf. If this happens, redirect the students to tackle at least one clover leaf as a group first. If they determine an effective strategy, they may choose to divide and conquer with the remaining clover leaves, as long as each group member understands and can explain the group's strategy.

As groups work on this task, circulate throughout the room and ask questions to check for understanding:

- How did you decide that this clover leaf could (or could not) make a complete clover without gaps or overlaps?
- Can you explain your drawing to me?
- What are you doing as you trace the clover leaf?
- How does the size of the clover leaf's angle help you determine whether or not it can make a complete clover without gaps or overlaps?
- What part of the clover leaf are you paying attention to when you decide whether or not you could use this leaf to make a complete clover?
- How did you use the measure of the clover leaf's angle to determine how many leaves will make a complete clover?
- Why did you decide to divide 360 by the measure of the angle? What does the quotient tell you?

Students may begin to recognize the possibility that leaves with other angle measures may create a complete clover. Watch for this idea to surface, especially taking note of any students who realize that factors may be reversed to create different more-leaf clovers. If these students finish all eight clover leaves in the task, consider prompts suggested in Differentiation to challenge their thinking.

At the end of this exploration, assign each group one clover leaf, and allow the groups five to ten minutes to prepare a poster presentation showing their thinking about their clover leaf. Be sure that the students present a range of strategies for clover leaves that do or do not make complete clovers. That is, in the Summarize portion of the lesson, students should see how a multiple or factor strategy relates to clover leaves that can or cannot be iterated to make a complete clover.

SUMMARIZE

Allow students five to ten minutes for a gallery walk to see the groups' strategies for solving this task. Groups should circulate together. Provide prompts for the students to think about as they consider each group's work:

- Do I understand this group's strategy?
- How is this strategy similar to or different from what we did for our clover leaf?
- Are there any similarities between this group's strategy and other groups' strategies?

After the gallery walk, ask students to return to their work areas and reflect on two final questions:

- How could you describe the different strategies that you saw during the gallery walk?
- How does (or could) the measure of the clover leaf's angle and its relationship to 360 degrees help you decide whether a leaf could make a complete clover without gaps or overlaps?

Bring the class back together to discuss these two questions. Highlight different strategies that the students used in their groups, revisiting posters as needed to make sure that the whole class understands each approach. In particular, highlight the connection between the measure of the clover leaf's angle and how it could be used to create a 360-degree angle, either by finding multiples of the smaller angle measure or by partitioning the 360-degree angle through division. Be sure that students are attending to precision through their use of mathematical language, such as *factor* and *multiple*.

If any groups extended their work by exploring one or more of the challenges below, provide an opportunity for them to share their findings with the whole class. This may allow students to make further connections to multiplication, division, multiples, and factors, and how these mathematical concepts relate to angle measurements.

DIFFERENTIATION

- If students struggle with tasks requiring fine motor skills, provide multiple copies of each clover leaf or copies that have been previously cut out.
- Provide differentiated support for students who struggle with measuring angles.
- Consider limiting clover-leaf choices to ones that create complete clovers, and ask groups to determine how many leaves will create the complete clover.
- Provide calculators for students who struggle with or get discouraged by computational demands.
- Challenge students to draw other clover leaves that will create complete more-leaf clovers.
- Challenge students to determine all the measures of clover leaf angles that could create complete clovers (all factors of 360).
- Extend students' thinking about the task's context by asking them to research questions raised during the Launch.
- Challenge students to find images of three-leaf clovers online, print these, and measure the angles. (Note that they are not 120-degree angles!)

Snowstorm!

The northeastern United States is getting another snowstorm! Sean, a fifth-grade student, decides that he will record how many inches of snow he gets in his backyard. Before he goes to bed, he measures and records the snow as $4\,3/4$ inches high. When he wakes up in the morning (snow day!), he measures again and records it as $12\,1/8$ inches high. How much snow fell overnight in Sean's backyard? Explain your reasoning.

CCSSM Standards for Mathematical Practice

Practice 2: Reason abstractly and quantitatively.

Practice 5: Use appropriate tools strategically.

CCSSM Content Standards

5.NF.A.2: Solve word problems involving addition and subtraction of fractions referring to the same whole, including cases of unlike denominators, e.g., by using visual fraction models or equations to represent the problem. Use benchmark fractions and number sense of fractions to estimate mentally and assess the reasonableness of answers. *For example, recognize an incorrect result $2/5 + 1/2 = 3/7$, by observing that $3/7 < 1/2$.*

Problem Discussion

In this task, students are asked to find an unknown addend in a word problem related to snowfall. Teachers in the primary grades may readily recognize this problem as an "add to—change unknown" problem, for which we know a starting amount, $4\,3/4$ inches, an unknown change that is being added to the starting amount, and a result, $12\,1/8$ inches. To solve this problem, students must identify the amount of change, or difference, between the two values. One equation associated with the meaning of this problem is $4\,3/4 + \square = 12\,1/8$. To solve this equation, the computation that can be carried out is subtraction:

$$12\,1/8 - 4\,3/4 = \square$$

However, given that students will be operating outside the familiar realm of whole numbers, they may not automatically recognize this as a subtraction problem. Instead, they may consider how much they need to add to the initial amount in order to reach the target amount. Of course, this missing addend approach demonstrates the inverse operations of addition and subtraction. The structure of the problem, however, may elicit alternative and unexpected problem-solving approaches.

Note the difference between the structure of this problem and another subtraction situation, in which one amount might be *taken away* from another. In such a case, we may start at the result (e.g., $12\,1/8$) and take away $4\,3/4$, but doing this does not match the context of the problem. Instead, if we use a number line, we can consider this "subtraction" situation as a "difference between two quantities" situation (see the diagram at the top of the next page).

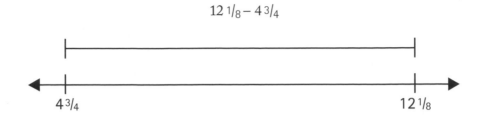

$$12\,^1/_8 - 4\,^3/_4$$

This particular context is chosen because of its alignment with a number line representation. If students have had opportunities in earlier years to perform addition and subtraction on the number line with whole numbers, then the snowfall context will provide an opportunity for them to extend their whole number strategies to working with mixed numbers, using an open number line as an appropriate tool (SMP 5).

Because this is an "add to" situation, students may approach it by identifying what needs to be added to $4\,^3/_4$ in order to reach $12\,^1/_8$. Consider the two open number line representations of possible solution strategies below:

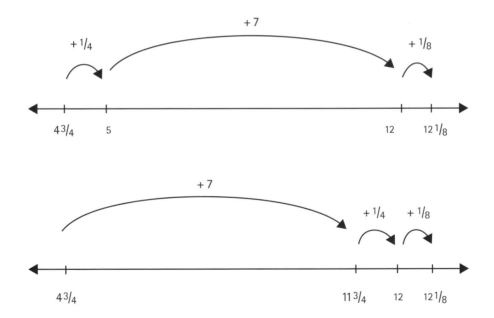

In each case above, the change amount can be determined by adding $7 + {}^1/_4 + {}^1/_8$, or the cumulative distances of the jumps. This sum provides the distance between the two values, or the difference between the two quantities.

Although other fraction models do not align with the context of this problem, students may choose to think about these fractional values with fraction circles, rectangles, or other area models. Regardless of how students choose to represent the fractions in this problem, they will eventually encounter the challenge of adding or subtracting fractions with unlike denominators (5.NF.A.2). If they are finding the sum of $7 + {}^1/_4 + {}^1/_8$, students may recognize from earlier fraction work that $^1/_4$ is equivalent to $^2/_8$ and exchange one fraction for the other in order to create fractional addends with the same denominator. Other students may recognize this as a "subtraction situation" from the outset and attempt to take away $4^3/_4$ from $12^1/_8$. This operation may be manipulated in multiple ways. For example, in lieu of the traditional algorithm, students may choose to use one of the following options to perform the subtraction (SMP 5).

- Subtract 5 from $12^1/_8$ to get $7^1/_8$ and add $1/_4$ to this difference to compensate for subtracting too much originally.
- Subtract 4 from $12^1/_8$ to get $8^1/_8$, and then subtract the remaining $3/_4$ in pieces, bridging the whole number by subtracting $1/_8$ and then $5/_8$.
- Subtract 4 from 12 to get 8. Subtract $3/_4$ from $1/_8$ (to get $-5/_8$). Combine 8 and $-5/_8$, or think about the problem as $8 - 5/_8$.

Subtraction solution strategies are not limited to those articulated above. Students may grapple in multiple ways with the fractions presented in the problem, reasoning about the fractional parts in terms of the context of the problem but also considering the fractions as abstract quantities that can be manipulated and operated on as such (SMP 2).

STRATEGIES

- Students may use an open number line to find the missing addend in $4^3/_4 + \square = 12^1/_8$. Jumps may be totaled by using manipulatives or identifying an equivalent fraction for $1/_4$.
- Students may use an open number line to take away $4^3/_4$ from $12^1/_8$. Landing points for the jumps may be found by using manipulatives, fraction number sense, or identifying equivalent fractions with the same denominators.
- Students may use fraction manipulatives to take away $4^3/_4$ from $12^1/_8$.
- Students may compute $12^1/_8 - 4^3/_4$ in a variety of ways, using fraction number sense and knowledge of equivalent fractions with common denominators.

MISCONCEPTIONS/STUDENT DIFFICULTIES

- Students may recognize the situation as an "add to" problem and add the two given quantities together.
- Students may misunderstand the context of the problem and think that the two measurements are separate snowfall amounts.
- Students may incorrectly apply an algorithm for adding or subtracting fractions by subtracting the numerators and the denominators.
- Students may use incorrect equivalent fractions in their reasoning or computation.
- Students may make computational errors in their open number line jumps or other computations.
- Students may apply correct strategies in an incorrect way. For example, a student may find the difference between the whole numbers to be 8. Then the student may find the difference between the fractions to be positive instead of negative: $5/_8$ instead of $-5/_8$.

Launch

Depending the usual winter weather in your region, begin this task by asking "How many of you have ever experienced a snowstorm?" or "How many of you remember the last snowstorm we had?" Have students share their experiences, and ask them if they remember how much snow fell in the last snowstorm. Ask students if they remember any big snowstorms in which more than a foot of snow fell. Discuss what would constitute a significant amount of snow to them; this will vary substantially according to the region where you and your students live.

Finally, ask students, "How do we usually measure snowfall in the United States?" Discuss the measurement of snowfall in inches and how many inches are equivalent to a foot of snow. Explain to students that the task they will be working on concerns a snowstorm and how much snow fell overnight in a particular storm. Have a student read the task aloud to the class. At each measurement of snow, display a picture that corresponds to the measure. As needed, review how to read a ruler, including measurements in quarter inches and eighths of an inch.

Ask students to talk in pairs or groups of three or four about what the problem is asking. Have them explain the context of the problem in their own words. Ask students if they have any lingering questions about the context of the problem. Identify the question that they need to answer and the expectations for presenting their solutions.

Explore

Have students work in groups of two to four on this task. Have multiple fraction manipulatives available—for example, fraction circles, fraction strips, and fraction squares. Students may also use other manipulatives in a novel way, so make available any other manipulatives that are present in the classroom (e.g., linking cubes, rulers, yardsticks).

As students first engage in the task in their groups, circulate throughout the room and pay attention to how they are making sense of the problem. Do some students automatically see it as a subtraction problem? Are other groups approaching it as a missing addend problem and attempting to add on to find this missing number? Are any groups misinterpreting the problem and attempting to add the two quantities together? Probe groups' thinking by asking questions. If a group is misinterpreting the problem, redirect the students' attention to the pictures provided. Ask, "What does this picture show in relation to the problem? What are you trying to find out about Sean's situation?"

As students work to find the difference between the two quantities, take note of the solution strategies and tools that they are using. Ask questions to check for understanding:

- How are you using this manipulative? Can you explain what you are representing in relation to this problem?
- Why did you choose this particular manipulative or tool? What does this tool allow you to do that another might not?
- How do you know that you are looking for the distance between these two points on the number line?

- Why are you subtracting $4^3/_4$ from $12^1/_8$?
- Can you figure out a way to add those jumps together? What makes it difficult?
- How did you decide to calculate the answer to your subtraction problem? What challenges did you encounter?

Have students prepare a poster of their solution strategy that provides a thorough explanation of how they solved the problem and why they made the choices they did.

SUMMARIZE

Explain to the students that they will be doing a gallery walk to examine the posters they have made. Ask them to attend to the following questions as they consider other groups' posters:

- Do you understand how and why this group solved the problem as they did?
- Do you see similarities or differences between groups' solution strategies, including yours?
- What questions do you have about a group's solution strategy?

Provide each group with a small set of sticky notes. Have them do the gallery walk as a group, writing comments or questions on sticky notes and leaving them with the other groups' posters. It may be helpful to emphasize that comments and questions on the sticky notes should be mathematical, thoughtful, and respectful. Circulate throughout the room during the gallery walk to make observations about the strategies that have been employed and to monitor students' behavior with the sticky notes.

At the end of the gallery walk, ask students to return to their own posters and examine the sticky notes that have been left for them. Provide some time for the groups to make sense of the notes and consider how they might respond to the questions and comments.

Engage the class in a discussion about the strategies that were used to solve the problem. Consider organizing the discussion around particular strategies. For example, all the work by groups that solved the problem by finding the quantity that needed to be added to the original snowfall amount to arrive at the final snowfall amount could be discussed together. If some groups solved the problem through subtraction, ask, "Does it make sense that we can use subtraction to find the missing amount that has been added? Why or why not?"

Highlight the tools that students have chosen to use for solving the problem as well. It might be beneficial to display a list of all the tools (e.g., open number line, fraction circles, equation) and ask students to reflect on the advantages and challenges of these tools. Connect this to SMP 5, and praise students for making choices about the tools that were available.

If any groups did not generate the correct answer to the problem, ask those students to share their strategies or examine where a mistake may have happened. Ask other groups if they made similar mistakes and how they were able to fix these mistakes.

Finally, highlight any examples of students' use of equivalent fractions in adding or subtracting the fractions. Note that this may be with fraction manipulatives or with the abstract fractions. Ask, "Why did you find it necessary to use an equivalent fraction? How did this help you?"

An introduction to the standard algorithm for adding or subtracting fractions is not appropriate at this time. Instead, indicate to the class that they will be continuing to consider how equivalent fractions might be useful for performing operations with fractions.

DIFFERENTIATION

- For students who are struggling with finding the difference between two mixed numbers with different denominators, ask them first to solve the problem by substituting $12\frac{1}{4}$ as Sean's morning snowfall measurement. Then, when they have solved that problem, ask them how they might apply their strategy or solution to the original problem.

- For students who are struggling, suggest that they use a yardstick to determine the new snowfall amount. If yardsticks are not available, and students would benefit from using a ruler, change Sean's morning snowfall measurement to $11\frac{1}{8}$ inches.

- Challenge students who have solved the problem successfully to write three similar problems of their own. One should be easier than the problem they just solved, one should be the same level of difficulty, and one should be harder. Ask them to solve the harder problem.

- To extend students' work on the task, write other problems involving mixed numbers with different denominators that are examples of different problem types. Ask students to solve these problems. For example:

  Add To—Result Unknown

  In a winter snowstorm, it snowed $3\frac{7}{8}$ inches by sunset. It snowed another $7\frac{1}{2}$ inches during the night. How much snow had fallen by morning?

  Compare—Smaller Unknown

  Westborough, Massachusetts, got $9\frac{3}{4}$ inches of snow in one December snowstorm. The nearby town of Hopkinton got $1\frac{7}{8}$ inches less snow. How much snow did Hopkinton get in the snowstorm?

Mardi Gras Parade

Kaelie has 600 doubloons in four different colors—gold, green, red, and purple—to toss from her float during the Mardi Gras parade. One-twelfth of her doubloons are gold, and 225 doubloons are green. What fraction of Kaelie's total number of doubloons are green? What fraction of her doubloons could be red? What fraction of her doubloons could be purple? How many doubloons of each color could Kaelie have on her float? Use pictures and equations to explain your thinking.

CCSSM Standards for Mathematical Practice

Practice 2: Reason abstractly and quantitatively.

CCSSM Content Standards

5.NF.A.1: Add and subtract fractions with unlike denominators (including mixed numbers) by replacing given fractions with equivalent fractions in such a way as to produce an equivalent sum or difference of fractions with like denominators. *For example, $2/3 + 5/4 = 8/12 + 15/12 = 23/12$. (In general, $a/b + c/d = (ad + bc)/bd$.)*

5.NF.B.4a: Interpret the product $(a/b) \times q$ as a parts of a partition of q into b equal parts; equivalently, as the result of a sequence of operations $a \times q \div b$. *For example, use a visual fraction model to show $(2/3) \times 4 = 8/3$, and create a story context for this equation. Do the same with $(2/3) \times (4/5) = 8/15$. (In general, $(a/b) \times (c/d) = ac/bd$.)*

Problem Discussion

In Mardi Gras Parade, students will apply their understanding of addition and multiplication of fractions in a real context. The context refers to *doubloons*, which are the coins often associated with Mardi Gras parades. If the term *doubloon* is challenging for students, change the term to *coin*. Students are given the total number of doubloons and told that $1/12$ of them are gold. To determine how many of the doubloons are gold, students will use reasoning related to division to find $1/12$ of 600 doubloons. They may solve the multiplication statement $(1/12) \times 600$ by partitioning the 600 doubloons into 12 equal parts by using division strategies or drawings (5.NF.B.4a), as shown in the Strategies section. Next, students are told that Kaelie has 225 green doubloons. Students must apply their understanding of fractions in a part-whole relationship to determine what fractional part of the coins the green doubloons represent. That is, they must realize that if the total number of doubloons is 600, then $225/600$ gives the fractional part that is green doubloons. Students will need to apply their understanding of equivalent fractions from grade 4 (i.e., $a/b = (a \times c)/(b \times c)$) either to simplify $225/600$ as $3/8$ or to express $1/12$ as $50/600$.

To determine the possible fractional amounts of red and purple doubloons, students must decompose the whole (600 doubloons) into four fractional addends. In doing so, they will add fractions with both like and unlike denominators (5.NF.A.1). For example, a student may see $50/600 + 225/600 = 275/600$ and realize they need two addends that total $325/600$. Likewise, a student may notice that $1/12 + 3/8 = 2/24 + 9/24 = 11/24$. Then they must decompose the remaining

$^{13}/_{24}$ into two addends. Students should be encouraged to record their fractional amounts in simplified form to make connections among strategies, drawings, and equations. For example, if different students find the same numbers of red and purple doubloons by using two or more of the equations shown below, the class discussion should include representations to verify that the equations are the same (SMP 2).

$^2/_{24} + {}^9/_{24} + {}^4/_{24} + {}^9/_{24} = 1$

$^{50}/_{600} + {}^{225}/_{600} + {}^{100}/_{600} + {}^{225}/_{600} = 1$

$^1/_{12} + {}^3/_8 + {}^1/_6 + {}^3/_8 = 1$

Using properties of operations, students will need to verify that the symbolic representations (i.e., the equations) represent the same quantities of each color of doubloon. For example, a student who uses the second equation above may notice that this representation explicitly gives them the total numbers of each color of doubloon. At the same time, students using equations 1 and 3 will need to understand the meaning of each fractional quantity. For example, in the first equation, students must recognize that $^2/_{24}$ does not mean that Kaelie has two gold doubloons, but rather that $^2/_{24}$ is the same as $^{50}/_{600}$, which results in 50 gold doubloons. Asking students to divide the 600 doubloons into 24 piles of equal size would give them a visual representation that might assist them in seeing this connection. Students will find that there will be 25 doubloons in each pile, and 2 of those 24 piles represent the gold doubloons; thus, $^2/_{24} = {}^{50}/_{600}$ (SMP 2).

STRATEGIES

- Students may find the number of gold doubloons by guessing the number of doubloons in each of the 12 partitions in the diagram below to find $^1/_{12}$ of 600 and then check that the total number of doubloons in the 12 partitions is 600. For example, they might guess that 20 doubloons are in each of the 12 partitions but then realize that accounts for only 240 doubloons.

- Students may find the number of gold doubloons by dividing 600 by 12 by using a missing factor approach and guessing and checking what factor they need to multiply 12 by to get 600.

- Students may find the number of gold doubloons by dividing 600 by 12 by recognizing that 60 divided by 12 is 5, so 600 divided by 12 is 50.

- Students may find the number of gold doubloons by dividing 600 by 12 by using repeated addition or repeated subtraction (i.e., 12 + 12 + 12 + … + 12 = 600)

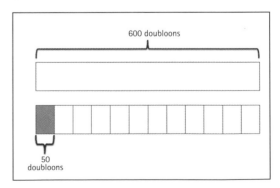

- Students may find the number of gold doubloons by dividing 600 by 12 by using long division.

- Students may find the number of gold doubloons by dividing 600 by 12 by using an area model or tape diagram to show the 50 doubloons in each of the 12 groups.

- Students may find the number of gold doubloons by considering a fraction that is easier to work with, such as $1/_6$. For example, a student may say, "$1/_6$ of 600 is 100, so $1/_{12}$ of 600 must be 50."

- Students may find the fraction of green doubloons by creating the fraction $225/_{600}$.

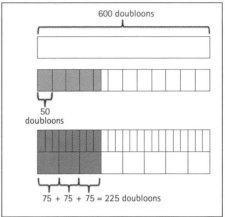

- Students may find the fraction of green doubloons by using their area model or tape diagram as shown to see that four and a half of the original 12 parts in the tape diagram total 225 (50 + 50 + 50 + 50 + 25), resulting in an equivalent fraction of $9/_{24}$.

- Students may determine the fraction of green doubloons by finding fractions equivalent to $225/_{600}$, such as $9/_{24}$ or $3/_8$, by repeatedly dividing the numerator and denominator by the same factor.

- Students may find possible numbers of red and purple doubloons by using the common denominator of 600 and finding two numbers that add to 325, such as 100 and 225.

- Students may determine possible numbers of red and purple doubloons by using a common denominator of 24 and finding two numbers that add to 13, such as 10 and 3.

MISCONCEPTIONS/STUDENT DIFFICULTIES

- Students may not understand that finding $1/_{12}$ of 600 is the same as partitioning 600 into 12 equal groups, resulting in finding 600 divided by 12.

- Students may struggle to determine equivalent fractions with large numerators and denominators.

- Students may not realize that the sum of the four fractional quantities representing the doubloons must equal a whole.

- Students may struggle to find and connect visual representations with their symbolic representations.

LAUNCH

Begin by asking students to share what they know about Mardi Gras. Below are some facts that could be used to help students understand the Mardi Gras celebration:

- Although Mardi Gras dates back thousands of years, the first Mardi Gras celebrations in the United States took place in 1699, when two French explorers held a celebration near what is now called New Orleans.

- The carnival celebration begins on January 6, which is the twelfth day after December 25.

- In French, *Mardi Gras* means *Fat Tuesday*. Fat Tuesday is the biggest day of the carnival celebration and can occur on any Tuesday between February 3 and March 9.

- Louisiana is the only state where the Mardi Gras festival is a legal holiday.

- Thousands attend the Mardi Gras celebration each year in New Orleans and experience the culture of the region.
- The first Mardi Gras parade was organized in 1857 and occurred in New Orleans.
- In the Mardi Gras parade, float riders often toss strings of beads or doubloons, which are brightly colored coins.
- *Doubloon* originates in the Spanish word for *double*, since a doubloon was worth twice as much as a gold coin.
- Purple, green, and gold are the traditional Mardi Gras colors. Purple stands for justice, green stands for faith, and gold stands for power.

Explain to students that during Mardi Gras parades, people on floats toss special coins to parade goers. These coins are called doubloons and are often purple, gold, green, or red. To assess students' background knowledge of part-whole relationships of fractions, pose the following scenario. "Suppose that you have 18 doubloons, and 6 are gold. Talk to your partner and decide what fraction of the doubloons are gold. Be sure to draw a picture to represent the fraction." As students discuss and represent the fraction by drawing area models or tape diagrams such as those below, ensure that the three possible answers ($6/18$, $3/9$, and $1/3$) are shared. Also focus on how the three fractions are the same size, even though the number and size of the parts differ (4.NF.A.1).

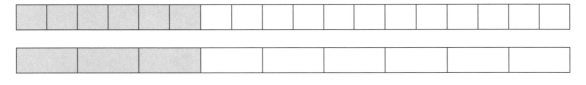

EXPLORE

Hand out the task, and have a student read it to the class. Ask students to discuss with a partner the information that is known and the information that is unknown. Next, ask students to solve the task with a partner. Ask the following questions to check for understanding:

- If there were only 24 doubloons on the float, how many would be gold? How do you know? Can you show me how a drawing could help you?
- Do you think the fraction of green doubloons is more than half or less than half of the total number of doubloons? Why?
- Does it matter if we find the number of gold doubloons before we find the fraction of green doubloons? Why or why not?
- Could the numbers of red and purple doubloons be the same? How do you know?
- What fraction of all the doubloons are green or gold? How do you know?
- How many doubloons are neither green nor gold? How do you know? How can this help you determine how many could be red and purple?

Summarize

Begin the summary by asking partners to share their strategies and the drawings they used to find the number of gold doubloons. (Possibilities are listed in Strategies.) Be sure to highlight those that have a pictorial representation, such as a tape diagram or area model (see below), and point out how these models relate to division. For example, encourage students to discuss how the models show both "1/12 of 600" and "600 partitioned into 12 equal-sized parts." To facilitate this discussion, ask questions such as the following:

- How did you know to divide your area into 12 pieces?
- How did you know how much each part represented?

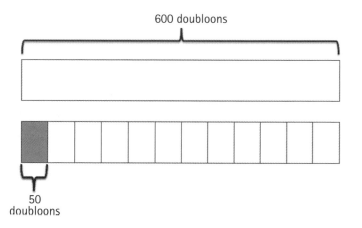

Next, ask students to share strategies for finding the fraction of green doubloons. If students leave the fraction as $^{225}/_{600}$, encourage them to simplify it. The picture below shows one strategy based on the diagram used to determine $1/_{12}$ of 600. In this strategy, students will need to add parts until they reach 225. Note that one part will need to be split in half in order to reach 225. Students may notice that $^9/_{24} \times 600 = 225$ green doubloons.

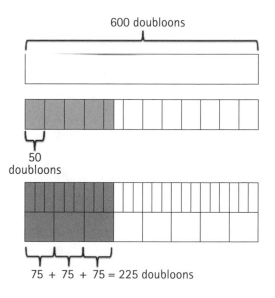

Students may use the preceding representation to further simplify $9/24$. The nine shaded parts can be grouped into three parts representing 75 doubloons each, showing $3/8 \times 600 = 225$ green doubloons.

Next, ask students to share what fractions of red doubloons and purple doubloons Kaelie could have on her float. Many solutions are possible. Allow students to share their solutions and methods for finding possible fractions of red and purple doubloons. Some students will focus on the total number of red and purple doubloons, while others will focus on the fractional part of the total that the red and purple doubloons represent. For example, as mentioned above in the Strategies section, students may reason in terms of doubloons, use a common denominator of 600, and find two numbers that add to 325, such as 100 and 225. Other students may reason in terms of the fraction of total doubloons and use a common denominator of 24 to find two numbers that add to 13, such as 10 and 3.

DIFFERENTIATION

- To support struggling students, give students visual fraction models that are partially completed, as shown below.

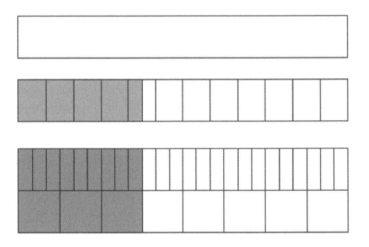

- To support struggling students, provide a fractional amount of red doubloons, such as $7/24$.
- To extend the task, provide students with additional constraints, such as "The fraction of red doubloons is more than the fraction of gold doubloons but less than the fraction of green doubloons."

Snow Removal

After 18 inches of snow fell overnight, two parking lots at Bushnell Elementary School needed to be cleared of snow. The teachers' parking lot is rectangular and measures 21 yards by 30 yards. The visitors' parking lot is also rectangular and measures 15 yards by 18 yards. If the open box bed of the dump truck used to remove the snow has dimensions of 12 feet by 9 feet by 6 feet, how many trips will the dump truck need to make to remove all the snow from both parking lots?

CCSSM Standards for Mathematical Practice

Practice 2: Reason abstractly and quantitatively.

Practice 4: Model with mathematics.

CCSSM Content Standards

5.MD.A.1: Convert among different-sized standard measurement units within a given measurement system (e.g., convert 5 cm to 0.05 m), and use these conversions in solving multistep, real world problems.

5.MD.C.5c: Recognize volume as additive. Find volumes of solid figures composed of two non-overlapping right rectangular prisms by adding the volumes of the non-overlapping parts, applying this technique to solve real world problems.

Problem Discussion

This task allows students to solve a task related to volume by using knowledge of the standard measurement system. Students are given the dimensions of two parking lots in yards, the depth of snow in inches, and the dimensions of the dump truck box in feet. Students must recognize the need to convert all measurements to the same unit (5.MD.A.1; SMP2). Once students decide which unit to use, they will then need to apply multiplication or division strategies to determine the volume of snow in each parking lot, as well as the volume of the dump truck box. Additionally, they will use this information to determine how many trips it will take the dump truck to remove the snow from both parking lots. Students must recognize that both the volume of snow that the dump truck box can hold and the volume of snow in the parking lots can be modeled using drawings of rectangular prisms. Equations can then be used for finding the volumes of these prisms (SMP 4). Students will also need to recognize that the depth of snow represents one dimension of a rectangular prism (SMP 2).

To determine the minimum number of trips, students must combine the volumes of snow from the two lots rather than supposing that the truck will remove the snow from one lot at a time (5.MD.C.5c). For example, by itself, the teachers' lot would fill $13\frac{1}{8}$ trucks, resulting in 14 trips. The visitors' lot by itself would fill $5\frac{5}{8}$ trucks, resulting in 6 trips. Solving the task this way would result in 20 total trips. However, if students combine the total volume of the two lots, the snow will fill 18 and $\frac{3}{4}$ trucks, resulting in 19 trips. The Summarize portion of the lesson should explore both strategies, since students will be encouraged to formulate their answer in the context of the problem and discuss the implications of the dump truck making an extra trip (SMP 2).

STRATEGIES

- Student may convert all measurement units to inches, feet, or yards to find the volume of the snow in the parking lots and the capacity of the dump truck box.
- Students may use the distributive property when finding the volume of the snow in one of the parking lot while using feet. For example, to find the volume of the snow in the teachers' lot (63 ft. × 90 ft. × 1.5 ft.), students may reason that 90 × 1.5 is the same as (90 × 1) + (90 × 0.5) = 90 + 45 = 135 cubic feet.
- Students may use an area model to find the area of the base of each rectangular prism. For example, to find the area of the visitor lot (15 yd. × 18 yd.), a student may use the area model shown below.

	10 +	8
10 +	100	80
5	50	40

- Students may use a standard algorithm to find the volumes of snow in the parking lots as well as the volume of the dump truck box.
- Students may determine the number of trips needed for each separate parking lot or combine the snow in the lots by using repeated addition or subtraction. For example, once students find the volume of snow in cubic yards, they may repeatedly subtract 24 (representing the 24 cubic yards that the dump truck box holds) until they get to zero or have a remainder that is less than 24.
- Students may use long division to find the exact answer.
- Students may use long division to find the whole number of trips, recognizing that the remainder indicates the need for an additional whole trip (i.e., the need to round up).

MISCONCEPTIONS/STUDENT DIFFICULTIES

- Students may struggle to recognize the 18 inches of snow as the height of the rectangular prism that models the snow in the parking lots.
- Students may not recognize the need to convert units.
- Students may incorrectly convert units (e.g., 21 yards as $21/3$ feet instead of 21 times 3 feet).
- Students may have difficulty with the multiplication and division required to solve this task.
- Students may not contextualize the remainder and instead give an answer that includes a fractional number of trips (e.g., 18 $3/4$ trips instead of 19 trips).

LAUNCH

Ask students to draw a solid figure that would have volume and describe how to find the volume of that shape. Have students share their shape and descriptions with a partner. Ask questions to check for understanding:

- Is your shape two-dimensional or three-dimensional?
- What is the name of your shape?
- How is volume different from area?
- What units do we use to measure volume?
- If you needed to find the volume of your shape, would the units for each length of your shape need to be the same? Why or why not?

EXPLORE

Hand out the task to pairs of students and read it with students. To provide context to the task, ask students to show with their hands how deep 18 inches of snow would be. Then ask students if they have seen snow being removed from a parking lot in a dump truck. If so, have the student describe this snow removal process. If not, show a short video of the process (https://www.youtube.com/watch?v=omCDE64AveU).

Ask students to reread the task, and then have the class work together to generate a list of important quantities that will help in solving the task. Students may use this information to complete the Reason Abstractly and Quantitatively Graphic Organizer for the task, shown below.

Reason Abstractly and Quantitatively Graphic Organizer	
What quantities are important?	What operations or equations will I use?
What pictures or drawings will help me?	What is my problem-solving process? (Show calculations.)

In pairs, students should devise a plan to solve this task by using the quantities in the class list. Ask questions to check for understanding:

- What do the edge lengths in your picture represent? Are all of the measurements the same unit? Does that matter? Why or why not?
- How many inches are in a foot? How many feet are in a yard? How does this information help you solve the problem?
- Does the order in which you multiply the edge lengths matter? Why or why not?
- How can you use the volume of the dump truck to help you solve the problem?

- I see you were repeatedly subtracting 24 from the total volume of snow. Will you explain why this makes sense in the context of this problem? Is there another operation that you can use?
- What does the remainder mean in this problem? What fraction of the dump truck bed does that remainder represent? How do you account for this fractional amount in the problem?

Circulate throughout the room to ensure that students have either a solution of 19 truckloads or a solution of 20 truckloads. Then have them complete the Time Order Map for the task (see below), outlining the steps they took during their problem-solving process.

Time Order Map
First we...
Next, we...
Then we...
Finally, we...
Our answer is _____ , and it makes sense because...

Summarize

To begin the process of summarizing, poll the students about the unit (inches, feet, or yards) into which they converted all the measurements. Next, ask students to discuss with a partner whether or not the unit used would change their answer. Encourage students to justify why or why not it would do so.

Next, ask students to share their solutions, keeping a record of the answers for all to see (solutions using inches, feet, and yards appear below). Depending on how students solved the task, two different solutions may be shared (solution 1: 20 trips; solution 2: 19 trips). If students treated the parking lots as separate entities, they would find that the teachers' lot would fill $13\,1/8$ trucks, resulting in 14 trips, and the visitors' lot would fill $5\,5/8$ trucks, resulting in 6 trips. Solving the task this way results in 20 total trips. However, if students combine the total volume of the two lots, the snow would fill $18\,3/4$ trucks, resulting in 19 trips.

Ask students who found a solution of 20 total trips to share their strategy with the class. Ask whether other students used different units and found the same answer. Focus attention on the size of the quantities involved in solving the problem, depending on which unit they used.

(Using feet will result in larger quantities than using yards; solutions calculated in different units are detailed below and on the next page, with the solution resulting in 19 trips appearing first, as path 1.) Next, ask students who found an answer of 19 total trips to share their strategy with the class. Ask students to turn and talk to their partner about the similarities and differences between the two solution strategies. Ask questions to check for understanding:

- Which volumes were found for each strategy?
- Were the volumes of the parking lots used in the same way for each strategy?
- Why do you think some groups chose to add the volumes of the snow in the teachers' and visitors' lots?
- If you pushed together all of the snow in the two parking lots, would you have the same amount of snow as you had before you did so? Why or why not?

Have students share the similarities and differences they see between the two strategies. They should recognize that in the first solution (20 total trips), students treated the snow in the parking lots as separate amounts of snow and did not fill the dump truck box completely on two of the trips. Encourage students to consider whether the two fractional amounts of snow left over in each lot could be combined into one or more truckloads. They should be asked to consider the implications of an extra trip in the real-life context of snow removal.

Solution using feet	
Teachers' lot:	1.5 ft × 90 ft × 63 ft = 8,505 ft³ of snow
Visitors' lot:	1.5 ft × 45 ft × 54 ft = 3,645 ft³ of snow
Dump truck box:	12 ft × 9 ft × 6 ft = 648 ft³ of space
Path 1:	8,505 ft³ + 3,645 ft³ = 12,150 ft³ of snow in all
	12,150 ft³ ÷ 648 ft³/trip results in 19 total trips

Note: Students may find the number of trips required for each separate lot (see the first two steps in path 2 below) and then add these numbers to arrive at 19 total trips.

Path 2:	8,505 ft³ ÷ 648 ft³/trip results in 14 trips
	3,645 ft³ ÷ 648 ft³/trip results in 6 trips
	14 trips + 6 trips results in a total of 20 trips

Solution using yards	
Teachers' lot:	0.5 yd × 21 yd × 30 yd = 315 yd³ of snow
Visitors' lot:	0.5 yd × 15 yd × 18 yd = 135 yd³ of snow
Dump truck box:	4 yd × 3 yd × 2 yd = 24 yd³ of space
Path 1:	315 yd³ + 135 yd³ = 450 yd³ of snow in all
	450 yd³ ÷ 24 yd³/trip results in 19 total trips

Note: Students may find the number of trips required for each separate lot (see the first two steps in path 2 below) and then add these numbers to arrive at 19 total trips.

Path 2:	315 yd³ ÷ 24 yd³/trip results in 14 trips
	135 yd³ ÷ 24 yd³/trip results in 6 trips
	14 trips + 6 trips results in a total of 20 trips

Solution using inches

Teachers' lot:	18 in × 756 in × 1080 in = 14,696,640 in³ of snow
Visitor's lot:	18 in × 540 in × 648 in = 6,298,560 in³ of snow
Dump truck box:	144 in × 108 in × 72 in = 1,119,744 in³ of space
Path 1:	14,696,640 in³ + 6,298,560 in³ = 20,995,200 in³ of snow in all
	20,995,200 in³ ÷ 1,119,744 in³/trip results in 19 total trips

Note: Students may find the number of trips required for each individual lot (see the first two steps in path 2 below) and then add these numbers to arrive at 19 total trips.

Path 2:	14,696,640 in³ ÷ 1,119,744 in³/trip results in 14 trips
	6,298,560 in³ ÷ 1,119,744 in³/trip results in 6 trips
	14 trips + 6 trips results in a total of 20 trips

DIFFERENTIATION

- To support struggling students, give all measurements in the same units.
- To support struggling students, change the 18 inches to 36 inches to eliminate fractional measurements.
- To support struggling students, provide diagrams of the rectangular prisms for students to label with the appropriate dimensions.
- To support struggling students, change the task to focus on the removal of snow from one parking lot.
- To extend this task, provide the volume of the truck's box bed in cubic feet instead of providing its dimensions in linear feet.

SPRING

Spring is the season that brings warmer weather, showers, and a chance to plant gardens. Various holidays and events celebrate these seasonal changes. This chapter contains several open-ended tasks that may encourage students to broaden their views of mathematical problem solving, justify their own reasoning, and understand the reasoning of others.

Two of the third-grade tasks in this chapter use racing contexts to develop mathematical concepts. The first task, Kentucky Derby, asks students to employ their skills with rounding and subtraction to find potential values related to this context. The second task requires students to reason about ways to construct a one-mile relay with fractional parts. In the final task for third graders, Peculiar Plantings, students explore various ways to partition a garden bed into halves and fourths.

Selling Umbrellas, the first fourth-grade task, challenges students to find factor pairs for two quantities to determine the possible number of umbrellas sold for a school fundraiser. The second task honors Earth Day by raising awareness of environmental challenges as students find surprising statistics and record them in multiple ways. The last fourth-grade task, May Day Maypole, requires students to reason about a non-unit fraction multiplied by a whole number.

In Relay Teams, fifth graders explore measures of center (mean and median) while adding decimals to the hundredths place. The final two fifth-grade tasks are fraction related, with students working in a garden context to find the area of a rectangle with fractional side lengths and considering springtime rainfall as they determine a mean of fractional amounts by using a line plot as a tool.

MATERIALS FOR EACH TASK, INCLUDING HANDOUTS, ARE AVAILABLE FOR DOWNLOADING AND PRINTING ON NCTM's WEBSITE AT NCTM.ORG/MORE4U BY ENTERING THE ACCESS CODE ON THE TITLE PAGE OF THIS BOOK.

DERBY DIFFERENCES

Some rounding occurred at the Kentucky Derby! Find exact quantities that could apply in the situations below.

1. In the Kentucky Derby, colts can carry approximately 130 pounds, and fillies can carry approximately 120 pounds. Colts can carry 5 pounds more than fillies.

2. After one minute, both horse A and horse B have raced approximately 990 meters of the course. Horse A is ahead of horse B at this point by 7 meters.

3. Two-day Kentucky Derby event tickets cost approximately $600 or $800. One of these two-day ticket packages costs $185 dollars less than the other.

Explain your reasoning for each situation. If you have time, find other possible answers.

CCSSM STANDARDS FOR MATHEMATICAL PRACTICE

Practice 7: Look for and make use of structure.

Practice 8: Look for and express regularity in repeated reasoning.

CCSSM CONTENT STANDARDS

3.NBT.A.1: Use place value understanding to round whole numbers to the nearest 10 or 100.

3.NBT.A.2: Fluently add and subtract within 1000 using strategies and algorithms based on place value, properties of operations, and/or the relationship between addition and subtraction.

PROBLEM DISCUSSION

In Derby Differences, students are asked to work backward from rounded or approximate quantities to identify exact values that will work in a given situation. Students have had some experience rounding quantities to the nearest 10 or 100 (3.NBT.A.1). However, they may not have had an opportunity to reason about rounded quantities and what values would round to a targeted number. For example, if a quantity has been rounded to 130 (as in the first situation), the original whole number quantity could have been 125, 126, 127, 128, 129, 130, 131, 132, 133, or 134. To think backward in this way, students will need to consider possible values that are less than, equal to, and greater than the rounded value. In short, what range of values would result in the same rounded quantity? This reasoning may be repeated for other rounded values, resulting in a shortcut for their thought processes as they engage in all three situations (SMP 8).

Multiple answers are possible for each of the situations in this task. In the first situation, the two values that round to 120 and 130 must be 5 pounds apart. If only whole number values are considered (which is appropriate for most third graders), then there are five possible solutions, as shown in the table below:

Colt's allowed weight (lbs.)	Filly's allowed weight (lbs.)	Difference
125	120	5
126	121	5
127	122	5
128	123	5
129	124	5

If the weight that a colt is allowed to carry is reduced any further, it will no longer round to 130. If the weight that a filly is allowed to carry is increased any further, it will no longer round to 120. Note that the actual weight restrictions for colts and fillies are 126 pounds and 121 pounds, respectively.

Three solutions are possible for the second situation, which requires a difference of 7 meters between the two horses. Note the pattern that is observed in each row of the table. As one value increases by 1, the other value increases by 1. Students may look for and use this pattern to maintain the difference between the two values (SMP 7).

Horse A's distance (m)	Horse B's distance (m)	Difference
992	985	7
993	986	7
994	987	7

The Kentucky Derby is typically a two-minute race for a distance of approximately 2000 meters. A reasonable halfway point has been approximated for these two horses, based on the assumption that the horses would run faster in the second half of the race.

In the final situation, the quantities have been rounded to the nearest 100, which allows for a greater span in possible quantities for each of the values. That is, any whole number from 550 through 649 will round to 600 when numbers are being rounded to the nearest 100. Maintaining a difference of 185 will somewhat restrict the number of possible solutions. For example, choosing $550, which is the minimum cost that would round to $600, as the cost of the less expensive package would make the cost of the more expensive package $735, but $735 would round to $700 rather than to $800, as the situation requires.

Eighty-five whole-number solutions are possible for the third situation, as shown in the table on the next page. Although it is not reasonable to ask students to find all possible solutions, they may be asked to find the most expensive possibility, the least expensive possibility, or a pattern that they could use to find other valid solutions (SMP 7 and SMP 8). Note that this

Less expensive package (in dollars)	More expensive package (in dollars)	Difference (in dollars)
565	750	185
566	751	185
567	752	185
⋮	⋮	⋮
648	833	185
649	834	185

situation is based on actual ticket options for the Kentucky Derby; current pricing and packages may be explored by students as an extension.

Strategies

- Students may guess and check values that meet the criteria for each situation. Students may also make adjustments to these guesses on the basis of the identified differences.
- Students may choose "friendly" or landmark numbers as one of the quantities for each situation and identify the second number on the basis of this choice.
- Students may list exact values that round to each given quantity. Then they may identify values from each list that are the required difference apart.
- Students may identify a value that rounds to the given quantity, find a value that is the required difference from that value, and check to see whether it meets the criteria of the problem.
- Once students have found a viable solution, they may consider how to find other solutions by adjusting both quantities by the same amount.

Misconceptions/Student Difficulties

- Students may struggle to understand how the solution quantities can be 5, 7, or 185 apart when the numbers they round to have a difference of 0, 10, or 200.
- Students may struggle to understand the idea of finding an exact value from a rounded value.
- Students may not consider the rounded value as a possible exact value of the solution (e.g., a solution of 125 pounds and 120 pounds is not viable, because 120 corresponds to the rounded value).
- Students may think that both values must be either greater than or less than the rounded value, making finding a valid solution impossible or challenging.
- Students may forget that a number with a 5 in the ones place or tens place rounds to the next ten or hundred, respectively.

- Students may think that the values in the third situation (600 and 800) are rounded to the nearest ten, making finding a valid solution impossible.
- Students may make computational errors when finding the differences between two quantities.

LAUNCH

Begin this task by asking students whether they know of any famous horse races. Students' experience with this topic may be quite limited; if so, share some information about the Kentucky Derby and supplement this information with online images. It may be surprising to many students that the Kentucky Derby is a fairly short race. Although it is one of the most famous sporting events in the United States, the race itself lasts only about two minutes!

Remind students of the work they have done during third grade on rounding numbers. Ask students, "Why is it helpful to round numbers? What do these rounded numbers tell us?" Also consider asking, "What information do we lose when we round numbers?" It might be helpful to have a brief discussion of the loss of precision when numbers are rounded and some cases in which this loss of precision makes it challenging to understand the situation. If possible, discuss a situation where knowing an exact amount might be beneficial. For example, what might an exact dollar amount be if we know that someone has approximately $20 in a wallet? Why might it be beneficial to know the exact amount?

Explain to students that the task asks them to generate exact amounts that will work in a situation for which they have been given rounded quantities. Display the problem and its initial directions, exposing one situation at a time. After the students have read each situation, ask them to turn to a neighbor to discuss what they know about that situation and what they want to know. Address vocabulary or contextual issues as they arise.

EXPLORE

Assign students to groups of three to work on this task. As the groups work, circulate throughout the room, and ask questions that check for understanding:

- How did you identify this number for this situation?
- What numbers round to 120? (130? 990? 600? 800?)
- What patterns do you see in the numbers that would round to the given numbers?
- Is yours the only solution to the problem?
- Do you see any patterns in your solutions?
- Do you think it might be possible to find another solution without repeating your whole problem-solving process?

Although the task does not ask students to find multiple solutions, make this a priority in the questioning, so that students are prepared to explore this idea during the Summarize portion of the lesson.

If some groups struggle to get started on a task, first ask them to share any ideas they have for getting started. Other questions to ask may include the following:

- If you know that a filly's allowed weight rounds to 120 pounds, what possible values could the weight be?
- What possible values could a colt's allowed weight be?
- What do you know about a filly's allowed weight in comparison with a colt's allowed weight?

Refrain from posing these questions at the outset. Instead, ask students how they are thinking of approaching the task so that your questions can build on students' current understanding.

Students may struggle especially with the final situation, in which there is a large gap between the targeted values, and the numbers are rounded to the nearest 100. Encourage students to persevere with this situation, even if they are not successful at finding a solution. Note that a straightforward solution is $600 and $785. If students find this answer quickly, ask them whether this problem has other solutions and how they might use their solution to find others.

Summarize

Once all the groups have completed at least two of the situations, bring students together as a class. Display blank tables set up like those in the Problem Discussion. Ask students to share solutions to the first situation. Use sticky notes to write these solutions in the table, or use another method to ensure that values can be moved and ordered easily within the table. Ask students to share how they arrived at each solution and to explain how they know that their solution meets the criteria of the situation. Have other students check the group's work and ask questions about the group's strategy as needed.

Have students share their solutions to the first situation until all solutions that were generated by the class have been exhausted. Take a moment to arrange the solutions in increasing or decreasing order. Ask, "What patterns do you see in this table? Do you think there might be solutions that we have missed?" Or, if all of the possible answers have been generated, ask, "How can we know that we have all the possible answers?" Highlight students' responses that attend to the extreme values that can be used before a number is rounded differently.

Follow this same sharing strategy for the second situation. Ask, "What is similar about these two problems?" Students may recognize that in both cases the numbers have been rounded to the nearest 10, and there is a difference of less than 10 between the two exact values.

Finally, ask students to share their answers to the third situation. (If several groups were unable to find a solution to this problem, consider allowing them five to ten minutes to revisit this situation. The groups that were successful might come together to think about how many possible solutions there are.) In discussing this last situation, trying to list all the possible solutions is unreasonable. Instead, put the answers in increasing or decreasing order, and ask the class, "Are there other solutions? How might we go about finding other solutions?" Try to elicit a class consensus that both numbers can be adjusted by the same amount to maintain the difference. Use two or three examples to demonstrate how this might work. Revisit this idea in light of the first two situations as needed.

DIFFERENTIATION

- If students struggle with making sense of the problem, have them work through the first situation in groups and discuss it as a class before sharing the other two situations.
- For the first situation, if students struggle with working backward from rounded numbers, help them generate a list of whole numbers that would round to 120.
- Challenge students to find all possible solutions to one of the situations.
- For the first situation, challenge students to identify two numbers that are 5 apart and would round to different values when rounding to the nearest 10.
- For the second situation, challenge students to identify two numbers that are 7 apart and would round to the same value when rounding to the nearest 10.
- Challenge students to write their own situational problem for another student to solve that is related to a spring sports event.
- Ask students to research other numbers that are relevant to the Kentucky Derby or other horse races. When would it be appropriate or helpful to round these numbers?

MILE RELAY

Jake, Mazie, and Carter are running as a team in the one-mile relay race. They are trying to decide what fraction of the mile each of them should run. In this race, runners do not need to run equal distances. Help Jake and his friends find three different ways they could each run a fraction of this race. Use a number line and equations to support your thinking.

CCSSM Standards for Mathematical Practice

Practice 2: Reason abstractly and quantitatively.

Practice 4: Model with mathematics.

CCSSM Content Standards

3.NF.A.3a: Understand two fractions as equivalent (equal) if they are the same size, or the same point on a number line.

3.NF.A.3b: Recognize and generate simple equivalent fractions, e.g., $1/2 = 2/4$, $4/6 = 2/3$. Explain why the fractions are equivalent, e.g., by using a visual fraction model.

3.NF.A.3c: Express whole numbers as fractions, and recognize fractions that are equivalent to whole numbers. *Examples: Express 3 in the form $3 = 3/1$; recognize that $6/1 = 6$; locate $4/4$ and 1 at the same point of a number line diagram.*

Problem Discussion

This task builds on students' knowledge of fractional parts of a whole. In the context of a mile-long relay race, students use a number line to represent distance. The number line "deepens students' understanding of the relative magnitude of fractions" (NCTM 2009a, p. 35). Specifically, the number line illustrates a length partitioned into equal parts and gives students an opportunity to visualize benchmark fractions as well as the relationships between fractions. In Mile Relay, students partition number lines into equal-sized parts to determine what fraction of the mile Jake, Mazie, and Carter can run. Students are likely to consider the scenario in which all three friends run the same distance, or $1/3$ of the mile. However, other options are possible, such as Jake running $1/4$ of a mile, Mazie running $1/2$ of a mile, and Carter running $1/4$ of a mile. Scenarios such as this allow for discussions related to equivalent fractions. For example, if two students come up with this scenario, one student may record Mazie's distance as $2/4$ instead of $1/2$ (see the Launch section for a visual model that could be used to compare these two ways of thinking). The number line model will assist students in understanding that two fractions are equal if they are at the same location on a number line (3.NF.A.3a). Thus, as students create their number lines, they will attend to the variety of ways to generate equivalent fractions (3.NF.A.3b), including fractions that are equivalent to the whole, such as $4/4$ (3.NF.A.3c).

This open-ended task also focuses students' attention on the use of the number line to model a real-world situation (SMP 4). After partitioning the number line into the desired number of equal-sized parts, students will then need to determine how many parts of one mile each friend might run. Below is a model using the number line to show the scenario in which Jake runs $2/6$ of the mile, Mazie runs $3/6$ of the mile, and Carter runs $1/6$ of the mile. Students working with this model must notice that the size of each interval is $1/6$ in order to determine each runner's total fractional part in the context of this situation (SMP 2). Labeling each interval as $1/6$ may help students who struggle to do this.

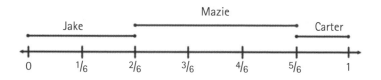

STRATEGIES

- Students may divide the race equally among the three friends and determine that each friend will run $1/3$ of the race.
- Students may use a guess-and-check strategy to find three fractions that sum to one whole.
- Students may partition the number line into fourths, sixths, or eighths and then find three fractional distances that sum to the whole.
- Students may choose fractions for two of the runners and then subtract their sum from 1 to find the third runner's fraction.

MISCONCEPTIONS/STUDENT DIFFICULTIES

- Students may struggle to find another solution besides each person running the same fractional amount of the mile ($1/3$ mile).
- Students may struggle to partition the number line into equal-sized parts.
- Students may not realize that they need common denominators to add and subtract fractions.
- Students may struggle to find equivalent fractions.
- Students may struggle to understand that the end points of two runners' segments are not the same as the fractional parts of the mile that each will run. For example, in the diagram above showing a number line model, students might say that Mazie will run $5/6$ of the mile instead of $3/6$ of the mile.

LAUNCH

Ask students whether they know that May is National Physical Fitness and Sports Awareness Month. Allow students to share ideas regarding what they do to stay active and why they think physical activity is important. Next, ask students whether they have ever been on a relay team or watched a relay race. If so, ask them to share their experience. If not, explain how a relay works and possibly have three or four students act out a relay to help students make sense of the context of a relay race.

Display a number line with 0 and 1 marked. Ask a student to mark where one-half would be. Next, ask students to talk with their partners about how they would determine where 1/4 and 3/4 would be on the number line. Have students share their strategies for partitioning the number line into fourths. To motivate students to recognize the labels on the number line as indicators of the distance from one point to the next, ask students how far it is from 0 to 1/4, 1/2 to 3/4, and so on. To engage students in thinking about equivalent fractions, ask whether there is a way to use fourths to label the 1/2 on the number line. Allow students to share their answers and record their thinking on the board. Below is an example of what your number line may look like at the conclusion of this discussion.

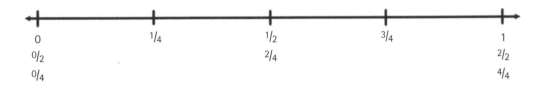

EXPLORE

Explain to students that they will be helping Jake and two friends figure out how far each of them will run in a one-mile relay race. Hand out the task and read it to students. Ask students to work with a partner to solve the task. Encourage students to use a variety of equal-sized units to partition the one-mile length. As students work, ask questions to check for understanding:

- How does your number line show that together the three friends will run a total of one mile?
- Could you partition the number line into a different number of equal-sized parts to find another way that the three friends could run this race?
- Can you think of a way in which all three friends could run the same distance? Can you show me this on the number line? How do you know they all would run the same distance?
- Can you think of a way in which two friends will run the same distance and the third will run a different distance? Can you show me this on the number line? How do you know that the two friends will run the same distance?
- Can you think of a way in which Jake will run the longest (shortest) distance? How do you know this is the longest (shortest) distance? Can you show me this on the number line?

SUMMARIZE

To summarize, ask if any groups partitioned the mile into thirds. If so, have these groups share how much of the mile each friend will run. (You may want to use number lines like those in the Differentiation section to display the work.) Next, ask students in groups that partitioned the mile into fourths to share their solutions. Allow students to show their work to the class, and take note of equivalent fractions as well as students' thinking concerning the distance that each friend runs. For example, when partitioning into fourths, as shown in the Launch section, students may think of $1/2$ as $2/4$. If two groups respond as shown below, be sure to ask the class whether these two scenarios are the same or different. Encourage students to use a number line to justify their reasoning.

Group 1: Jake, $1/4$ Mazie, $2/4$ Carter, $1/4$

Group 2: Jake, $1/4$ Mazie, $1/2$ Carter, $1/4$

Continue this process for sixths and eighths, allowing multiple groups to share different scenarios for the race. Note that $1/5$, $1/7$, and so on are also fractions that students may use to solve this task. Ask questions such as the following to check for understanding:

- Is there another way to record Jake's $3/6$ of a mile? How do you know $3/6$ is equivalent to $1/2$?
- Is the length from $1/6$ to $3/6$ the same as or different from the length from $4/6$ to $6/6$? How do you know?
- I see that one group has a scenario in which Jake will run $3/6$ of the mile, and another group has a scenario in which Jake will run $3/8$ of a mile. In which scenario do you think Jake will run farther? Why?

To conclude this discussion, ask students to discuss with a partner which of the partitions—thirds, fourths, sixths, or eighths—could result in a scenario in which each friend would run the same fractional amount. Have students share their answers to be sure that they have identified partitions of thirds and sixths as possible scenarios because both denominators are divisible by 3. Next, ask students to work with another partner to determine why they think these partitions could result in each friend running the same distance. Students should share their thinking with the whole class.

DIFFERENTIATION

- To support struggling students, provide fraction tile manipulatives and let students use the concrete manipulatives to create their number lines.
- To support students who struggle to partition the number line into equal-sized parts, provide number lines already partitioned into fourths, thirds, sixths, eighths, and so on, as shown on the next page.
- To support struggling students, supply Jake's fractional part of the mile for each of three scenarios.
- To extend the task, ask students to create only situations in which each student runs the same distance, and ask them to discuss what they notice about the denominators in each solution.
- To extend the task, ask students to create their own relay team with as many racers as they would like and determine what fraction of the one-mile race each student would run.

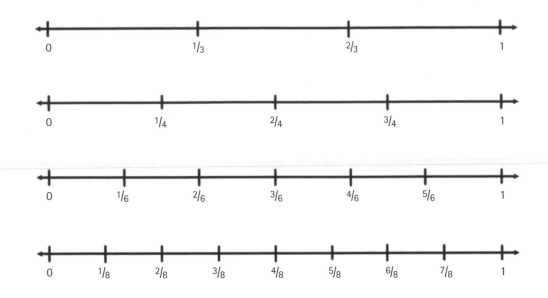

• To extend the task, ask students to write a letter to Jake, Mazie, and Carter, describing how they should divide up the mile and explaining why they think this is the best way.

PECULIAR PLANTINGS

Penelope has two square garden beds that she would like to plant with vegetables:

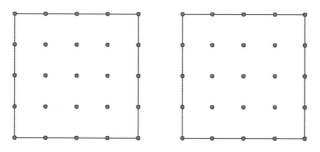

- In one of the garden beds, she wants to split the space into two parts to share equally between carrots and tomatoes.
- In the second garden bed, she wants to split the space into four parts to share equally among onions, lettuce, beans, and celery.

Penelope is a bit peculiar, however. She wants to plant her vegetables in spaces that do not look the same as one another. For each garden bed, find three ways to split the bed so that the vegetables are sharing the garden bed equally, but their spaces don't look the same. Explain how you know that the spaces are equal in size.

CCSSM Standards for Mathematical Practice

Practice 3: Construct viable arguments and critique the reasoning of others.

Practice 5: Use appropriate tools strategically.

CCSSM Content Standards

3.G.A.2: Partition shapes into parts with equal areas. Express the area of each part as a unit fraction of the whole. *For example, partition a shape into 4 parts with equal area, and describe the area of each part as 1/4 of the area of the shape.*

Problem Discussion

Peculiar Plantings asks students to partition squares into noncongruent halves and fourths. In this context, Penelope is peculiar; she does not want the spaces for each of her vegetables to look the same—that is, to be congruent. Instead, she would like halves and fourths of equal area but with shapes that look different. Consider one familiar way of partitioning a geoboard into halves, as shown on the right.

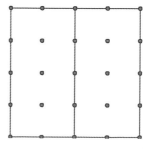

This partitioning of the square does not meet Penelope's peculiar standards, because the two spaces for the carrots and tomatoes are the same size and shape—they are congruent.

Instead, students are asked to partition the square into halves that are equal in area but are not congruent. There are many ways to partition the square into noncongruent halves of equal area. Consider the following example:

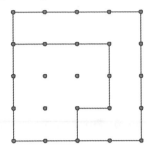

Each of these halves is composed of 8 square units. Students can determine or demonstrate this by further partitioning the halves into smaller rectangles, finding the area of these rectangles, and adding the areas together. Or students can partition each half into individual square units and count the number of square units (8) in each (SMP 3). In this task, students describe their halves and fourths in relation to the area of the total shape (3.G.A.2). As long as each half is equivalent to 8 square units and each fourth is equivalent to 4 square units, students will have found planting possibilities that meet Penelope's peculiar criteria.

Partitioning the square into noncongruent fourths will be challenging. Students will need to explore partitioning the space by using triangles or halves of unit squares, while thinking about the areas of these shapes. Consider the three possibilities below:

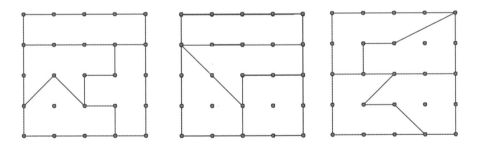

For students who struggle with finding four different-shaped fourths of the square, consider changing the criterion to "no more than two planting areas that are the same shape." This modification will allow students to find a solution without partitioning unit squares into triangles, as in the possibility shown below:

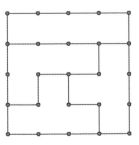

Students should use appropriate tools for this task (SMP 5). First, they should have access to geoboards and rubber bands to explore equipartitioning the area of the square into halves and fourths. Second, they may also choose to use the formula for the area of a rectangle as they determine the areas of the polygons that they have created. Students may also choose to use other tools that are available in the classroom. For example, instead of equipartitioning a given space, they may choose to create a garden bed of 16 square units with color tiles or snap cubes (with each color representing a different vegetable). Then they can record these results on the geoboard spaces on the activity sheets provided.

STRATEGIES

- Students may use color tiles or snap cubes to construct a square with an area of 16 square units, using different colors to represent different vegetables. The required number of each color may be selected ahead of construction, and then these pieces may be joined together to make a larger square.
- Students may use geoboards to identify familiar ways to partition the square into halves and fourths. Then they may alter these ways by adding units to one part and taking away an equivalent number of units from another part.
- Students may use geoboards to construct sections of the required area, knowing that half of a geoboard will require 8 square units ($1/_2$ of 16) and that a fourth of a geoboard will require 4 square units ($1/_4$ of 16).
- Students may skip the use of geoboards and instead use the geoboard diagrams on the activity sheet to construct their answers in a way that coincides with the two geoboard strategies above.

MISCONCEPTIONS/STUDENT DIFFICULTIES

- Students may have the misconception that parts of a whole need to be congruent for them to be halves or fourths of a whole.
- Students may not see parts as congruent if the shapes are oriented differently. For example, if an L shape is rotated, they may not see it as congruent to another L shape.
- Students may calculate the total area of the geoboard as 25 square units by counting the pegs along each side as unit measures of the length and coming up with a 5 × 5 square.
- Students may think that the entire garden bed does not need to be planted.
- Students may measure the perimeters of the parts of the whole that they construct rather than the areas of the parts in square units.

LAUNCH

Open this task by asking students whether they have ever had an opportunity to plant a garden. Have students share their experiences, and ask them what types of plants they planted. Also ask them to recall and share the shape of the garden bed.

Next, display a geoboard to the class, and ask them to imagine that this geoboard is a garden bed that needs to be planted. Explain that this garden bed needs to be shared equally between two vegetables: carrots and tomatoes. Ask a student to use a rubber band to demonstrate one way that the geoboard could be divided into two same-sized parts. (Students are very likely to generate a familiar visual of a geoboard divided into congruent halves, either by connecting the midpoints of two opposite sides or by constructing a diagonal.) Ask the class to name each of these parts as one half, or $1/2$. Write these terms on the board.

Ask the class, "How do you know that each of these parts is one-half of the whole garden bed?" Have students turn and talk with a neighbor, and then ask individual students to share their thinking. Answers may include the idea that there are two equal-sized parts or that each of the parts is made up of 8 unit squares. Ask students to reflect on the other students' reasoning by asking, "Does that make sense to you?"

Finally, introduce the Peculiar Plantings task to the class and discuss Penelope's peculiarity. Ask the students, "Why wouldn't the arrangement that we have here work for Penelope's garden?" Provide an opportunity for students to share their reasoning about this question, but do not allow them to talk about other possibilities. Instead, explain that they will be working in groups to generate alternative ideas for planting the garden beds.

EXPLORE

Arrange students in groups of three to work on this task. Each group should be provided with enough geoboards and rubber bands so that each student has his or her own set of tools. Also supply a cup of square tiles and a cup of snap cubes to each group. Explain that they can choose their own materials to work with in their groups, but ultimately they will need to record their three ideas on the activity sheets provided. Emphasize the importance of explaining their reasoning or proving that the parts they have created are one-half or one-fourth of the whole garden bed.

As students work, circulate throughout the room, asking questions to check for understanding (while also monitoring behavior with rubber bands!):

- Are the parts that you have made the same shape? How do you know that they are (or are not)?
- Are the parts that you have made the same size? How do you know that they are (or are not)?
- How do you know that this part is one-half (or one-fourth) of the whole garden bed?
- How can you adjust this part to make sure that it is one-half (or one-fourth) of the whole garden bed?

If some groups struggle to get started, consider posing questions that may build on the discussion from the Launch portion of the lesson:

- How could you adjust the rubber band in ways that might change the shape but keep each side one-half of the whole?
- How many square units should half of the garden bed cover? How do you know?
- Can you use a rubber band to create a shape that covers 8 square units?

Students will struggle to create noncongruent fourths of the geoboard until they consider triangles as an alternative. Allow this struggle to take place before intervening; this is a valuable opportunity for students to develop spatial reasoning. After some time, say, "I wonder if it's impossible to do this without using triangles. What do you think?"

SUMMARIZE

For this portion of the lesson, student groups should be paired to explain and justify their reasoning to another group. Have group members share responsibility for presenting solutions, with each student from each group presenting one of the group's solutions for each of the garden beds, so that each student has an opportunity to prove that the group created halves or fourths by counting or compiling the square units. Students in other groups should be encouraged to ask questions to clarify thinking. Consider generating some sentence starters if the students find critiquing one another's reasoning challenging.

After the group pairing and sharing, ask students to summarize as a class how a particular portion of a geoboard can be shown to be one-half or one-fourth of the whole. Confront any lingering misconceptions by asking, "Is it possible to have two halves of the whole that do not look the same?" Ask the same question regarding fourths. Require students to explain their reasoning beyond a simple yes.

Finally, ask students to work by themselves to partition an additional garden bed into noncongruent fourths and explain their own partitioning (More4U contains a sheet for this purpose). Use students' work to create a class display of a variety of ways that a geoboard can be partitioned into different-shaped fourths.

DIFFERENTIATION

- For students who struggle to find three different ways to partition the garden bed into fourths, allow them to work with no more than two congruent planting sections (see the Problem Discussion).
- Students can be challenged to find a way to partition the square equally for three vegetables. When they discover the challenge of this (each third would need to be equivalent to 5 1/3 square units, ask them to design a rectangular garden bed on a geoboard that could be easily partitioned into thirds.

Selling Umbrellas

The fourth graders at La Crescent Elementary School were selling umbrellas to raise money for a class trip. Alexis and Kelsey sold the most umbrellas. Alexis's total sales were $120, and Kelsey's were $96. They sold each umbrella for the same price. What could have been the price of an umbrella? How many umbrellas did each student sell? Use pictures and equations to support your answer.

CCSSM Standards for Mathematical Practice

Practice 7: Look for and make use of structure.

CCSSM Content Standards

4.OA.B.4: Find all factor pairs for a whole number in the range 1–100. Recognize that a whole number is a multiple of each of its factors. Determine whether a given whole number in the range 1–100 is a multiple of a given one-digit number. Determine whether a given whole number in the range 1–100 is prime or composite.

4.NBT.B.6: Find whole-number quotients and remainders with up to four-digit dividends and one-digit divisors, using strategies based on place value, the properties of operations, and/or the relationship between multiplication and division. Illustrate and explain the calculation by using equations, rectangular arrays, and/or area models.

Problem Discussion

Selling Umbrellas requires students to reason with factors and multiples of whole numbers (4.OA.B.4) to determine the price for each umbrella if two students sold $120 and $96 worth of umbrellas at the same price per umbrella. That is, this task allows students to determine whether a whole number is a multiple of a given whole number by "interpreting prior knowledge of division in terms of the language of multiples and factors" (Common Core State Standards Writing Team 2011, p. 30). To solve this task, students may list multiples of numbers by using a variety of multiplication strategies (e.g., skip counting, repeated addition, arrays, area models) to check whether 120 and 96 are both multiples of that number. For example, students may list multiples of 6 and see that both 96 and 120 are in the list by skip counting by 6 (i.e., 6, 12, 18, 24, 30, 36, 42, 48, 54, 60, 66, 72, 78, 84, 90, **96**, 102, 108, 114, **120**). Or you might prompt students to use manipulatives such as counters or blocks to determine what arrays they can make with a total of 96 and 120 counters or blocks.

Another possible strategy involves systematically listing the factors of both 96 and 120 to determine which factors the lists have in common. For this strategy, students may use a variety of division models, including repeated subtraction, properties of operations, place value concepts, arrays, area models, or a missing factor approach (4.NBT.B.6). For example, students may use an area model along with the distributive property, as shown below, to determine that 6 is a factor of 96 by decomposing 96 into two addends that they recognize are divisible by 6. That is, a student may notice that 6 divides both 60 and 36 evenly, resulting in the equations 6 × 16 = 96 and 96 ÷ 6 = 16 (SMP 7).

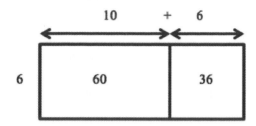

Using a variety of multiplication and division strategies, students may find that there are eight possible whole-dollar selling prices for the umbrellas, as shown in the table below. To allow additional practice with the division strategies outlined above, students can be asked to determine how many umbrellas Alexis and Kelsey sold for a given selling price. It is important for students to interpret the meaning of factors and multiples in their equations and models. For example, if they generated the equations 6 × 16 = 96 and 96 ÷ 6 = 16, they need to recognize that 6 and 16 are factors of 96, and 96 is a multiple of both 6 and 16. Students must then interpret these equations in the context of the situation to make a statement such as "Kelsey could have sold 16 umbrellas for $6 each, resulting in a total of $96."

Price per umbrella (in dollars)	Number of umbrellas sold by Alexis	Number of umbrellas sold by Kelsey
1	120	96
2	60	48
3	40	32
4	30	24
6	20	16
8	15	12
12	10	8
24	5	4

This task also offers a context for students to communicate their understanding of the difference between factors and multiples. For example, students will note that when they multiply two factors of the number, the product will be a multiple of each of the factors (SMP 7). Through discussion in the Summarize section, students will be encouraged to notice the structure of factors and multiples. For example, if 8 is a factor of 96, so are 2 and 4 (SMP 7). Other patterns in the table may be discussed, including, for example, the pattern that emerges in the number of umbrellas sold if the price of each umbrella is doubled. If the price doubles, half as many umbrellas are sold.

STRATEGIES

- Students may use trial and error to find which numbers evenly divide both 120 and 96.
- Students may systematically search for all factor pairs of both 120 and 96 by checking whether 2 is a factor, then 3, then 4, and so on.
- Students may begin by listing multiples of numbers, looking for both 120 and 96 in each list (i.e., The multiplies of 6 are 6, 12, 18, 24, 30, 36, 42, 48, 54, 60, 66, 72, 78, 84, 90, **96**, 102, 108, 114, **120**).
- Students may use division strategies, such as repeated subtraction, long division, or decomposing the number into two addends (96 = 60 + 36), and look for common factors of these addends (i.e., 6 is a factor of both 60 and 36. Since 10 × 6 = 60 and 6 × 6 = 36, 6 × 16 = 96.)
- Students may find the difference of $24 between Alexis's and Kelsey's total sales ($120 − $96) and list the factors of 24, which are 1, 2, 3, 4, 6, 8, 12, 24.

MISCONCEPTIONS/STUDENT DIFFICULTIES

- Students may multiply 120 by 96.
- Student may add 120 and 96 and find numbers that evenly divide 216.
- Students may have difficulty finding all factors of each number.
- Students may confuse the terms *factor* and *multiple*.
- Students may have difficulty finding quotients with equations involving divisors of 12 and 24.

LAUNCH

Ask students whether they have ever sold items for a fundraiser. Allow them to share what these items were and what the fundraiser was raising money for. Next, tell students about a time you sold something for a fundraiser. Tell them how much each item cost and how many you sold. For example, you might say, "When I was in fourth grade, I sold tins of popcorn for $8 each. In one day I collected $192. How many tins of popcorn did I sell?" Have students work individually to solve this task. Next, ask students to share their answers and division strategies (see the Problem Discussion and Strategies sections for possible strategies). To focus on the academic language of *factor* and *multiple*, ask students to tell a partner one factor and one multiple of 8. Share a few of their answers with the class. Next, display the sentence frames below and have students complete them.

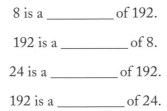

8 is a _____ of 192.

192 is a _____ of 8.

24 is a _____ of 192.

192 is a _____ of 24.

Throughout this discussion, ask questions to check for understanding:

- What do you notice about factors?
- What do you notice about multiples?
- Are factors always smaller than the number? Explain.
- Can a number be both a factor and a multiple of a given number? Explain.

EXPLORE

Hand out the task and read it to students. Ask students what information is important. Be sure that they understand that each umbrella was sold for the same amount. Have students work individually to solve this task. Ask questions to check for understanding:

- How do you know 2 is a factor of both numbers?
- I see you have 4 as an answer. Why does this number make sense as a possible price of each umbrella?
- Why are we looking for factors of 96 and 120 instead of multiples of these numbers?
- Can you find another number that is a factor of both 96 and 120?
- Would a selling price of $10 work? How do you know?

SUMMARIZE

To bring the task to completion, ask students to work in small groups of three or four to compare solutions. Challenge groups to find all solutions and prove they have indeed found all possible solutions, as shown in the table on page 133. Their justifications may include arguments such as, "We listed all factor pairs of both numbers, and these were the only ones they had in common," or "We found all the numbers that evenly divided 96 and checked to see if they also evenly divided 120." Select groups to share a solution and explain why that solution is valid, using equations and models. Allow groups to continue sharing until all eight solutions have been discussed. If no groups share a particular solution, such as $1, ask students if this amount would work and explain why or why not. As groups share solutions, encourage the use of the terms *factor*, *multiple*, *product*, and *quotient*. Ask questions to check for understanding:

- What do you notice about the factors of 120?
- If we know that 8 is a factor of a number, what other numbers are also factors? (2 and 4.) Does this work for other numbers such as 6 or 12? (Yes. For example, if 6 is a factor of a number, then 2 and 3 must also be factors of that number.)
- Using this reasoning, how could you explain why 10 is not a factor of both 96 and 120 (e.g., 2 is a factor of both 96 and 120, but 5 is not a factor of 96, so 10 is not a factor of both 96 and 120).
- What do you notice happens to the number of umbrellas sold if the price is cut in half?

To conclude the task, ask students to choose the selling price they think is the most reasonable and explain to the class why it seems so.

DIFFERENTIATION

- To support struggling students, lower the sales numbers to $60 and $48.
- To support struggling students, provide manipulatives for students to use to represent each dollar. These can be used to subtract repeatedly to find factors of each number.
- To support struggling students, allow students to complete the task with a partner.
- To extend the task, add a third student's total sales of $180.
- To extend the task, ask students to find the total sales for two students so that there are only three possible solutions or two possible solutions.
- To extend the task, tell students that someone solved the task by finding the factors of the difference of 120 and 96. Ask students to determine whether this strategy would work and explain why or why not.

Surprising Statistics

Research topics related to Earth Day, and find two statistics that surprise you. Use a recording sheet to record each statistic, and write the value as a numeral, with a number name, and in expanded form. Explain why each of your statistics is surprising to you, and what you think we should do about it.

Example

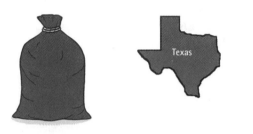

My Statistic: One estimate of the size of the North Pacific Garbage Patch is 540,000 square miles, twice the size of the state of Texas.
Numeral: 540,000
Number Name: Five hundred forty thousand
Expanded Form: 500,000 + 40,000
Why this statistic is surprising to me, and what I think we should do about it!

CCSSM Standards for Mathematical Practice

Practice 3: Construct viable arguments and critique the reasoning of others.

CCSSM Content Standards

4.NBT.A.2: Read and write multi-digit whole numbers using base-ten numerals, number names, and expanded form. Compare two multi-digit numbers based on meanings of the digits in each place, using >, =, and < symbols to record the results of comparisons.

Problem Discussion

Surprising Statistics is an open-ended task that is intended to increase students' awareness of environmental issues and simultaneously engage them in making sense of large numbers. Students are asked to represent these numerical statistics in multiple ways: as numerals, with number names, and in expanded form (4.NBT.A.2). The Summarize portion of the lesson provides an opportunity to compare the statistical values, using the different representations of the numbers (SMP 3). Students may also recognize that some comparisons of numbers lack meaning when the values are considered in context. For example, 540,000 < 380,000,000,000 is a meaningful numerical comparison, but it may not be meaningful when these quantities are considered in context. The first value, 540,000, which appears in the example given with the task, refers to an estimate of the size in square miles of the Great Pacific Garbage Patch, and the second value, 380 billion, refers to the number of plastic bags used annually in the United States.

Human impact on the environment is multifaceted, although fourth-grade students may have limited knowledge of this fact. Elementary school students' experiences with Earth Day may be limited to generic assertions that it is important to reduce, reuse, and recycle. This task provides an opportunity for students to broaden their horizons about the environment and understand quantifiable statistics related to human impact on our planet's ecosystems. Because students' knowledge of the environment may be limited, consider brainstorming researchable topics during the Launch portion of the lesson. Potential topics include the following:

- Size of garbage patches in the ocean (Great Pacific, North Atlantic, and Indian Ocean)
- Number of plastic bags used by a nation each year or by the world each day
- Number of plastic bottles used per minute, per day, per year in a country
- Countries involved in celebrating Earth Day
- Number of different marine species affected by plastics in the ocean
- Gas mileage for different models of automobiles
- Number of acres of rain forest destroyed annually
- Amount of oil used to produce plastic bags or plastic bottles
- Population estimates of endangered species
- Water usage, such as the number of gallons used by an average family per day

Values such as these should be relatively easy for students to find online.

This task also enables students to make sense of large numbers and identify situations in which these numbers are applied. Students will need to make sense of these values to present their findings to their peers. They will need to reason about why a statistic is surprising and what actions might be appropriate to change the statistic to lessen the negative impact on the environment (SMP 3).

STRATEGIES

- Students may identify statistics represented as a numeral or number name and represent this quantity in other forms.

- Students may identify statistics represented as a combination of a numeral and number name (e.g., 380 billion) and represent this quantity in other forms.
- Students may refer to place value charts to make sense of large numbers.
- Students may label the periods within the statistics (e.g., billions, millions, thousands, etc.) to make sense of a large number.
- Students may make comparisons between their statistic and another known quantity to make sense of the value or size of the statistic.

Misconceptions/Student Difficulties

- Students may struggle to understand quantities written as a combination of a numeral and number name (e.g., 380 billion).
- Students may struggle to remember place value positions for millions, billions, trillions, and so on.
- Students may have difficulty representing a numeral as a number name, especially with large quantities. For example, a student may write 540,000 as "five hundred thousand, forty thousand."
- Students may be able to compare quantities found in various statistics but struggle to recognize that comparisons between the values in context may lack meaning.

Launch

This task can be launched either by asking students what they know about Earth Day or by asking them what they know about statistics. Both, however, should be discussed, highlighting the purpose of Earth Day (awareness and protection of our environment) and the applicable definition of statistics (numerical facts, data). If possible, present a local statistic related to Earth Day. For example, "Sixteen out of 17 classrooms at our school are participating in Earth Day activities." Discuss the meaning of this local statistic, whether or not it is surprising to students, and how they might plan to improve the statistic.

Next, explain that the students will be researching statistics related to Earth Day, with a special challenge to look for large numbers. Ask the class to generate ideas about potential topics. Supplement this list with topics of local interest or ideas from the list found in the Problem Discussion. Consider selecting a few of these and asking the students to make estimates of what they might expect.

Finally, ask a student to read the task aloud to the class. Share the example provided. As needed, discuss the Great Pacific Garbage Patch; some online investigation may be warranted. Then ask the class how they might write the numeral 540,000 as a number name and in expanded form. Have students share their thinking, and record the correct answers on a display of the recording sheet. Ask the class why this statistic is surprising to them, and what humans could do to make this environmental situation better. Summarize their ideas on the recording sheet.

Explore

Assign students to pairs to complete their research, and make sure that they record their two different statistics. If possible, make sure that each pair has access to the Internet. If needed, generate a list of search terms or websites that students might explore. Provide two copies of the recording sheet to each pair, and have additional recording sheets available to support students who want to document more than two surprising statistics.

As students work, circulate throughout the room, asking questions to check for understanding:

- What number have you found that surprises you?
- How do you say that number?
- How would you write that number in expanded form? What place values are important in this number?
- Why is this statistic so surprising?
- Your statistic seems to be a combination of a number name and a numeral. How can you use the information provided to write it as each?
- How did you decide how many zeroes you needed for your number?
- How did you decide where to put commas in recording your numeral?

Also take note of the values that students are finding. They will have an opportunity to compare and order some of these values in the Summarize portion of the lesson. It might be helpful to select values from students' work that are close to one another or that refer to something similar (e.g., plastic bags and plastic bottles, sizes of oceanic garbage patches).

If students struggle with saying numbers correctly (and therefore writing the number names), writing numbers in expanded form, or writing a number with its appropriate place value structure, provide support by referring them to a place value chart or having them construct a place value chart as a small group. Helping students attend to the period values (thousands, millions, billions, trillions…) may assist them in making sense of some of these large quantities.

Summarize

Ask the students to come together with their recording sheets to discuss their surprising statistics as a class. Have each partner in a pair present one of the pair's statistics. Ask each pair of students to share how they translated their number from the way it which it was presented in the statistic to the corresponding numeral, number name, and expanded form. Also, ask each pair to explain why they think this statistic is surprising, and what human actions might be taken to support the environment and change the statistic.

As student pairs present, ask their peers to attend to the presenters' reasoning, ask questions respectfully, and reflect on their own about the meaning of the statistic. For most students, conceptualizing such large quantities will be challenging. As needed, discuss the place value positions used in the numbers, and emphasize the meaning of content standard 4.NBT.A.2.

After all pairs have shared one of their statistics, ask them to discuss as a class how they would compare and order these quantities. Arrange data from the recording sheets in order from least to greatest on the board as students discuss their comparisons (e.g., "I know that 540 billion is less than 3 trillion). Again, ask students to justify their reasoning, and highlight any use of the numerals, number names, or numbers in expanded form. Have peers critique their reasoning, allowing for as much of the discussion as possible to occur between students.

Finally, ask students to do a gallery walk to take in the statistics that were not shared. Then ask students to share what they have learned about their environment and one thing related to one of these statistics that they will try to change to have a positive impact on the environment.

DIFFERENTIATION

- For students who struggle with time or focus, provide a specific Web address for them to explore.
- For students who struggle with task completion or writing, require that they complete only one surprising statistic recording sheet.
- For students who struggle with place value understanding of large numbers, provide a place value chart, or review place value during the Launch portion of the lesson.
- Challenge students to find multiple statistics related to the same topic (e.g., number of plastic bags used annually by different countries, size of the oceanic garbage patches) and order their statistics.
- Challenge students to find other statistics related to a specific statistic. For example, if they find the size of the Indian Ocean Garbage Patch, what state is of comparable size?
- Challenge students to find surprising statistics related to other topics that interest them (e.g., sports, other countries).

May Day Maypole

Ms. Higgins's class is preparing a traditional maypole to celebrate May Day. The students need $^2/_3$ of a spool of ribbon for each ribbon coming down from the top of the maypole. If they want to make a maypole with 16 ribbons, how many spools of ribbon should Ms. Higgins buy for the class? Support your explanation with drawings, manipulatives, or equations.

CCSSM Standards for Mathematical Practice

Practice 4: Model with mathematics.

Practice 8: Look for and express regularity in repeated reasoning.

CCSSM Content Standards

4.NF.B.4c: Solve word problems involving multiplication of a fraction by a whole number, e.g., by using visual fraction models and equations to represent the problem. *For example, if each person at a party will eat $^3/_8$ of a pound of roast beef, and there will be 5 people at the party, how many pounds of roast beef will be needed? Between what two whole numbers does your answer lie?*

Problem Discussion

In May Day Maypole, students are asked to determine how many spools of ribbon should be purchased to decorate a maypole. Each ribbon requires $^2/_3$ of a spool, and the class needs to drape 16 ribbons from the top of the maypole. Students will reason that shorter lengths of ribbon may be joined to make a ribbon for the maypole. Thus, the amount of ribbon that is needed is $16 \times {}^2/_3$ (written in this order to represent 16 sets of $^2/_3$). Students may think about this task in terms of multiplication of a fraction by a whole number (4.NF.B.4c). However, if students have not encountered this type of problem before, it is likely that they will model it in a way that is more aligned with repeated addition (SMP 4).

Students may use a variety of tools to represent their thinking in this task. Consider the first of the diagrams shown at the top of the next page, in which $^2/_3$ is represented by two shaded linking cubes out of three cubes. These shaded cubes represent the amount of ribbon needed from one spool for one maypole ribbon; the cube representing the remaining $^1/_3$ of a spool is shown as white. Each set of two shaded cubes can make one maypole ribbon. However, the white cubes representing the remainders from each spool can also be joined together to make additional maypole ribbons. Students may recognize that two spools of ribbon can make three maypole ribbons. They can repeat this reasoning to make three additional maypole ribbons with each pair of spools until they have accounted for fifteen maypole ribbons with ten spools (SMP 8). One additional spool will be needed to make the sixteenth maypole ribbon. Using the linking cubes in this case makes it clear that $^1/_3$ of a spool will be left over. Note that some students may use trial and error as they attempt to account for sixteen maypole ribbons. In addition, students may need to recreate the representation to count the total number of spools, shown by a different arrangement of cubes on the right.

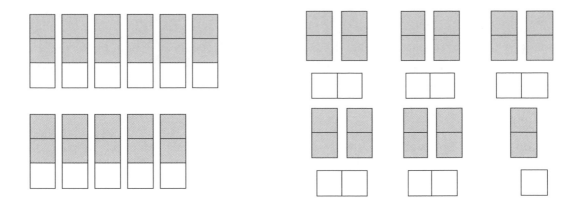

The line of reasoning outlined in the preceding paragraph is slightly different from the one illustrated in the diagrams below, although it also uses linking cubes. This time, linking cubes in only one color are used; all the cubes in the diagrams are shaded alike to show this. The diagram on the left shows sixteen sets of two linking cubes that represent the $2/3$ of a spool required for each ribbon. Each cube again represents $1/3$ of a spool. To determine the number of spools needed, students can regroup these thirds into sets of three to represent a complete spool. In doing so, they will determine that $10\,2/3$ spools are needed. They may have to reason further to determine that 11 spools must be purchased to allow enough ribbon for 16 maypole ribbons.

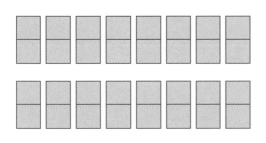 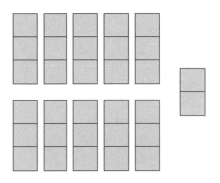

Finally, students may reason through this problem abstractly, by determining the total quantity when 16 two-thirds are added together (see below). Some support with manipulatives may be necessary for students to determine partial sums (e.g., $2/3 + 2/3 + 2/3 = 2$), but their final representation may be purely abstract. If so, it will be important to determine students' underlying reasoning as they determined the total sum.

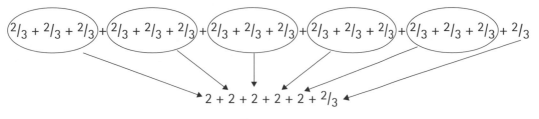

$$10\,2/3 \text{ spools}$$

Note that this task provides opportunities for students to think about how the final answer relates to the context of the problem. In some shops, it may possible to buy portions of spools. Students who know this may defend a final answer of 10 $2/3$ spools of ribbon. However, students are more likely to reason that the teacher must purchase complete spools. In this case, 10 spools will not provide enough ribbon, but 11 spools will be sufficient.

STRATEGIES

- Students may represent 16 groups of $2/3$ with manipulatives (e.g., for each group of $2/3$, 2 linking cubes, 2 fraction pieces) and regroup these to make wholes with $3/3$.
- Students may represent $2/3$ as part of a whole (e.g., 2 blue linking cubes attached to 1 red linking cube), repeat, and regroup the extra $1/3$ from each whole to create the required 16 ribbons. Then they may form wholes of $3/3$ to count the number of spools needed.
- Students may make 16 jumps of $2/3$ on a number line, marking each landing spot until reaching 10 $2/3$.
- Students may add sixteen addends of $2/3$. To do this, they may look for quantities that create whole numbers; for example, three addends of $2/3$ sum to 2. They may repeat this reasoning, clustering three $2/3$ addends to create partial sums of 2. Note that students may support this repeated reasoning with the use of manipulatives.
- Students may think about $16 \times 2/3$ as $(16 \times 2) \times 1/3$.
- Students may consider the quantity of spools that is needed (from strategies identified above) and reason that a whole number of spools (11) must be purchased.

MISCONCEPTIONS/STUDENT DIFFICULTIES

- Students may think that 16 spools are needed, reasoning that the extra ribbon on each spool is waste.
- Students may find it difficult to understand how the extra ribbon might be joined to create another ribbon for the maypole.
- Students may create 16 two-thirds and then erroneously consider each of these "wholes" (i.e., a whole ribbon) as a whole spool.
- Students may make computational errors or misapply algorithms. For example, students may multiply both the numerator and denominator of $2/3$ by 16.

LAUNCH

Begin this task by asking students how many of them have heard of May Day. This holiday is not as popular in North America as it is in other parts of the world, so students may have limited knowledge to share. If this is the case, share some information about the holiday, and take some time to record questions that the students have and would like to explore. These questions can be pursued by students during other class time.

Explain to the students that one of the ways that May Day has been celebrated is by dancing around a maypole. Show some images that represent this tradition, pointing out the pole itself, and the ribbons draped from the top of the pole. Rich descriptions of maypole dancing and its cultural connections can be found online. Before the lesson, identify links to appropriate sites for the class to explore. A possible option is to discuss the layered histories of May Day—the traditional, historical May Day celebrations and the holiday's connections with socialism, communism, and the labor movement. Students may also be familiar with the emergency call "Mayday!" These connotations can provide opportunities for additional exploration for students.

Set the mathematical context of this problem by explaining that a class is making a maypole to celebrate May Day. Have a student read the task aloud, and ask students what they know about the problem from this reading. Display their thoughts—for example, "The class needs to make 16 ribbons."

Ask the students to think by themselves about a way that they could represent $2/3$ of a spool. Have students talk to an elbow partner about their ideas. Then, as a class, collect the multiple suggestions of ways that $2/3$ can be represented. Record these as drawings when appropriate. If students refer to a manipulative, demonstrate $2/3$ with the manipulative for the class to see. Students may use a variety of manipulatives, such as linking cubes, fraction circles, fraction rectangles or squares, or color chips. Be sure that all ideas are shared and given equal attention in displays that remain visible as students work on the task.

Before asking students to begin work on this problem, ask them what they are trying to find out. Have several students restate this in their own words. Ask students to make a prediction as well. Predictions may be a range of values (e.g., 10–15 spools), or they may be single values (about 10 spools). Remind students that they will be expected to explain their solutions and represent their thinking with drawings, manipulatives, or equations.

EXPLORE

Allow all students five to ten minutes of individual work time for this task. Have multiple manipulatives and other materials available at each table. Provide any fraction manipulatives that students have worked with earlier (e.g., fraction circles, fraction strips) as well as other manipulatives or tools that could be used to represent aspects of the problem (e.g., linking cubes, open number lines, color chips, construction paper). Do not expect a complete answer at the end of this individual work time. Rather, this time should give individual students a way to begin reasoning about the problem that they can then bring to partner or group work.

If students struggle to get started, ask them questions about their understanding of the problem and how they might use manipulatives and other tools to represent what they know:

- How is the number $2/3$ important to the problem?
- How could you use something at your table to represent $2/3$ of a spool of ribbon?
- How many ribbons does Ms. Higgins's class want to prepare for the maypole?
- How could you use something at your table to represent the 16 ribbons that need to be made?

If students wonder whether the extra ribbons from spools can be combined, interrupt the individual work to discuss this dilemma. Bring the class to a consensus that for the purposes of the problem, remaining ribbon from spools can be combined (perhaps by sewing or taping) to create ribbons for the maypole. It is better if students reason on their own about the idea that the $1/3$ remaining from two spools of ribbon could create another maypole ribbon.

After the individual work time, ask students to work with a partner or their table groups to share their thinking thus far. Ask them to share one by one, giving each student an opportunity to speak. Then ask students to continue to work on solving the problem, either individually, pursuing their own solution strategies, or working in pairs or groups. Regardless of the students' choices, all students should continue to use their peers as resources and take advantage of opportunities throughout the remaining time to share and critique one another's thinking.

As students continue to work, circulate throughout the room. Note that students may use manipulatives in similar ways but pursue divergent strategies. Ask questions such as the following to elicit their solution strategies and check for understanding:

- Can you explain how you're representing the problem here?
- How does this represent one ribbon?
- How does this represent one spool of ribbon?
- Can you tell me how you know that two spools can make three ribbons?
- Is there a way that you can extend this knowledge to figure out how many spools you would need for 6 ribbons? For 9 ribbons?
- I see that you have indicated that the teacher needs to purchase $10\,2/3$ spools of ribbon. Is it possible to buy $2/3$ of a spool of something?
- Can you tell me how you combined these quantities in your equation? How did you know that 3 two-thirds would make 2?

Students may exhibit some confusion as they refer to different wholes during the Explore phase. For example, they may refer to $2/3$ but consider this as a whole spool, rather than a whole ribbon for the maypole. Assist students in clarifying their language and conceptions as they explain their thinking. Additional questioning may be necessary as they come to understand the problem more deeply.

Ask students to make posters showing their final solutions, either individually or with other students. If students are still working and have not come to a final solution, ask them to make a poster of their work thus far, and perhaps indicate a question that they have about how to proceed. Allow displays to lie flat, so that students can use their manipulatives to support their reasoning. When students have finished their displays, group these to show similar strategies together in the room.

Summarize

Give students five to ten minutes for a gallery walk throughout the classroom, focusing on the different strategies that were used. Then ask students to think about how different models were used in the solution strategies. Ask, "What different kinds of manipulatives were used?" and "How were these manipulatives used?" Allow some time for students to discuss each manipulative model of the problem and how each was used. Note that although different students may have used the same model, they may have used it in different ways to find a solution to the problem. Have students who used each of these models discuss their solution strategy if it is being misinterpreted or needs clarification.

Ask, "How did students use fractions and operations to solve the problem?" Give students some time to discuss each of the computational strategies that were used. Take any available opportunities to discuss the connections between the computational work and the manipulatives. For example, if a student grouped three two-thirds together to create two whole spools, make sure that the connection between this computation and using two spools of ribbon to create three maypole ribbons with manipulatives is highlighted and discussed.

This problem provides an opportunity to involve students in some early proportional reasoning. If students recognize that 2 spools will create 3 maypole ribbons and then use this ratio to determine the number of spools required for 15 maypole ribbons, examine this reasoning as a class. If there is time, ask questions such as the following:

- If 2 spools of ribbon will make 3 maypole ribbons, how many maypole ribbons will 4 spools make?
- How many spools would it take to make 9 maypole ribbons? How do you know?

Proportional reasoning is not the content focus for this task, however. Limited time should be spent in efforts to highlight this particular mathematical reasoning.

DIFFERENTIATION

- A less challenging task would be to change the amount of a spool needed to make a ribbon from $2/3$ to a unit fraction, such as $1/3$.
- The task could be changed so that the number of maypole ribbons needed is a multiple of 3; this change would avoid the need to reason about needing to buy a whole number of spools.
- For students who struggle to envision this task, provide a spool of ribbon for them to manipulate. It may be helpful to mark off thirds of the ribbon before using the spool with the class.
- Ask students who solved this problem by using manipulatives to think about how they might solve it with an equation or how they might represent their earlier thinking with an equation.
- Ask students to write and solve a similar problem.
- Challenge students to determine what quantities of maypole ribbons could be made that would create no ribbon waste (multiples of 3).

Relay Teams

The spring track coach at Lawrence School is trying to put together two balanced relay teams with four girls on each team. Each girl will have to run 200 meters. The coach has recorded the three best times in seconds for each girl in the table below. Use this information to create two balanced relay teams, and predict how long it will take each team to run the entire race. Justify your reasoning.

Name	Time 1	Time 2	Time 3
Emerald	30.08 sec	31.24 sec	29.13 sec
Grace	25.75 sec	25.68 sec	25.9 sec
Kendall	28.65 sec	32.04 sec	33.15 sec
Maria	24.5 sec	24.05 sec	23.88 sec
Janiqua	29.55 sec	23.65 sec	29.41 sec
Kim	26.98 sec	26.52 sec	27.21 sec
Stephanie	34.1 sec	33.64 sec	33.15 sec
Olivia	22.13 sec	23.6 sec	22.85 sec

CCSSM Standards for Mathematical Practice

Practice 1: Make sense of problems and persevere in solving them.

Practice 3: Construct viable arguments and critique the reasoning of others.

CCSSM Content Standards

5.NBT.A.3b: Compare two decimals to thousandths based on meanings of the digits in each place, using >, =, and < symbols to record the results of comparisons.

5.NBT.B.7: Add, subtract, multiply, and divide decimals to hundredths, using concrete models or drawings and strategies based on place value, properties of operations, and/or the relationship between addition and subtraction; relate the strategy to a written method and explain the reasoning used.

Problem Discussion

This task is open-ended and provides students with opportunities to reason about decimal values to the hundredths place, add decimals together, and make comparisons (5.NBT.A.3b; 5.NBT.B.7). Students will analyze data for each runner and make conclusions about how fast they might expect each runner to run in her 200-meter leg of the relay (SMP 1).

To do this, students may choose the fastest time for each runner (the lowest time in seconds). However, they may recognize that there is great variation in the times of some runners (e.g., Janiqua), so choosing the fastest time may not truly represent the runner's performance in a race. Students may also choose to use the median (middle number) for each runner as a way to represent each runner's potential more accurately. Note that either of these strategies requires comparison of decimals to the hundredths place (5.NBT.A.3b). Some values have been purposefully chosen to challenge students in these comparisons. With Maria, for example, students may struggle to identify which value—24.5 or 24.05—is actually the smaller value. They will need to consider the place value of the digit 5 in each of these numbers to make a successful comparison.

Alternatively, students may estimate an average, although they may not be mathematically familiar with the terminology or methods for finding a mean. The table below contains an additional column with the average computed for each runner:

Name	Time 1	Time 2	Time 3	Average
Emerald	30.08 sec	31.24 sec	29.13 sec	30.15 sec
Grace	25.76 sec	25.68 sec	25.9 sec	25.78 sec
Kendall	28.65 sec	32.04 sec	33.15 sec	31.28 sec
Maria	24.5 sec	24.05 sec	23.87 sec	24.14 sec
Janiqua	29.55 sec	23.65 sec	29.42 sec	27.54 sec
Kim	26.98 sec	26.52 sec	27.2 sec	26.9 sec
Stephanie	34.1 sec	33.64 sec	33.15 sec	33.63 sec
Olivia	22.13 sec	23.6 sec	22.85 sec	22.86 sec

Unless students are already familiar with a method for computing the mean, they are more likely to estimate values that are close to those in this final column.

Once a representative value has been identified for each runner, different combinations of four of these values can be generated to determine fairly balanced teams. This can be done by playing with the numbers and trying to find sums of four that are close to one another. This will vary depending on the representative values that students are using. Thus, students will need to construct their own viable arguments for their methods, as well as make sense of and critique the reasoning of others (SMP 3).

If the means from the table above are used, one potential combination for relay teams might be the following:

  Team 1: Emerald, Maria, Stephanie, Olivia (110.78 seconds total)

  Team 2: Grace, Kendall, Janiqua, Kim (111.5 seconds total)

Other combinations might be determined by trial and error. Students might make exchanges of runners between teams to produce total values that are closer together, thus creating an opportunity to engage in algebraic reasoning. Because there are multiple ways of finding a representative value for each runner and combining these values together, the opportunities for students to construct viable arguments for different answers abound.

Strategies

- Students may choose the fastest time to serve as a representative value for each runner.
- Students may choose the middle time (median) to serve as a representative value for each runner.
- Students may estimate a mean for each runner. (If students are familiar with a method for finding the actual mean, they may use this.)
- Students may use trial and error to combine four representative values into teams until they have created teams with similar total values.
- Students may use a manipulative to combine the runners' representative values (e.g., base-ten blocks).
- Students may combine runners' representative values by using strategies based on the place value meaning of digits. Students may also combine whole numbers of seconds and then combine the partial seconds by using strategies based on place value.
- Students may compare decimals by using a manipulative (e.g., base-ten blocks), a diagram, or strategies based on place value.

Misconceptions/Student Difficulties

- Students may find the notion that the smaller value represents a faster—and better—time challenging to understand.
- Students may struggle with comparisons of numbers with place values to the tenths and hundredths (e.g., 24.5 and 24.05). A misconception that the number with more digits is larger may surface.
- Students may struggle to decide on a method for identifying a representative value for each runner.
- Students may think that they must find two teams with total times that are *equal*, rather than two teams with total times that are *close*.
- Students may struggle to add decimal values or may make computational errors.

Launch

Students are likely to have varied experiences with races—more specifically, relays—so begin this task by asking students to share what they know about running races, track events, or relay races (e.g., the Olympics.). Some helpful information to counter misconceptions may come out of this discussion. For example, ask, "In a running race, how is the winner decided? What is compared to determine the winner?" Discuss the format of relay races as well; consider showing the class a video of a relay race so that they can see baton passes and how the race as a whole is completed.

Next, display the task for the students, and ask them to read it to themselves. Have them identify any challenging vocabulary and elicit their input on these terms before providing clarification. Then, have students share what they know from their reading of the problem.

Make a list of their contributions on a whiteboard or other display. For each, ask other students if they agree with the information or where they see it in the task itself.

If needed, take some time to clarify the measurements for each of the trial runs. Students may not realize that times for running races are often measured to hundredths of a second. Therefore, it may be helpful to clarify what a particular time measurement (e.g., 31.24 seconds) means in the context of the problem.

Finally, explain to students that they will be working in groups of three or four to solve this problem. Provide base-ten blocks and any other place value manipulatives or models that students are familiar with or accustomed to using.

Explore

Have students share ideas for tackling the problem with their group members when they first get into groups. Before each group proceeds with an idea, have them check in with you and articulate their plans. There is no need to intervene at this point. Instead, this is a helpful opportunity for the group to demonstrate consensus with a public plan.

As groups begin their work, circulate throughout the room, and ask questions to assess students' understanding:

- Can you explain why you are using these times for each of the runners?
- Why did you choose the fastest time? Do you think it is safe to ignore the other two times?
- Why did you choose the middle time? Why didn't you choose the fastest time for each runner?
- How are you deciding whether or not the relay teams are fairly balanced?
- Do you think it's possible to get two relay teams that are perfectly balanced?
- What kind of variation might you expect in the real race?
- How reasonable do you think your total race time predictions are?
- Can you explain your strategy for adding these numbers together?
- Can you explain your strategy for comparing the race times?
- Are there other combinations for teams that might be similarly balanced?

As students respond to these questions, make sure that they can justify the reasoning behind their selection of the representative values for each runner, as well as demonstrate and explain how they are comparing and computing with decimals. Take note of groups that have used similar strategies in selecting representative times for the runners, since students in these groups may have a unique opportunity to critique one another's reasoning about the formation of the relay teams.

When it appears that most or all of the groups have established at least one set of fairly balanced relay teams, ask each group to make a poster or whiteboard display of their teams, estimates of total time for the race, and the reasoning behind their decisions.

SUMMARIZE

Organize presentations for this task by asking groups with similar reasoning for the runners' representative values to present back-to-back, possibly in the following sequence:

- Groups that used the fastest time to represent each runner.
- Groups that used the median time to represent each runner.
- Groups that estimated a mean, although this terminology may not be familiar to them.
- Groups that calculated a mean running time for each runner.

This sharing is an opportunity for students to critique one another's reasoning for choosing these representative values.

Use this discussion to raise drawbacks to each method. For example, choosing the fastest time for each runner may be unrealistic, especially if the fastest time is significantly different from the other times. Discussing these drawbacks is important, yet so is realizing that the debate may have no resolution, since any method has drawbacks. This is simply an opportunity to discuss representative values and different approaches for thinking about data.

These presentations are also the time to bring out the strategies used for comparing and computing with decimals. There may be some variation in these strategies. Be sure that students have thoroughly explained any use of manipulatives or models, connections to place value, and algorithms. Ask questions that guide students to make connections among strategies by focusing on how manipulatives and models connect to place value, and how the structures of algorithms are based on place value. If this is the first time that students have been asked to compare or add with decimals, ask them to investigate some strategies that their group did not use, highlighting the strategies' connections to place value.

DIFFERENTIATION

- For students who struggle with comprehending the multiple data points that have been provided for each runner, consider providing only one trial time for the task.
- For students who struggle with addition with decimals, provide calculators for checking their work or for exploring different teams' configurations.
- Challenge students to make two teams that are very unbalanced. Have them explain how they know that these teams are unbalanced.
- Challenge students to research the world record for women's 4 × 200m relay. Ask them how the time of the fastest team from the group of runners in Relay Teams might compare with the world record. What improvement might each runner need to make in her time to challenge the world record?

Planting a Garden

Students at Wishek Elementary School are planning a school garden. They have 10 yards of fencing for the exterior of a square garden. The interior of the garden will then be divided into equal-sized square units so that each student will be able to choose one plant for his or her square unit plot. How many students will have a square plot? Use pictures to show your work.

CCSSM Standards for Mathematical Practice

Practice 2: Reason abstractly and quantitatively.

Practice 4: Model with mathematics.

CCSSM Content Standards

5.NF.B.4b: Find the area of a rectangle with fractional side lengths by tiling it with unit squares of the appropriate unit fraction side lengths, and show that the area is the same as would be found by multiplying the side lengths. Multiply fractional side lengths to find areas of rectangles, and represent fraction products as rectangular areas.

Problem Discussion

This problem builds on students' knowledge of fraction multiplication as well as their understanding of area and perimeter. In the context of dividing a garden plot into equal-sized square plots, students must first use the perimeter (10 yards of fencing) to determine the dimensions of the resulting square garden plot. Next, students use these dimensions ($2\frac{1}{2}$ yards by $2\frac{1}{2}$ yards) to create a diagram of equal-sized square units into which this plot can be subdivided. To do this, students must realize that the largest possible square unit would have a side length of $1/2$ yard (see the diagram on the right). The resulting square unit would, therefore, have an area of $1/4$ square yards.

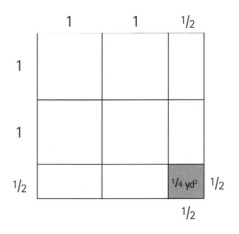

Students will use this information to partition the garden plot into unit squares that measure $1/2$ yard by $1/2$ yard, as shown at the top of the next page on the right (SMP 4, 5.NF.B.4b). Through classroom discussion, they will be encouraged to notice that the area of the original garden plot is represented by these 25 square units, each of which has an area of $1/4$ square yards. In the Summarize portion of the lesson, students will investigate the relationship between multiplying the garden plot's fractional side lengths (i.e., $2\frac{1}{2}$ yards $\times$ $2\frac{1}{2}$ yards $= {}^{25}/_4 = 6\frac{1}{4}$ square yards), as shown on the left on the next page, and partitioning and finding the number of $1/4$ square yards, as shown on the right. That is, the area of twenty-five $1/4$ square yards is the same as that of four large 1-yard by 1-yard squares, four 1-yard by $1/2$-yard rectangles, and a small $1/2$-yard by $1/2$-yard square (which is $1/4$ of the large square) (SMP 2, 5.NF.B.4b).

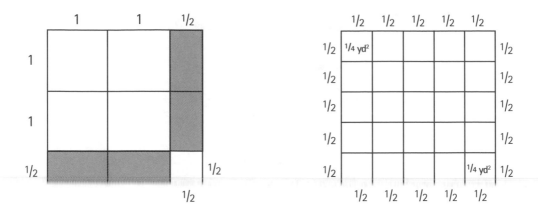

The area models shown above (SMP 4) provide students with an efficient way to explore different strategies for multiplying with fractions greater than 1 (Van de Walle, Karp, and Bay-Williams 2010). Another strategy may include changing the mixed numbers to fractions whose numerators are greater than their denominators and applying the standard algorithm for multiplying fractions. For example, students may see $2^1/_2 \times 2^1/_2$ as $^5/_2 \times ^5/_2$, which is the same as $^{25}/_4$, as shown in the area models above. If students understand that $2^1/_2$ is the same as $2 + ^1/_2$, they may use the distributive property to help solve this task (i.e., $2^1/_2 \times 2^1/_2 = (2 + ^1/_2) \times (2 + ^1/_2) = 4 + 1 + 1 + ^1/_4 = 6^1/_4$).

Strategies

- Students may use a guess-and-check strategy to determine the side lengths of the square.
- Students may divide 10 yards by 4 to get $2^1/_2$ yards for the length of each side of the square.
- Student may use grid paper to represent the square garden.
- Students may sketch the square garden and partition the garden into square and rectangular units (e.g., 1-yard by 1-yard squares, 1-yard by $^1/_2$-yard rectangles, $^1/_2$-yard by $^1/_2$-yard square).
- Students will use the square unit of $^1/_2$ by $^1/_2$ and partition the entire garden into square units of this size.

Misconceptions/Student Difficulties

- Students may struggle to determine the length of each side of the square.
- Students may not realize that the length of the sides of a square can be a fractional value.
- Students may not realize that to find the total area of a shape, the area units must be the same size.
- Students may struggle to find the area of one of the $^1/_2$ by $^1/_2$ square units.
- Students may struggle to connect the area of the square to the number of $^1/_4$ square yards into which the square can be partitioned.

LAUNCH

Begin by asking students whether they have planted a garden or know anyone who gardens. If so, have students share what types of plants were in the garden as well as the shape of the garden. Tell students that many gardens are in the shape of rectangles and squares. Draw a rectangular garden with an area of 24 square units, and ask students to verify that the area is 24 square units by counting the square units. Next, ask students to describe the dimensions of each square unit. Students should explain that each unit is a square with dimensions of 1 unit by 1 unit. Ask students to find the perimeter of their rectangle and show a partner the perimeter units to verify that their perimeter is correct.

Pose questions such as the following to check for understanding:

- What is important to count when finding area?
- What is the shape and size of each area unit?
- What is important to count when finding perimeter?
- What is the shape and size of each perimeter unit?

Next, ask students to consider the actual length of the square units. Students need to understand that a unit can be of any length, including fractional lengths or whole numbers greater than 1. Ask, "Do you think if you measured the length of one of your square units, you would get 1 inch or 1 centimeter? What do you think you would find if you measured the length of a square unit?"

EXPLORE

Distribute the task to students, along with 1-inch grid paper, and ask students to sketch the outline of a square garden with a perimeter of 10 inches. Students should then share their representations with a partner and show their partner that the perimeter is indeed 10 inches. Next, ask students if they think other ways of representing the garden are possible. Students should realize that there is just one square with a perimeter of 10 units.

Next, reread the task aloud, highlighting the need for equal-sized square units for each one of the students' plants. As the students work individually to partition the garden into these equal-sized square units, ask questions to check for understanding:

- Do all of the area units need to be the same shape? Why?
- Do all of the area units need to be the same size? Why?
- Which square is the smallest square in your representation?
- How many of the small squares do you think would fit into this square unit (point to the 1 × 1 square unit)? How many small squares do you think would fit into this rectangle (point to the 1 × $^1/_2$ rectangle)?
- How could you partition the shape so that all the units are squares of the same size? What are the dimensions of these square units? How do you know?

SUMMARIZE

Ask students to work with a partner to discuss their strategies for finding the total number of plants that can be put in the garden. Next, ask a selection of students to share their strategies for partitioning the garden into equal-sized square units. Pose questions to check for understanding:

- What information did you use to decide how to partition the garden into square units?
- What are the dimensions of the square units? How do you know?

To conclude the task, focus on the how the area of the entire garden is related to the twenty-five $^1/_4$ square yards that the students found. The series of pictures below should be displayed to help students make this connection. Display the pictures and ask students if each picture represents the same area of the garden and to explain how they know.

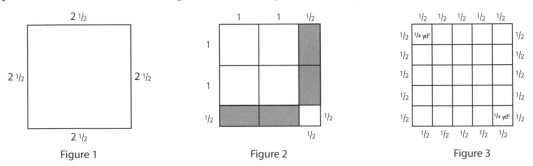

Figure 1   Figure 2   Figure 3

Ask students how they would find the area of each shape. To find the area of the square in figure 1, students must recognize that they need to use the area formula and multiply the length and width of the square to arrive at $^{25}/_4$, or $6\,^1/_4$, square yards. To determine the area in figure 2, students may combine the four gray $1 \times {}^1/_2$ rectangles into two 1×1 square yards. Adding these two square yards to the four square yards results in 6 square yards with an additional $^1/_4$ square yard, for a total of $6\,^1/_4$ square yards. This strategy can be linked to the distributive property of multiplication over addition—that is, $(2 + {}^1/_2) \times (2 + {}^1/_2) = 4 + 1 + 1 + {}^1/_4 = 6\,^1/_4$. To link these strategies to the area of figure 3, which shows twenty-five $^1/_4$ square yards, students should be asked to discuss how the twenty-five $^1/_4$ square yards are equivalent to both $^{25}/_4$ square yards and $6\,^1/_4$ square yards. Key points in this discussion may include the following:

- $^{25}/_4$ = 25 divided by 4, which is 6 with a remainder of 1.
- $^{25}/_4$ is 25 times as much as $^1/_4$.
- Each square yard can be partitioned into four $^1/_2$ by $^1/_2$ squares, resulting in four $^1/_4$ square yards per square yard.

To conclude the task, ask students to determine which plant they would plant in their plot with an area of $^1/_4$ square yard.

DIFFERENTIATION

- To support struggling students, provide 1-unit squares, 1- by $1/2$-unit rectangles and $1/2$ by $1/2$ square tiles to build the garden.

- To support struggling students, provide grid paper with the garden and measurement already shown.

- To extend this task, ask students whether they could use square units of other sizes to divide the garden (e.g., $1/4 \times 1/4$ square units, $1/8 \times 1/8$ square units) and to draw a picture to show their thinking.

April Showers

The city of Bellingham saw rainfall on each of the first six days in April. Caleb wants to know how many inches of rain would have fallen each day if the daily amounts of rainfall were redistributed equally among the days. Use the daily rainfall totals below to help Caleb.

Day 1	Day 2	Day 3	Day 4	Day 5	Day 6
1 in.	1 1/8 in.	3/4 in.	1 1/4 in.	3/4 in.	3/8 in.

CCSSM Standards for Mathematical Practice

Practice 5: Use appropriate tools strategically.

CCSSM Content Standards

5.MD.B.2: Make a line plot to display a data set of measurements in fractions of a unit ($1/2$, $1/4$, $1/8$). Use operations on fractions for this grade to solve problems involving information presented in line plots. *For example, given different measurements of liquid in identical beakers, find the amount of liquid each beaker would contain if the total amount in all the beakers were redistributed equally.*

Problem Discussion

The goal of this task, aligned with the selected standard (5.MD.B.2), is to encourage students to create a line plot, use tools to represent the amount of rainfall per day, and reason with equivalent fractions to compare and order fractional quantities. To create the line plot, students must recognize that the smallest unit of measure is $1/8$ inch (5.MD.B.2). Next, students will need to compare fractions to place each rainfall amount on the line plot. As shown below, students will need to use eighths to rename each fraction. Doing so builds on equivalent fraction concepts from previous grades (3.NF.A.3 and 4.NF.A.2).

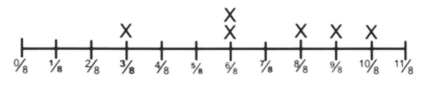

inches of rainfall

Students will then need to use tools such as manipulatives, string, operations on fractions, or the line plot to determine how to redistribute the rainfall amounts equally among the six days (SMP 5). Students may use manipulatives to represent each eighth of an inch of rain and recreate the line plot with these manipulatives. Students can then use trial and error to redistribute manipulatives until each day has the same number of manipulatives, with each representing 1/8 inch of rainfall. This process is illustrated in steps 1–3 below:

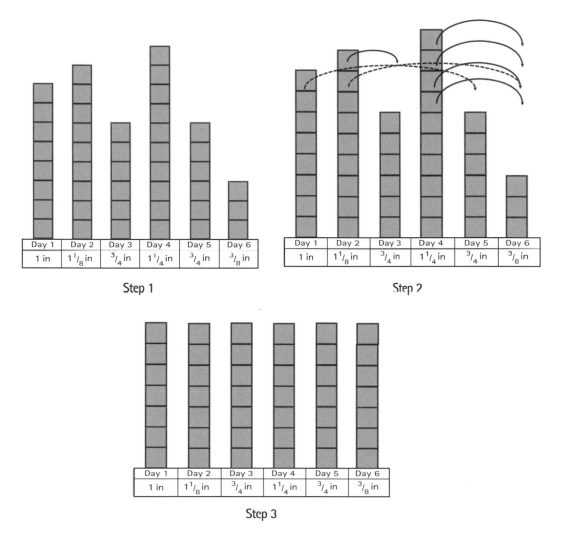

Day 1	Day 2	Day 3	Day 4	Day 5	Day 6
1 in	$1\frac{1}{8}$ in	$\frac{3}{4}$ in	$1\frac{1}{4}$ in	$\frac{3}{4}$ in	$\frac{3}{8}$ in

Step 1

Day 1	Day 2	Day 3	Day 4	Day 5	Day 6
1 in	$1\frac{1}{8}$ in	$\frac{3}{4}$ in	$1\frac{1}{4}$ in	$\frac{3}{4}$ in	$\frac{3}{8}$ in

Step 2

Day 1	Day 2	Day 3	Day 4	Day 5	Day 6
1 in	$1\frac{1}{8}$ in	$\frac{3}{4}$ in	$1\frac{1}{4}$ in	$\frac{3}{4}$ in	$\frac{3}{8}$ in

Step 3

Students may also find the total amount of rainfall by combining all 42 of the manipulatives, with each representing an eighth of an inch of rain, to determine that 5 and 2/8 inches of rain fell in all. They may then use a fair-sharing approach to division and "share" the manipulatives, one at a time, fairly among the six days. This would result in dividing 42 by 6 and giving seven 1/8 inches of rain to each day.

Another strategy involves operations on fractions and recognizing the need to divide by 6. For example, students may add fractions to find a total amount of rainfall of 42/8 inches and then share this total equally among the six days, resulting in 7/8 inches per day.

Students may also use the line plot created in the Launch section and add or subtract eighth inches of rainfall until all days end up with the same rainfall value. One possible sequence to accomplish this redistribution of rainfall follows in steps 1–4.

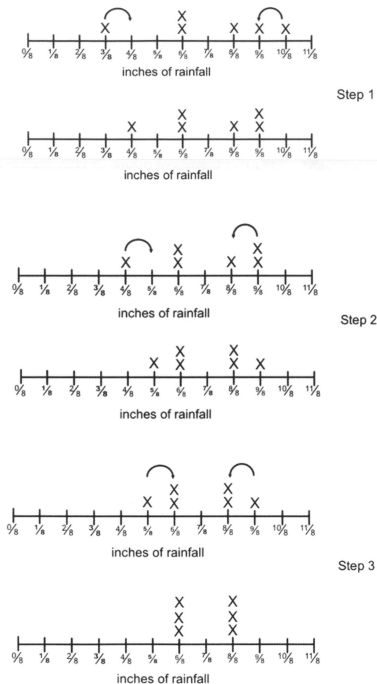

Step 1

Step 2

Step 3

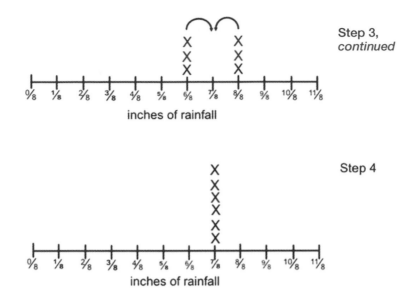

Step 3,
continued

inches of rainfall

Step 4

inches of rainfall

Students may also use string to represent the total amount of rainfall. For example, students can measure and mark each day's rainfall on a piece of string, resulting in a string with a length of 5 1/4 inches. Next, students need to partition this length into six segments of equal length. As shown below, folding the string into thirds and then halves will result in six segments of string, each measuring 7/8 inch. Note that students may conclude that the answer is one inch or just under one inch. During the Summarize portion of the lesson, the limitations of using the string method can be discussed. For example, the elasticity of the string, together with imprecision in measurement, may cause variation in students' answers.

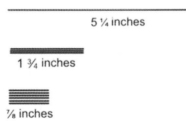

5 ¼ inches

1 ¾ inches

⅞ inches

STRATEGIES

- To create the line plot, students may first plot 1 inch and the two 3/4-inch rainfall totals and then partition each unit further into eighths to plot the remaining rainfall totals.

- To create the line plot, students may use eighths to rename all the fractions and plot these fractions by comparing numerators.

- To create the line plot, students may use a strip of paper representing two units and fold to find halves, fourths, and eighths. They may then use this strip to represent each day's rainfall.
- To redistribute the rainfall equally, students may use manipulatives to represent each eighth of an inch of rain and use trial and error to redistribute manipulatives until each day has the same number of manipulatives, with each representing $1/8$ inch of rainfall.
- To redistribute the rainfall equally, students may use string to represent the total amount of rainfall and then fold the string into six segments of equal length and determine the length of each.
- To redistribute the rainfall equally, students may use their line plot to add or subtract eighth inches of rainfall until all days end up on the same rainfall value.

MISCONCEPTIONS/STUDENT DIFFICULTIES

- Students may not recognize the need to rename all the fractions in eighths.
- Students may struggle to rename all the fractions in eighths.
- Students may struggle to understand what it means to redistribute the inches of rainfall equally.
- Students who choose to use manipulatives to represent each day's rainfall total may struggle to understand that each block must represent an eighth of an inch of rain.
- Students who choose to use the string to represent the total amount of rainfall for the six days may struggle to use a ruler to measure to the nearest eighth of an inch.
- Students may struggle to add fractions with unlike denominators.

LAUNCH

Before the lesson, determine which month is the wettest (rainiest) for your city or town. Label four corners of your classroom with a different month, including the wettest month. Ask students to go to the corner of the room that represents the month they think is the wettest. Ask students to share why they think they have chosen the correct month. Next, hand out the task and read it with the students. Ask them to begin the task by creating a line plot representing the rainfall for the six days. As students create the line plot, pose questions to check for understanding:

- How did you know where to place $3/4$?
- How many eighths are in $1\frac{1}{8}$? How do you know?
- Which is greater, $1\frac{1}{8}$ or $1\frac{1}{4}$? How do you know?
- How do you know your line plot represents all six days of rainfall?

Ask students to share their line plots with two or three others to ensure that everyone has created the same line plot.

EXPLORE

Reread the task, and ask students to talk to a partner about what it is asking them to do—specifically, what it means to "redistribute equally." Students should then share their thinking. Be sure that they understand that each of the six days would need to have the exact same amount of rainfall to help Caleb. Provide manipulatives and string, and have students work with a partner to solve the task. As students work, ask questions to check for understanding:

- Do you think the answer will be less than one inch or greater than one inch? Why?
- How much rain fell in all? How do you know? How could you use the string to represent this?
- If the string represented the total amount of rainfall, how could you divide the string into six segments?
- How could you use the manipulatives to represent each day's rainfall total? How many inches of rain does each manipulative represent?
- Once you redistribute the amounts of rainfall equally, what will your line plot look like? (All the marks will be above the same number.)
- Will the total amount of rainfall be different from what it was before the inches of rainfall were equally redistributed? How do you know?
- If you subtract $1/8$ inch from day 2, what would you have to do make sure the total amount of rainfall for the six days does not change? (Add $1/8$ to another day to keep the total amount of rainfall the same.)

SUMMARIZE

Ask students to share their solutions and strategies with another group. Have students discuss similarities and differences between strategies. Next, select groups to share with the whole class, beginning with a group that used manipulatives and followed by a group that used the line plot. If no group used the line plot, discuss this strategy next. These two strategies demonstrate how the average acts as a balance point for the values. Through this discussion, focus attention on how moving the manipulatives (or Xs on the plot) is the same as adding or subtracting $1/8$. Ask students, "If you moved one block (or X) forward $1/8$, what did you have to do to another block (or X)? Why?" Students may have used a trial-and-error strategy to realize that moving one of the lower amounts forward $1/8$ resulted in needing to move one of the higher amounts backward $1/8$ to ensure that the total amount of rainfall in the six days remained the same. Next, ask students who used the string to share their strategy. Focus the conversation on how students determined that they needed to divide the string representing the total amount of rainfall into six equal segments.

To conclude, ask students to discuss with their groups how each of the three methods redistributed the rainfall equally among the six days. Select students to share their group's reasoning with the class.

DIFFERENTIATION

- To support struggling students, provide a number line partitioned into eighths.
- To support struggling students, remove the need for eighths and use rainfall totals of $1/4$, $1/2$, $3/4$, $3/4$, 1, and $11/4$.
- To extend the task, add a day having 0 inches of rainfall.
- To extend the task, ask students to change one of the day's rainfall totals so that when the rainfall is equally redistributed among the six days, the result is $3/4$ inch of rain per day.

SUMMER

Tasks set in summer contexts afford opportunities for students to apply what they have learned throughout the year in novel ways. Various seasonal activities and summer holidays, such as Flag Day and the Fourth of July, are used as contextual backdrops for the mathematics content in this chapter's tasks. Teachers may choose to use tasks from the previous grade level to start the school year or tasks from the current grade level to round out students' learning for the year.

Three third-grade tasks revisit mathematical concepts of multiples, fractions, and area and perimeter. In the first task, students are asked to find a common multiple to determine a possible end point for a fireworks show. The second task challenges students to identify and draw five fractions that may represent activities or situations found at a state fair. The third task, Strawberry Farm, challenges students to find two ways to construct rectangular plots with 80 meters of fencing.

The first fourth-grade task, Recycling Bikes, is a multilayered problem involving division with whole numbers. The second task requires fourth graders to identify and order fractional parts of rectangular flags. In the third task, Dollars for Decking, fourth-grade students compare two types of decking material for the construction of a new deck.

Students are asked to reason about multiplying fractions in Roller Coasters, the first fifth-grade task. The next task for fifth graders applies division of whole number by a fraction in the context of a whale-watching adventure. The final fifth-grade task, Polar Bear Exhibit, offers students an opportunity to explore connections between the factors of whole numbers and the volumes of rectangular prisms.

MATERIALS FOR EACH TASK, INCLUDING HANDOUTS, ARE AVAILABLE FOR DOWNLOADING AND PRINTING ON NCTM'S WEBSITE AT NCTM.ORG/MORE4U BY ENTERING THE ACCESS CODE ON THE TITLE PAGE OF THIS BOOK.

FOURTH OF JULY FIREWORKS SHOW

The city of San Francisco is planning a very special fireworks show for the Fourth of July. In addition to their standard fireworks, the organizers are including special fireworks that will go off at specific times, as shown in the table:

Firework	Timing
White Chrysanthemum	Every 2 minutes
Blue Bloom	Every 3 minutes
Red Explosion	Every 5 minutes

If the organizers want to start and end the fireworks show with all three of these special fireworks going off together, how long could the fireworks show be? Explain your reasoning.

CCSSM STANDARDS FOR MATHEMATICAL PRACTICE

Practice 1: Make sense of problems and persevere in solving them.

Practice 5: Use appropriate tools strategically.

CCSSM CONTENT STANDARDS

3.OA.C.7: Fluently multiply and divide within 100, using strategies such as the relationship between multiplication and division (e.g., knowing that 8 × 5 = 40, one knows 40 ÷ 5 = 8) or properties of operations. By the end of grade 3, know from memory all products of two one-digit numbers.

3.OA.D.9: Identify arithmetic patterns (including patterns in the addition table or multiplication table), and explain them using properties of operations. For example, observe that 4 times a number is always even, and explain why 4 times a number can be decomposed into two equal addends.

PROBLEM DISCUSSION

This task requires students to examine and extend arithmetic patterns and consider when these patterns have common intersection points, or common multiples (3.OA.D.9). Students may use multiplication to determine the terms in the arithmetic pattern (e.g., 4, 8, 12, etc. are all successive multiples of 4) (3.OA.C.7), or they may skip count to find the terms. This provides an opportunity to revisit the connection between skip counting and multiplication that third graders have studied throughout the school year.

The use of tools is important to this task (SMP 5). Students may find it helpful to organize their thinking in a table or an organized list. If they choose to use a table, they may focus on individual minutes and the types of special fireworks that go off at each of these points, as shown in the table on the next page.

Time (in minutes)	White	Blue	Red
0	*	*	*
1			
2	*		
3		*	
4	*		
5			*
6	*	*	
7			
8	*		
9		*	
10	*		*
11			
12	*	*	
13			
14	*		
15		*	*
16	*		
17			
18	*	*	
19			
20	*		*
21		*	
22	*		
23			
24	*	*	
25			*
26	*		
27		*	
28	*		
29			
30	*	*	*

Notice that the fireworks show could end after 30 minutes, which is the least common multiple of the numbers 2, 3, and 5. Shows could be longer; every multiple of 30 minutes is a possible solution. However, 30 minutes may be the most reasonable answer for an expected duration for a fireworks show.

An organized list of multiples for each value is also an appropriate and useful tool for finding the common time for the fireworks, as illustrated below:

> White Chrysanthemum: 2, 4, 6, 8, 10, 12, 14, 16, 18, 20, 22, 24, 26, 28, 30, 32, 34, 36, 38, 40...
>
> Blue Bloom: 3, 6, 9, 12, 15, 18, 21, 24, 27, 30, 33, 36, 39, 42...
>
> Red Explosion: 5, 10, 15, 20, 25, 30, 35, 40, 45...

Even if students have not been introduced to this particular strategy, they may intuitively develop organized lists and use these to look for common multiples. If the idea of using an organized list does surface spontaneously, naming this tool for students and discussing its merits can be valuable.

Students may also take a logical approach to the task, using divisibility tests or knowledge about multiples of particular numbers. For example, they may recognize that all even numbers (White Chrysanthemums) end in 0, 2, 4, 6, or 8. All multiples of 5 (Red Explosions) end in 0 or 5. Therefore, the common time must end in a 0, since that is the ending digit shared by multiples of 2 and 5. By examining multiples of 10—10, 20, 30, and so on—students can determine which of those values are also multiples of 3 (Blue Blooms). Thirty is the first value that meets this criterion.

This task is a challenging application of the multiplication concept that third graders have studied throughout the year. It also prepares them to think about concepts that they will explore more deeply in fourth grade when they "gain familiarity with factors and multiples" (4.OA.B.4) and "generate and analyze patterns" (4.OA.C.5) (NGA Center and CCSSO 2010, p. 29). Students may think that they have found a solution at several points (e.g., 12 minutes, 15 minutes), only to discover that that time fails for one of the special types of fireworks. Students will need to persevere—and potentially correct faulty facts or addition—to determine the solution (SMP 1).

STRATEGIES

- Students may choose values for the time (either systematically or randomly) and check to see whether the value is divisible by 2, 3, and 5.
- Students may make lists of times that each special firework goes off and check the lists to see which values are the same.
- Students may make a table that marks the times that each of the special fireworks goes off. Then they will use this table to find a common time for all three special fireworks.
- Students may use logic or observation to determine common multiples in values (e.g., multiples of 10 are common multiples of 2 and 5, multiples of 6 are common

multiples of 2 and 3). They may determine whether or not these common multiples are also multiples of the third value.

- Students may multiply the three values together ($2 \times 3 \times 5 = 30$) to determine a common multiple of the three values.

MISCONCEPTIONS/STUDENT DIFFICULTIES

- Students may think that they should begin at 1 minute with each of the patterns (i.e., White Chrysanthemum: 1, 3, 5, 7…).
- Students may determine times that two of the three special fireworks will go off simultaneously but neglect the third special firework.
- Students may make errors in skip counting or multiplication.
- Students may not extend their lists or table far enough to identify a common multiple for the three values.

LAUNCH

Introduce this task by asking students how many of them plan to watch a fireworks show on the Fourth of July. Have students share their plans for the holiday. Explain that the problem they will be working on is related to a fireworks show with special fireworks going off in a predictable pattern.

Display the problem for the students, and ask them to read it silently. Have them turn to an elbow partner and, one by one, exchange information about the problem. For example, one student might say, "I know that there are three types of special fireworks." His or her partner might respond, "I know that the White Chrysanthemum goes off every 2 minutes." After they have discussed all that they know about the problem, ask them if they have any questions about the information provided. Should questions arise, have students turn to a neighbor to discuss them with each other before discussing them as a class.

One question that is likely to arise is related to when each type of firework goes off for the first time—at how many minutes. It will be helpful to clarify for the students that all three fireworks will go off at the beginning of the show—they can call this "0 minutes." If the question does not arise, be sure to bring it up before students begin working on the problem.

EXPLORE

Assign students to groups of three for this task. Provide any materials that students might find helpful (e.g., graph paper, linking cubes, colored pencils). Allow the groups several minutes to begin tackling the problem before asking questions that check for understanding:

- Can you explain to me how you're setting up your table? What information do you think you still need to add?
- I see that you have listed multiples of 2. Why is this helpful to you?
- What are you looking for in your table to help solve the problem?

- What are you looking for in your listings of multiples of 2, 3, and 5 to help solve the problem?
- Have you identified any values that won't work? How do you know?
- How do you know that you need to look for a value with a 0 in the ones place?
- Why did you multiply the values together? What does that tell you about this situation?
- How do you know that the first time the three special fireworks go off together after the beginning of the show is at 30 minutes?

Take note of the strategies that students are using to assist with sequencing of the discussion during the Summarize portion of the lesson.

Have each group make a small poster or other display of their presentation strategy. Offering organizational or presentation-related suggestions as students work on their posters may be helpful. For example, suggesting column headers for a table or descriptors for lists of multiples may prompt them to consider the communication aspects of an explanation. Consider questions such as "How could you make it clear that I am looking at times when the White Chrysanthemums will be going off?" Explain that someone should be able to make sense of their work, even when the students aren't there to explain it.

By the end of the Explore section, have several groups ready to present their strategies, with one group representing each strategy that has surfaced. Consider asking students who are typically more reluctant to share their work to do so during the class discussion. If they are uncomfortable, ask them if they would be willing to let you share their work.

SUMMARIZE

Have student groups present their solution strategies in a sequence that makes sense according to the strategies that have surfaced. Although more concrete to more abstract is one sequencing possibility, students may also benefit from seeing an abstract strategy and attempting to make sense of it as concrete strategies are presented. For example, if one group solved the problem by multiplying the time intervals, say, "Let's see if we can make sense of why this might work as we look at other strategies."

As groups present their strategies, be sure to make connections between the time intervals and where they surface in each strategy. Questions to consider include the following:

- Group A made a list of multiples of 2. Where do you see these multiples of 2 in group B's table?
- Let's look at two of the special fireworks: Red Explosion and Blue Bloom. When do they go off at the same time? Where can you see that in the list of multiples? Where can you see that in the table?
- When do the White Chrysanthemum and Red Explosion fireworks go off together? How does this connect with the strategy of looking for a number that has a zero in the ones place?

- When do the White Chrysanthemum and Blue Bloom fireworks go off together? What do you notice about these values? Why does this make sense?
- This group chose to select different numbers and see if each time interval divided the number. What does this tell you? How does the strategy of multiplying 2, 3, and 5 address this group's challenge of finding a number that works?

At this time, be sure to highlight and name specific tools that students found helpful. Invite students to discuss how a table was a helpful tool for organizing the information. Also encourage them to discuss how making an organized list of multiples enabled them to find times that were shared by the special fireworks. Consider listing these as "helpful tools" in a display in the classroom to support SMP 5.

Finally, address any generalizations or conjectures that may have arisen during the whole-class discussion. For example, one group may ask if the strategy of multiplying 2, 3, and 5 together will always work. If time permits, allow some exploration of this with additional numbers (e.g., 2, 3, and 4, or 2, 5, and 7). Does it always work? Does it always give the *first* time that the values overlap? If time does not allow an exploration of this kind, post this and other questions or conjectures in the classroom for students to explore when time is available.

DIFFERENTIATION

- If students struggle to find an intersection of the multiples of the three numbers, consider removing Blue Bloom as a special firework. Instead, have students find all the times that White Chrysanthemum and Red Explosion will go off at the same time in a 30-minute show.
- For students who struggle to understand the context of the problem and the resulting pattern, consider beginning to list the times that the White Chrysanthemum fireworks will go off.
- For students who solve this problem quickly, provide another set of time intervals, and ask them to solve this problem in a different way.
- If students solve this problem quickly by multiplying the time intervals together (2 × 3 × 5), ask them if this always works. Have students formulate a conjecture. Ask them to consider the intervals of 2, 3, and 4 minutes to test their conjecture (2 × 3 × 4 = 24, but the least common multiple is 12). Ask why their conjecture doesn't work in this case or whether they can identify the conditions under which their conjecture is true.
- Extend this task by asking students which special fireworks would be going off at another interval (e.g., 102 minutes) if the pattern were extended.

State Fair Fractions

Chloe has been invited to go to the state fair with her best friend. Chloe's parents remind her that she has some math challenges to do over the summer. They give her permission to go to the fair with her friend, but she has to look for fractions while she is there!

When Chloe returns home after a wonderful time at the fair, her parents ask her if she was able to find any fractions.

"So many!" replies Chloe. "Where should I begin?"

What are some fractions that Chloe may have found during her visit to the fair? Identify at least five different fractions that Chloe may have found. Write a sentence for each fraction, and draw pictures to represent your fraction scenarios.

CCSSM Standards for Mathematical Practice

Practice 4: Model with mathematics.

Practice 6: Attend to precision.

CCSSM Content Standards

3.NF.A.1: Understand a fraction $1/b$ as the quantity formed by 1 part when a whole is partitioned into b equal parts; understand a fraction a/b as the quantity formed by a parts of size $1/b$.

Problem Discussion

State Fair Fractions asks students to model the real world with mathematics (SMP 4). More specifically, this task requires students to identify situations that can be effectively represented with fractions. The task is open-ended, and students can draw on many contexts within the state fair. With multiple models for fractions, the solution possibilities are endless.

In this task, it is possible that students will be attracted to identifying fractions that demonstrate *part of a whole*. For this meaning of fractions, Van de Walle, Karp, and Bay-Williams (2013) identify three models: area (sometimes referred to as region), length, and set:

1. In an area model, the *whole* is the total area of a region, and the *parts* are defined as parts of that whole area with equal area. The fraction is "the part of the area covered, as it relates to the whole unit" (p. 292).
2. In a length model, the *whole* is a unit of linear measure, and the *parts* are defined as parts of that linear unit with equal length. Thus, the fraction represents the number of equal distances as it relates to a whole unit of linear measure.

3. In a set model, the *whole* is a collection of objects, and the *parts* are defined by an "equal number of objects." The fraction is "the count of objects in the subset, as it relates to the defined whole" (p. 292).

Students may have had opportunities throughout third grade to identify fractions by using manipulatives or pictures (e.g., 1/3 of the circle is green or shaded—area model; 2/5 of the vehicles are trucks—set model). This task, however, asks them to imagine scenarios in which fractions might be relevant and demonstrate how the fraction models the scenario.

Consider how fractions might effectively model scenarios related to three common attractions at a state fair: animals, games, and food.

	Area/region	Length	Set
Animals	Straw or hay covered about 2/3 of the floor of the llamas' stall.	The horse ran 2 1/2 times around the course before the rider could slow it down.	Two-sevenths of the goats were kids.
Games	If I could land the bean bag in the square that was 1/9 the size of the large square, I would win a prize.	When the woman struck the lever with the mallet, the puck rose 3/4 of the way to the bell.	I used 4/4 of my quarters on the throwing rings game.
Food	I ate 1 1/3 elephant ears.	The line for cotton candy was 1/2 as long as the line for deep-fried Snickers.	Three-fifths of the family ate hot dogs at the fair.

Of course, a state fair offers many other contextual possibilities, such as competitions, rides, concerts, and shopping opportunities. Students should be encouraged to explore different contexts and imagine how fractions might be "seen" throughout the state fair.

Although students may be inclined to think of part-to-whole fraction relationships, other fraction constructs may arise, such as division, operator, and ratio (Van de Walle, Karp, and Bay-Williams 2013, p. 291), and watching for these is important:

- Division: The group of 5 people had to share 100 ride tickets, so each person got 100/5 tickets.
- Operator: I used 1/4 of my 20 tickets on one ride (1/4 of 20 is 5 tickets).
- Ratio (either part-part or part-whole): The ratio of boys to girls on the Ferris wheel was 3/4. The ratio of boys to people on the Ferris wheel was 3/7.

If different constructs arise during the Explore portion of the lesson, make note of these to bring up during the class discussion in the Summarize section.

As students work on this task, they will find it necessary to attend to precision (SMP 6). Their fractions will refer to different wholes (in the case of the part-to-whole fraction construct), and they will need to attend to appropriate labeling and communication of the whole.

Similarly, they will need to make sure that the parts that are being referred to are equal in size. In some cases, approximations will be appropriate (e.g., straw or hay covered about 2/3 of the floor of the llamas' stall). It may be worthwhile to discuss why it is sometimes necessary to approximate, and how a reasonable approximation might be made.

STRATEGIES

- Students may use images from state fairs to construct relevant fractions.
- Students may imagine state fair scenarios in which fractions might be relevant.
- Students may construct fractions by using area, length, or set models and consider how these fractions might relate to a state fair context.
- Students may use their own experiences with state fairs to recall relevant situations involving fractions.

MISCONCEPTIONS/STUDENT DIFFICULTIES

- Students may be inhibited by the context if they have never been to a state fair.
- Students may identify only situations in which unit fractions are relevant.
- Students may identify only fraction situations related to area/region.
- Students may fail to make the fractional parts equal in size or quantity.
- Students may consider using only fractions that fall between 0 and 1, ignoring fractions greater than 1 or equivalent to 0 or other whole numbers.

LAUNCH

Begin this task by asking the class, "How many of you have ever been to a state fair?" If no one has, find a state fair or county fair website. Explore the images, the map of the fair, and the calendar of events. Highlight some of the events or experiences that third graders might find enticing, such as rides, games, food, and animals. If some students have attended a state fair, ask them to share their experiences, but also supplement their descriptions with a state fair website.

Choose one image from the state fair website, and ask, "Can anyone see a fraction in action in this picture?" Be sure to select an image that might present several opportunities for students. Be prepared with some fractions for the image in case students are having trouble getting started (e.g., 4/7 of the prizes are pink, 2/3 of the people have their hands in the air on the ride.)

Introduce the task to the students by reading the scenario about Chloe's "assignment" to find fractions at the state fair. Ask students to turn to an elbow partner and have one partner summarize the problem in his or her own words. The other partner should summarize what they are being asked to do. Have a short discussion about the product that is expected: each fraction is to be included in a clear sentence, with a picture to illustrate it.

Explore

Students should form groups of two or three, either by self-selection or through teacher assignment. If some groups have no students who have attended a state or local fair, consider allowing them to use a computer to look up activities that are typical of state fairs. This may help students get started, and they should also be encouraged to generate fractions that are not already visible in online images.

As students work, circulate throughout the room, taking note of the fraction constructs that students are using, as well as the fractions that they are generating. For groups that are focused on fractions that model area/region scenarios, ask, "You've also learned about fractions of sets, and fractions on a number line—length models. Could you think of how these kinds of fractions might be used in a scenario?" If students are focused on unit fractions or only on fractions between 0 and 1, ask, "Could you imagine a scenario where there might be a fraction equal to zero or a whole number, or a number greater than 1?" In this way, encourage students to think beyond any unnecessary constraints that they may be imagining.

At each group, ask questions to check for understanding:

- Can you explain how your fraction relates to your picture?
- What is the whole?
- How is the whole partitioned?
- How did you determine what your numerator would be?
- How did you determine what your denominator would be?
- Is it important that the parts are equal sizes?
- Can you think of an equivalent fraction that you could use to represent this scenario?
- What other fractions could you use with this scenario (or picture)?
- Do you think this fraction is approximate or exact? How do you know?

As students review their own work, help them attend to precision. Be sure that their fractions are not "naked numbers" but are part of a phrase or sentence that articulates the whole and indicates to which part of the whole the fraction refers.

Have students make individual posters ($4\,1/4 \times 5\,1/2$ in. or $8\,1/2 \times 11$ in.) for each of their scenarios to share during the Summarize portion of the lesson.

Summarize

Begin the whole-class discussion by identifying and displaying two fraction posters that are similar in what they refer to. For example, fractions of circles (area/region) are commonly used; choose two from different groups and ask the class, "How are these fractions similar?" Students should quickly recognize that the fractions both refer to parts of a whole when the wholes are circles. Ask the two groups to explain briefly what their fractions describe, revisiting comprehension questions identified above as needed. Then ask the class, "Did

any other groups use fractions of circles?" Display all similar posters and allow the students some time to look at each of them. Continue the discussion by highlighting a few of these fractions, especially those that may be uncommon because they are values greater than or equal to 1. In each case, have students from the group that created the poster briefly discuss their fractions and what they represent. Allow a free exchange of questions from the rest of the class.

Move on to a different category, such as fractions that refer to parts of a whole when the wholes are rectangles (including squares). Repeat the earlier process for this category. Continue this process with new categories until most of the posters have been sorted into categories. A few posters may remain. Discuss each of these as a class to determine whether there is a category in which they might be placed or whether a new category is necessary. If any category has been overlooked by the entire class (e.g., fractions of sets), offer two examples yourself, and ask, "How are these fractions similar?" Have students return to their groups to identify another fraction that belongs in this category.

Finally, ask students to pay attention to fractions in their own world throughout the summer. Challenge them to find a fraction a day in some of the fun things that they do.

DIFFERENTIATION

- If there is an alternative local event that is very popular, replace the state fair with this event.
- For students who struggle to generate fictional fractions, provide images from state fair websites that they can use to identify fractions.
- Consider limiting the number of fractions that students need to identify to three.
- Consider providing different contexts for which students need to identify fractions (e.g., games, rides, food).
- Consider challenging students (after they have completed five scenarios) to find types of fractions or fraction models that they are missing, such as fractions of sets, whole number fractions, and fractions greater than 1.
- Ask students to research statistics on their state fair and generate some fractions that are related to these statistics. Approximations may be particularly important for this challenge.

STRAWBERRY FARM

At a strawberry farm, berries will be planted in two rectangular fields. The farmer has 80 meters of fencing to surround the fields. Find at least two ways the farmer can plan his fields, and the total area of each plan. Use pictures and equations to explain your thinking.

CCSSM STANDARDS FOR MATHEMATICAL PRACTICE

Practice 4: Model with mathematics.

Practice 8: Look for and express regularity in repeated reasoning.

CCSSM CONTENT STANDARDS

3.MD.C.7a: Find the area of a rectangle with whole-number side lengths by tiling it, and show that the area is the same as would be found by multiplying the side lengths.

3.MD.C.7b: Multiply side lengths to find areas of rectangles with whole-number side lengths in the context of solving real world and mathematical problems, and represent whole-number products as rectangular areas in mathematical reasoning.

3.MD.D.8: Solve real world and mathematical problems involving perimeters of polygons, including finding the perimeter given the side lengths, finding an unknown side length, and exhibiting rectangles with the same perimeter and different areas or with the same area and different perimeters.

PROBLEM DISCUSSION

This open-ended task builds on students' understanding of perimeter as the distance around an object and how to find area by counting unit squares (3.MD.C.5 and 3.MD.C.6). First, students must use the given perimeter fencing of 80 meters and the fact that the strawberry fields will consist of two rectangles to create a diagram of the fields. Students will need to make assumptions about whether the fields are adjacent and whether side lengths are realistic in the context of strawberry fields (SMP 4). For example, students are likely to create fields of different shapes and sizes. They may, for instance, create a plan with two adjacent rectangles in the shape of an L or a T, as shown on the next page. Other students' plans may contain two non-adjacent rectangular fields, as also shown. To create these fields with a total fenced perimeter of 80 meters, students will need to use addition and subtraction strategies to determine the side lengths of their rectangular shapes (3.MD.D.8).

Once students have decided on the dimensions for their two rectangular fields with a total fenced perimeter of 80 meters, they will need to determine the area of each rectangular field. Students may use a variety of strategies to find these areas. For example, they could tile their diagrams with square units and count them (3.MD.C.7a), multiply the side lengths of the fields (3.MD.C.7b), use repeated addition, or work with properties of operations. A strawberry field with dimensions of 12 meters by 14 meters, for instance, would have an area given by 12×14, which is the same as $12 \times 7 \times 2$ or $(12 \times 10) + (12 \times 4)$. If students multiply the side

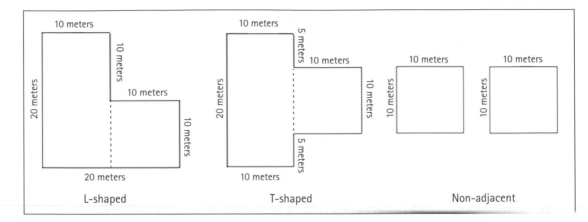

10 meters		10 meters		5 meters		
20 meters	10 meters	20 meters	10 meters	10 meters	10 meters	10 meters
	10 meters		10 meters	10 meters		
20 meters	10 meters	10 meters	5 meters	10 meters	10 meters	10 meters
L-shaped		T-shaped		Non-adjacent		

lengths of the fields, they will be asked to verify the resulting area by tiling the areas with square units. Similarly, if students use a tiling approach to find the area, they will be asked to explain how the length of the sides of the rectangle could be used to verify the area of the fields.

As students share their diagrams with one another and the class, they will be encouraged to discuss the relationship between the perimeters and areas of the different fields. This open-ended task also allows students to explore a context in which shapes with the same perimeter may have different areas (3.MD.D.8). During the Summarize section, students may notice that making adjacent rectangles eliminates the need to fence all four sides of each rectangular field as must be done with two separate rectangular fields. The change to adjacent rectangles makes it possible to increase the side lengths of one or both of the adjoining rectangles, thereby potentially increasing the area. This is evident in the L-shaped field as compared with the non-adjacent fields in the figure above. When the separate rectangles are joined in the L shape with a total perimeter of 80 meters, one side length of the original 10-meter by 10-meter rectangle increases to 20 meters. This increases the total area by 100 square meters. In testing a variety of fields, students will use concrete cases to help them conclude that shapes with the same perimeter may or may not have equal areas (SMP 8). Through repeated reasoning, students may also notice patterns that arise in two non-adjacent rectangles, such as the fact that increasing one side length by a given amount involves decreasing the other side length by that same amount (SMP 8). (See the tables below and on the next page for examples of this pattern.)

Rectangle 1				Rectangle 2			
Length (meters)	Width (meters)	Perimeter (meters)	Area (square meters)	Length (meters)	Width (meters)	Perimeter (meters)	Area (square meters)
10	10	40	100	10	10	40	100
10	10	40	100	11	9	40	99
10	10	40	100	12	8	40	96
10	10	40	100	13	7	40	91

Rectangle 1				Rectangle 2			
Length (meters)	Width (meters)	Perimeter (meters)	Area (square meters)	Length (meters)	Width (meters)	Perimeter (meters)	Area (square meters)
11	9	40	99	10	10	40	100
12	10	44	120	9	9	36	81
13	11	48	143	8	8	32	64
14	12	52	168	7	7	28	49

STRATEGIES

- Students may create separate non-adjacent rectangles.
- Students may create adjacent rectangles resulting in an L- or T-shaped field.
- Students will use a trial-and-error method to find possible side lengths that result in a perimeter of 80 meters.
- Students may create two separate but identical rectangles and divide the perimeter in half, using 40 meters for each rectangle's perimeter.
- Students may count square tiles to determine the area of each field.
- Students may multiply the lengths of the sides of their fields to find the area of each field.

MISCONCEPTIONS/STUDENT DIFFICULTIES

- Students may have difficulty finding combinations of side lengths that sum to 80.
- Students may draw two adjoining rectangles and count the length of the adjacent sides as part of the total perimeter.
- Students may confuse the formulas for perimeter and area.
- Students may not draw precise rows and columns when tiling the strawberry fields to verify or find the area of each rectangular field.

LAUNCH

Ask students if they have ever picked strawberries at a strawberry farm. If so, ask them to describe the rows of strawberries. If not, display a picture of a strawberry farm and ask students why they think there is a space between the rows.

Tell students that in this task a strawberry farmer has 80 meters of fencing. Next, ask students to use their hands to show the length of a meter. Ask them to share what they know about the perimeter of a shape. Students should note that the perimeter is the distance around a shape. Ask students how they would find the perimeter of the classroom in meters and predict whether that perimeter is more or less than 80 meters. Either have the answer prepared or, if time permits, have students estimate the perimeter and share their estimation strategies with the class. Next, ask students to share what they know about area. They should respond that area is the number of unit squares that cover a shape without overlaps or gaps. Students should then be asked to describe how large one square meter would be and predict the area of their classroom. Either have the answer prepared or allow students to find the area.

EXPLORE

Hand out the task and read through it with students. Have students work with a partner to draw diagrams of two different ways the farmer can plan the strawberry fields with a total of 80 meters of fencing. Ask questions to check for understanding:

- Which is represented by the 80 meters—the perimeter or the area of the rectangular fields? How do you know?
- How are the perimeter and the area different? Show me what you would count to find the area of the entire field.
- Why did you choose to draw your rectangles with two separate (or connected) rectangles?
- How do you know that your plan shows a total fenced perimeter of 80 meters? Show me what you counted.

SUMMARIZE

To summarize, ask students to share their diagrams and answers with another pair of students. Ask them to take note of the shape of the plan and to verify that the other pair's plan has a perimeter of 80 meters. Next, ask the two pairs to take turns explaining to each other how they found the area of the field for each of their plans.

As a whole class, have pairs of students share their diagrams and explain their thinking. Include pairs that used two separate rectangular fields as well as pairs that used two adjacent rectangular fields. If students do not share one of these strategies, engage them in a discussion about the merits of such plans. For example, if students did not use T- or L-shaped fields, draw one on the board (fully labeled examples appear on the next page) and ask students if this is a reasonable shape for the two rectangular fields. Students could be asked to determine the lengths of the sides of this shape. As students share their diagrams and explanations, ask questions to check for understanding:

- Why did you use two adjoining rectangles instead of two separate rectangles (or vice versa)?
- When finding the area of the fields, what did you count?
- If someone used a square field: Do you think a square field meets the task's requirement "berries will be planted in two rectangular fields"?

Next, ask students why they think some pairs found different areas for their plans, even though the perimeters are the same. Some students may notice that the adjoining rectangles eliminate the need to fence some parts of the rectangles' perimeters, as compared with two separate rectangular fields. Have students share their predictions and give examples showing when the same fenced perimeter results in different areas (as in the adjoining rectangles in the T-shape and the non adjacent rectangles in the first diagram below) and when the same perimeter results in the same area (as shown in the L-shaped and the T-shaped rectangles in the second diagram below). If no group was able to find either the T-shaped or the L-shaped scenario, draw a diagram of one of these scenarios, and ask the students to verify that the perimeters are the same and the areas are the same.

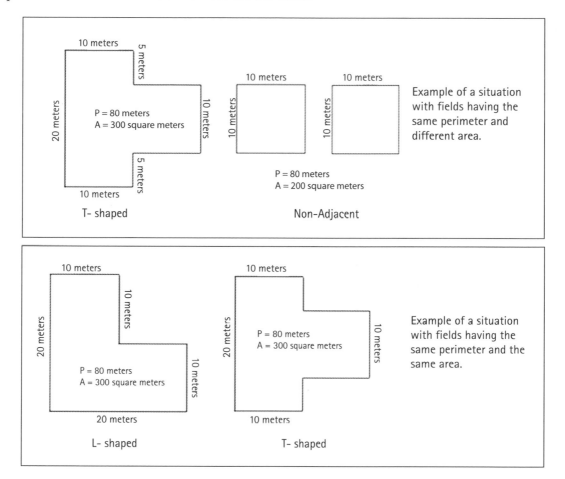

To conclude the task, ask students to complete the following statement by selecting "always," "sometimes," or "never," and encourage them to justify their reasoning:

Two shapes with the same perimeter will _____ have the same area.

DIFFERENTIATION

- To support struggling students, provide centimeter grid paper or square tiles.
- To support struggling students, modify the task to have the farmer making a strawberry field consisting of one large rectangle instead of two strawberry fields consisting of two rectangles.

- To support struggling students, provide rectangles with missing side lengths for them to find.
- To extend this task, give students the area of a field and ask them to make a diagram showing its perimeter.
- To extend this task, tell students that the rows of strawberries in each rectangular field are 3 feet apart, and each row of strawberries is 2 feet wide. Ask them to use equations and drawings to help the farmer find the area that is covered by strawberries.

RECYCLING BIKES

The city of La Crosse collected 623 bikes from the community. The city needs to decide how to transport and donate the bikes to students in the 5 elementary schools in La Crosse. Use equations or drawings to support your answers to the following questions:

a. How many bikes should be delivered to each school?

b. If the city's trucks can carry 9 bikes at a time, how many trips will it take to deliver the bikes to each of the elementary schools?

CCSSM STANDARDS FOR MATHEMATICAL PRACTICE
Practice 2: Reason abstractly and quantitatively.

CCSSM CONTENT STANDARDS
4.NBT.B.6: Find whole-number quotients and remainders with up to four-digit dividends and one-digit divisors, using strategies based on place value, the properties of operations, and/or the relationship between multiplication and division. Illustrate and explain the calculation by using equations, rectangular arrays, and/or area models.

PROBLEM DISCUSSION
In this open-ended task, students examine whole number division and give particular attention to the meaning of the remainder in two different situations. "Students should not just think of remainders as 'R 3' or 'left over.' Addressing what to do with remainders must be central to teaching with division" (Van de Walle, Karp, and Bay-Williams 2013, p. 161). Students are first asked to use a sharing interpretation of division to distribute 623 bikes among 5 schools. This results in 124 bikes for each school, with 3 bikes remaining. Therefore, students will need to determine a reasonable way to deal with the 3 remaining bikes. Students could choose to give an extra bike to three schools or choose another option that they deem reasonable. Next, students are asked to determine how many trips the city trucks will need to take to deliver the 124 bikes to a school. This repeated subtraction interpretation of division results in 13 trips with 9 bikes and another trip with the other 7 bikes, or 14 trips to deliver 124 bikes to one elementary school. If a student decides to give all 3 remaining bikes to one school, delivering the 127 bikes to that school will result in 14 trips with 9 bikes and another trip with just 1 bike, for a total of 15 trips.

These two tasks require students to use division strategies and representations to find and support their solutions (4.NBT.B.6). For example, students may use place value understanding, a missing factor approach, or area models to support a standard algorithm for the division involved in this task (see the Summarize section for examples of a variety of strategies that students may use). "By reasoning repeatedly about the connection between math drawings and written numerical work, students can come to see multiplication and division algorithms as abbreviations or summaries of their reasoning about quantities" (Common Core State Standards Writing Team 2015, p. 14). In particular, students will reason about the quantities involved in this context to determine how to deal with the remainders (SMP 2). In part (a) the remainder of 3 bikes can either be discarded so that each school receives the same number of bikes or be distributed to the schools however the students decide. In part (b) the remainder requires students to round up to ensure that all the bikes are delivered to one of the schools.

STRATEGIES

- Students may use a sharing approach and distribute the bikes to each of the 5 schools either one at a time or in groups of 5, 10, or another number.
- Students may use a missing factor approach to determine what they need to multiply 5 by in order to get close to 623 with less than 5 remaining.
- Students may use a variety of division algorithms to find the quotient and remainder (see the Summarize section).
- Students may use an area model to find the missing length of a side of a rectangle with area of 623 or an area close to this value.
- Students may use properties of whole numbers and reason as follows: 623 = 600 + 20 + 3, and 600 ÷ 5 = 120, 20 ÷ 5 = 4, and there are 3 bikes left over.
- Students may use a repeated subtraction approach to find the quotient. For example, students may repeatedly subtract 9 from 124 until they are left with 7 bikes.

MISCONCEPTIONS/STUDENT DIFFICULTIES

- Students may struggle to divide a three-digit dividend.
- Students may struggle to interpret the meaning of the digits in their quotient.
- Students may have difficulty interpreting the remainders in the context of the problem.

LAUNCH

Ask students to share information about items that they recycle. If students do not mention bicycles, explain to them that some communities recycle bicycles and bicycle parts by donating them to groups of people who fix up the bikes. The recycled bikes are then donated to people in need. Ask students to share what they think recycling or fixing up a bike might involve. Students' ideas may include putting on new tires or a new chain, adding new brakes, repainting, replacing broken parts, and so on. Next, tell students that in La Crosse (or your local community), people donate bikes to be reconditioned and then given to elementary students. Pose the following problem:

> If 104 new bike tires were donated by a local bike shop, how many bikes can receive new tires? Use pictures and equations to support your answer.

As students share their answers, call their attention to the variety of strategies. For example, students may use a missing factor approach to determine what they must multiply 2 by in order to get 104 by reasoning "2 × 5 = 10, so 2 × 50 = 100, and I will need 2 more groups of 2 to make 104." Students may also use properties of operations and think of 104 as 100 + 4 and divide 100 by 2 and 4 by 2 to arrive at 52 total bikes. Another strategy that students may use is an algorithm to divide 104 by 2. Questions like, "How many groups of 2 can be taken from 104?" can be used to help students connect the steps of the algorithm to the place value concepts involved in the algorithm. Students may interpret this question as a repeated subtraction approach to division and use a drawing that shows 52 groups of 2. Alternatively, students may create an area model like the one below:

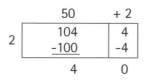

As students share their strategies, ask questions to check for understanding:

- How did you know that this was a division problem?
- Could you write a multiplication problem to represent this situation?
- What does 5 (or 2) mean in the quotient?
- Are there any bike tires left over? How do you know?

EXPLORE

Hand out and read the task to students. Have students work individually on the problem. As they work, ask many of the same questions as in the Launch to check for understanding:

- How did you know that this was a division problem?
- Could you write a multiplication problem to represent this situation?
- What does each digit in the quotient mean?
- Is there a remainder? What does it mean?
- How do you think the city should deal with the remaining bikes?
- How does your picture relate to your equation?

Before students move on to part (b), ensure that they have arrived at an answer of 124 bikes for each of the 5 elementary schools with 3 remaining bikes. Allow students to deal with the remainder in a manner that seems reasonable to them. Once students have completed both parts of the task, ask them to share their answers and strategies with a partner. Partners should discuss—

- how their solutions are similar and how they are different;
- how their drawings supported their solutions; and
- how they dealt with the remainders.

SUMMARIZE

To summarize, ask students to share their solutions to part (a) with the class. Have students share until all their solution strategies and drawings have been discussed. Students should also describe how they chose to deal with the 3 left-over bicycles. Examples of possible solution strategies appear on the next two pages. If students overlook some of these strategies, display them and discuss their merits with the class.

	Area Model
$?$ $100 \quad + \quad 20 \quad + \ 4$ 5 | $\begin{array}{c c c} 623 & 123 & 23 \\ -500 & -100 & -20 \ \ 3 \\ \hline 123 & 23 & 3 \end{array}$ Remainder of 3	I wanted to find the missing side length of a rectangle with an area close to 623 with one side length of 5. I knew if the missing side length was 100, then the total area would be 500, so I had 123 left. I know 5×20 is 100, so if the missing side length was 120, I would have an area of 600 with 23 left. Because 5×4 is 20, I know that the missing side length is 124, and 5×124 is 620, with 3 left.

	Sharing Interpretation
$\begin{array}{r} 124 \text{ R}3 \\ 5\overline{)623} \\ -5 \\ \hline 12 \\ -10 \\ \hline 23 \\ -20 \\ \hline 3 \end{array}$	I want to share 623 bikes equally among the 5 schools. I know 623 is 6 groups of 100, 2 groups of 10, and 3 ones. I can give each school a group of 100 bikes, which is 500 total bikes shared. This leaves me with one group of 100 bikes. So I put the bikes in groups of 10, giving me 12 groups of 10. I shared 2 groups of 10 to each school. This was 100 more bikes. Now I have 2 groups of 10 bikes, plus 3 more bikes, to share. I know I can share 20 bikes evenly by giving 4 bikes to each school, so I have 3 bikes remaining that could not be shared equally among the 5 schools.

	Missing Factor
$5 \times 100 = 500$ $5 \times 10 = 50$ $5 \times 10 = 50$ $5 \times 4 = \underline{20}$ 620	I wanted to find what I should multiply 5 by to get close to 623 with less than 5 bikes remaining. I know that $5 \times 100 = 500$, and $5 \times 10 = 50$, so 5×120 is $5 \times 100 + 5 \times 10 + 5 \times 10$, or 600. So they can share 120 bikes fairly among the 5 schools with 23 bikes left over. I know 5×4 is 20, so they can share 4 more bikes to each of the 5 schools with 3 left over. So I know $5 \times 124 = 5 \times 120 + 5 \times 4$, or 620. This means 623 divided by 5 is 124 with a remainder of 3. So each school can get 124 bikes, and there are 3 bikes left.

	Repeated Subtraction
$\begin{array}{r} 4 \\ 10 \\ 10 \\ 100 \end{array}$ $5\overline{)623}$ $\begin{array}{r} -500 \quad \text{100 groups of 5} \\ \hline 123 \\ -50 \quad \text{10 groups of 5} \\ \hline 73 \\ -50 \quad \text{10 groups of 5} \\ \hline 23 \\ -20 \quad \text{4 groups of 5} \\ \hline 3 \end{array}$	I needed to know how many times I could subtract 5 from 623. I took away 100 groups of 5 from 623, which is $623 - 500 = 123$. I then took 10 more groups of 5 away giving me $123 - 50 = 73$. So I knew I could take another 10 groups of 5 away, leaving me with 23 bikes. So I took 4 groups of 5 away, which was $23 - 20$, giving me 3 bikes left over.

	Place Value Concepts
$60 \div 5 = 12$ $600 \div 5 = 120$ $20 \div 5 = 4$ $620 \div 5 = 124$	I decomposed 623 into 600 + 20 + 3. I knew that 60 divided by 5 was 12, since 50 divided by 5 is 10, and 10 divided by 5 is 2. This means that 600 divided by 5 is 120. I then took 20 divided by 5, which gave me 4. So I know 620 divided by 5 is 124. I would still have 3 bikes left.

Next, ask students to share their solutions to part (b) with the class. Have students continue to share until all their solution strategies and drawings have been discussed. Students should also describe how they chose to deal with the bikes that could not be transported in a full truckload (either 7 or 8 bikes—or possibly just 1 bike—depending on how they dealt with the remainder in the first part of the task). Below are examples of possible solution strategies for transporting 124 bikes to one school. Again, if students do not share all of these strategies, consider displaying them and discussing their merits with the class.

	Tape Diagram
124 9 9 9 9 9 9 9 9 9 9 9 9 9 7 ↑ Remainder of 7	I wanted to know how many groups of 9 were in 124, so I kept adding 9 until I got close to 124. I added 13 groups of 9, which gave me 117. This means that it will take 13 full trips to deliver 117 bikes. I had 7 bikes left over, which means that it will take 14 total trips to deliver the 124 bikes to the schools.
	Repeated Subtraction
$\begin{array}{r} 3 \\ 10 \\ 9\overline{)124} \\ \underline{-90} \\ 34 \\ \underline{-27} \\ 7 \end{array}$ 10 groups of 9 3 groups of 9	I wanted to find out how many times I could subtract 9 from 124. I took away 10 groups of 9. So 10 trips would deliver 90 of the bikes, leaving 34 bikes. I then knew I could take away 3 more groups of 9, or take 3 more trips to deliver 27 bikes, so I would be left with 7 bikes. This means the city would take 13 trips with 9 bikes and one more trip with 7 bikes.
	Missing Factor
$9 \times 10 = 90$ $9 \times 2 = 18$ $9 \times 1 = 9$ $9 \times 13 = 117$	I need to find how many groups of 9 would be close to 124 with less than 9 bikes left. I knew 10 trips would deliver 90 bikes, since this is 10 groups of 9. If they took 2 more trips with 9 bikes, this would deliver 18 more bikes. So we have delivered 90 + 18 = 108 bikes with 14 bikes left. So they can take one more trip to deliver 9 bikes and one more trip to deliver 7 bikes. This means it will take 10 + 2 + 1 + 1 = 14 total trips.

To conclude the task, ask students to consider how they dealt with the remainder in the two parts of the task. Ask, "Did you deal with the remainder in the same way in each part? Why or why not?" Students should note that in part (a) they either discarded the remainder or gave extra bikes to some of the schools. By contrast, in part (b), they needed to round up the total number of trips to ensure that all the bikes were delivered.

DIFFERENTIATION

- To support struggling students, provide manipulatives to represent the number of bikes.
- To support struggling students, reduce the number of bikes from 623 to 62.
- To extend the task, ask students to create story situations involving division in which they must deal with the remainders by rounding up, rounding down (discarding), or representing the quotient with a fractional amount.
- To extend this task, ask students to write a letter to their city, explaining the benefits of recycling bikes in their community.

FLAG DAY

Help determine the Flag Day parade lineup by ordering the flags below from the flag with the least amount of gray to the flag with the greatest amount of gray. Use drawings and fractions to justify your answer.

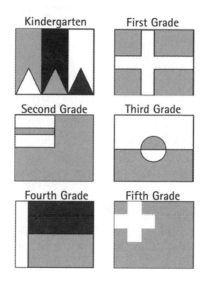

CCSSM Standards for Mathematical Practice

Practice 2: Reason abstractly and quantitatively.

CCSSM Content Standards

4.NF.A.1: Explain why a fraction a/b is equivalent to a fraction $(n \times a)/(n \times b)$ by using visual fraction models, with attention to how the number and size of the parts differ even though the two fractions themselves are the same size. Use this principle to recognize and generate equivalent fractions.

4.NF.A.2: Compare two fractions with different numerators and different denominators, e.g., by creating common denominators or numerators, or by comparing to a benchmark fraction such as $1/2$. Recognize that comparisons are valid only when the two fractions refer to the same whole. Record the results of comparisons with symbols >, =, or <, and justify the conclusions, e.g., by using a visual fraction model.

Problem Discussion

The Common Core State Standards expect third-grade students to "understand a fraction $1/b$ as the quantity formed by 1 part when a whole is partitioned into b equal parts; understand a fraction a/b as the quantity formed by a parts of size $1/b$" (3.NF.A.1). In this task, students will extend their understanding of these ideas. Flag Day requires students to find the

fractional part of a whole by selecting a unit and partitioning a shape into equal-sized units. "Helping students identify the unit, or whole, and connect it with a fractional part is an essential part of developing and deepening their understanding of the meaning of fractions, as well as laying the foundation for their future computational work with fractions" (Chval, Lannin, and Jones 2013, p. 31). Building on this partitioning of a shape, students will determine the fractional part of a flag that is shaded gray and then compare and order fractions with different numerators and different denominators (4.NF.A.2). Students may choose to compare fractions by using same numerators, same denominators, benchmark fractions, or equivalent fractions. This task also builds on students' understanding of the idea that area is additive (3.MD.C.7d). That is, for the kindergarten flag, students will need to compose two gray shapes into one rectangle to see that the gray rectangle is 1/3 of the flag.

Each flag is the same size, thus representing the same whole. "To help students better understand the role of the unit in fractions, it is important to make this role explicit" in classroom discussion (Battista 2012, p. 8). For example, students should be encouraged to explain by using statements such as, "1/2 of this flag is greater than 1/3 of that flag because the flags are the same size." The unit that students use to partition each flag may vary. Thus, classroom discussion will focus on explaining why two fractions are equivalent by considering how the number and size of the units differ but still result in the same fractional amount of gray (4.NF.A.1). As students work to partition each flag, the discussion will focus on the need for units of equal size. Some students may draw in each individual unit while others may build from the existing lines in the shape and draw in horizontal and vertical lines to create rows and columns of units. The examples on the left and right below show how two students might use different-sized units to partition the fifth-grade flag and generate the fractional quantities of 25/30 and 5/6, respectively. Note that the arrows in the fraction models that follow indicate how a student might translate representations to visualize equivalent fractions.

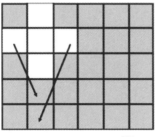

Visual fraction model for 25/30

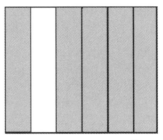

Visual fraction model for 5/6

As students make sense of the two fractions, they will reflect on and use reasoning related to the meaning of the numerator and denominator as parts of a whole (SMP 2). Through classroom discussion, these types of visual fraction models will assist students in explaining fraction equivalence. Students may explain, "Each of the bigger pieces is split into five smaller pieces, " "There are groups of five small pieces in each of the bigger pieces," or "Each bigger piece has five times as many pieces as the smaller piece." These statements can then lead students to reason, "There are five groups of five gray units out of six groups of five units total." This later statement can provide a connection to justify that

$$\frac{5}{6} = \frac{5 \times 5}{6 \times 5} = \frac{25}{30}.$$

Likewise, students may reason that they are putting the smaller pieces together to form bigger pieces to generate equivalent fractions by dividing the numerator and denominator by the same number.

STRATEGIES

- Students may visually estimate which flag has more or less gray.
- Students may select a unit and draw in equal-sized units to fill the space to find the fraction of the flag that is gray.
- Students may extend existing lines to create rows and columns of square units to find the fraction of the flag that is gray.
- Students may use rectangular units to find the fraction of the flag that is gray.
- Students may compare fractions by using reasoning based on common numerators, common denominators, or benchmark fractions.

MISCONCEPTIONS/STUDENT DIFFICULTIES

- Students may have difficulty creating equal-sized units to partition the flags.
- Students may miscount the number of equal-sized units.
- Students may not realize that it is not necessary to construct and count the square tiles in the flags and struggle to deal with the triangular and circular parts of the flag.
- Students may use whole number strategies when comparing fractions (e.g., $5/12$ is larger than $4/5$ because 12 is a larger number than 5).

LAUNCH

Ask students what they know about Flag Day. Interesting facts about this holiday include the following:

- In the United States, Flag Day is celebrated on June 14.
- Flag Day is often celebrated with a parade.
- Flag Day celebrates the adoption of the U.S. flag, which occurred on this day in 1777.
- June 14 is the same day that the Army celebrates its birthday.
- Flag Day is not an official federal holiday.
- On June 14, 1937, Pennsylvania was the first state to celebrate Flag Day as a state holiday.

Next, ask students to think about the flags they have seen from other countries. Ask, "What colors do you see most often in those flags?" Allow students to share ideas about the colors that they frequently see in flags from around the world. Students will probably offer colors such as red, white, blue, black, yellow. If possible, display three flags from around the world—for example, Ukraine, Nigeria, and Mauritius—and ask students to share which color they think makes up the largest part of each. Ask students to turn to a partner and discuss the similarities and differences among these three flags. Allow students to share their thinking with the class. Students may share that each flag is partitioned into smaller rectangles of the same size. Half of Ukraine's flag is yellow, and the other half is blue. One third of Nigeria's flag is white, and the remaining two thirds are green. Mauritius's flag is divided into fourths.

EXPLORE

Tell students that an elementary school created six flags, one for each level, kindergarten through grade 5, for a Flag Day celebration. Explain that one student thinks the flags should be arranged in the parade in order by how much of the flag is gray. Distribute the task and ask a student to read it aloud. Have students work with a partner to order the flags from the one with the least amount of gray to the one with the greatest amount of gray. Ask questions to check for understanding:

- How can you partition the flag to show that your visual estimates are accurate?
- What is important about the size of each unit that you have created?
- How can you use your partitioning to find the fractional amount of the flag that is gray?
- How could you use the total number of unit squares to find the fractional amount of the flag that is gray?
- How do you know $1/2$ is greater than $1/3$?
- How do you know $5/6$ is greater than $5/12$?
- How can you show that $25/30$ is equivalent to $5/6$ (refer to the fifth-grade flag).
- Can you show me another way to show that $2/3$ of the flag is gray (refer to the first-grade flag).

Once pairs have agreed on the order of the flags, ask them to cut out and paste the flags in order on a piece of paper. Between each pair of flags, have students explain how they determined which of the two flags had a smaller or larger amount of gray.

SUMMARIZE

To summarize, ask partners to work with another pair of students to compare their strategies for finding the fractional part of each flag that is gray. To share strategies, begin with the kindergarten flag and conclude with the fifth-grade flag. The discussion for each flag may include the following:

Kindergarten

- Students are likely to use a visual strategy, noting that each triangle is the same size and visually sliding the triangles to the left to justify that $1/3$ of the flag is gray.
- Students may also partition the flag into 30 equal-sized square units, as shown at the top of the next page, and see that 10 of these are gray.
- Encourage students to discuss how they know that $10/30$ is the same as $1/3$.

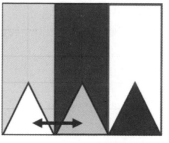

Visual fraction model for 1/3

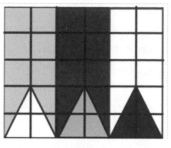

Visual fraction model for 10/30

First Grade

- Students may partition this flag into 30 equal-sized units and find that 20 of the 30 are gray.
- Students may also rearrange the white squares as shown below to see three equal-sized rectangles of which two rectangles are gray.
- Encourage students to discuss how they know 20/30 is the same as 2/3, using the visual fraction models to show

$$\frac{2}{3} = \frac{2 \times 10}{3 \times 10} = \frac{20}{30}.$$

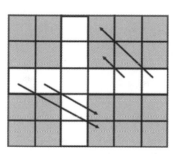

Visual fraction model for 20/30

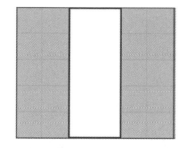

Visual fraction model for 2/3

Second Grade

- Students may partition the flag into 30 equal-sized pieces and combine half units to create whole units (as shown on the left in the set of diagrams below).

Visual fraction model for 24/30   Visual fraction model for 48/60   Visual fraction model for 96/120

- Students will then notice that 24 of the 30 squares are gray.
- Students may partition the flag into 60 rectangular units (as shown in the center in the previous set of diagrams) and see that 48 of the 60 are gray.
- Students may divide the flag into 120 square units (as shown on the right in the previous set of diagrams), and see that 96 are gray. Encourage students to discuss how they know each partitioning produces equivalent fractions that can also be represented as $4/5$. You may use the strategy pictured below to show that $4/5$ of the flag is gray.

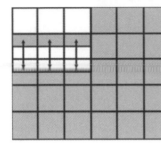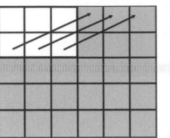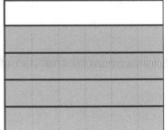

Third Grade

- Students may visually flip or rotate the gray semicircle onto the white semicircle and see that half of the flag is gray.

Fourth Grade

- Students may partition the flag into 30 equal-sized pieces (see below on the left) and count the total number of gray units to arrive at 12.5.
- Students may partition the flag into 60 rectangular units (see below in the center) once they realize that in a partitioning into 30 square units some of the square units are half gray. They will then find that 25 of these 60 rectangles are gray.
- If students partition the flag into 60 rectangular units after realizing that a partitioning into 30 square units results in some units that are half gray, they may further partition these rectangles into squares (see below on the right) to see that 50 of the 120 units are gray.

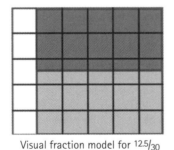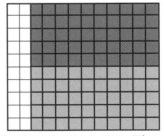

Visual fraction model for $12.5/30$ Visual fraction model for $25/60$ Visual fraction model for $50/120$

- Encourage students to discuss how they know each partitioning produces equivalent fractions that can also be represented as $5/12$. You may use the two strategies pictured at the top of the next page to show $5/12$.

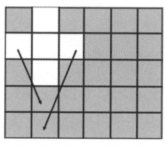

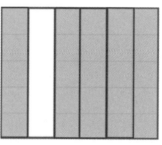

Fifth Grade

- Students may partition the shape into 30 equal-sized pieces (see below on the left) and find that 25 of the 30 units are gray.
- Encourage students to discuss how they could rearrange the square units to show $5/6$ (see the results below on the right).

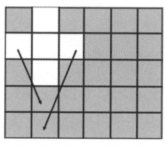

Visual fraction model for $25/30$

Visual fraction model for $5/6$

Next, ask partners to work in their larger groups to share the order of their flags and justify their reasoning. Once individual groups agree on the order, ask the whole class to decide which flag should be first in the parade lineup (least amount of gray). If groups disagree, ask them to justify why one flag has less or more gray than another flag. Continue this process until all flags have been placed in the parade lineup. The lineup from least to most gray should be kindergarten, fourth grade, third grade, first grade, second grade, fifth grade. To compare fractional parts, students may use a variety of strategies:

- Common numerators (e.g., $5/12$ is less than $5/6$ because twelfths are smaller pieces of the same whole)
- Common denominators (e.g., $1/3$ is less than $2/3$ because two $1/3$ pieces are more than one $1/3$ piece of a whole)
- Benchmark fractions (e.g., $5/12$ is less than $1/2$ because $6/12$ is the same as $1/2$)
- Closer to 1 (e.g., $4/5$ is less than $5/6$ because $4/5$ is $1/5$ away from a whole, and $5/6$ is $1/6$ away from a whole)
- Equivalent fractions (e.g., $2/3$ is less than $4/5$ because $2/3$ is the same as $4/6$)

To conclude the task, ask students to create a flag that would fall between the first and last flags (or any other two flags) in the parade lineup. Have students share their flags and the fractional amount of the flag that is gray.

DIFFERENTIATION

- To support students who struggle to partition the flags into equal-sized units, give them the task in the alternate version, which shows the flags with grid lines (available at More4U).

- To support students who struggle to partition the flags into equal-sized units, provide a ruler.

- To support students who struggle to partition the flags into equal-sized units, remove the second- and fourth-grade flags.

- To extend the task, ask students to justify where in the parade lineup they would place their flag.

- To extend the task, ask students to predict whether the order would change if the flags were lined up according to the total area of the flag that is white. Have students find the area of each flag that is white to check their prediction.

DOLLARS FOR DECKING

This summer, the McCool family is building a new deck on the back of their house according to the diagram shown:

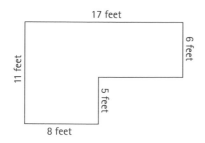

They are considering two possibilities. They may build the deck of treated wood, in boards that are 12 feet long and 4 inches wide. Each board costs $8.28. Or they may build it of cedar, in boards that are 12 feet long and 6 inches wide. Each of these boards costs $12.18. How much would it cost to use treated wood to build the deck? How much would it cost to use cedar to build it? Show your work on posters, and be prepared to explain your reasoning.

CCSSM STANDARDS FOR MATHEMATICAL PRACTICE

Practice 2: Reason abstractly and quantitatively.

Practice 6: Attend to precision.

CCSSM CONTENT STANDARDS

4.MD.A.2: Use the four operations to solve word problems involving distances, intervals of time, liquid volumes, masses of objects, and money, including problems involving simple fractions or decimals, and problems that require expressing measurements given in a larger unit in terms of a smaller unit. Represent measurement quantities using diagrams such as number line diagrams that feature a measurement scale.

4.MD.A.3: Apply the area and perimeter formulas for rectangles in real world and mathematical problems. *For example, find the width of a rectangular room given the area of the flooring and the length, by viewing the area formula as a multiplication equation with an unknown factor.*

PROBLEM DISCUSSION

Dollars for Decking is a complex task that incorporates many mathematical ideas that fourth graders have learned throughout the school year. This task involves a real-world application of computing the area of rectangles (4.MD.A.3), made challenging in part because of the linear dimensions provided for the two types of decking. Students are also asked to make connections between the price of a board of decking material and the amount of material needed (4.MD.A.2). To do so, they will need to perform various operations related to whole numbers and decimals. Because the computation is not the mathematical focus of the task and students may not yet have learned these skills, it is recommended that students have access to calculators for these computations.

The McCools' deck can be partitioned into two rectangles to find the area, by drawing a line horizontally or vertically:

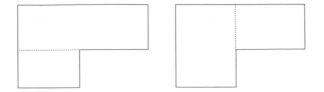

The resulting dimensions of the rectangles, given in feet (6 × 17 and 5 × 8; 11 × 8 and 6 × 9), can be used to calculate the total area of the deck as 142 square feet. Students may calculate the total area of the deck in other ways, such as partitioning the rectilinear figure into more than two rectangles, or considering the area of a larger rectangle (11 × 17) and subtracting the missing portion.

After determining the area, students will find that the challenge becomes how to use this measurement to calculate the cost of the decking material. Unlike some flooring materials, the cedar and treated wood are not priced in terms of square feet, so students may reason about the number of square feet that are covered by an individual board for each of the materials. For example, a 12-foot board of treated wood that is 4 inches wide could be sectioned into three equal lengths of 4 feet. Laying these next to each other as in the diagram below would demonstrate that one board could cover a rectangle that is 1 foot by 4 feet, or 4 square feet.

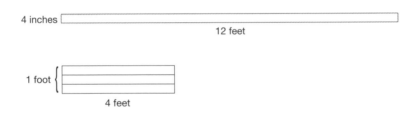

With similar reasoning about the cedar boards, students may determine that one cedar board could cover a rectangle that is 1 foot by 6 feet, or 6 square feet.

Students may then divide the total number of square feet by the number of square feet covered by one board of each type to determine the number of boards needed for each type of material for the deck:

Treated wood: 142 ÷ 4 = 35.5

Cedar: 142 ÷ 6 = 23.666…

Assuming that it is impossible to purchase portions of whole boards, students will need to revisit the context to reason that they need the next whole number of boards for each type of material: 36 of treated wood and 24 of cedar (SMP 2). Each of these quantities can then be multiplied by the price per board to determine the cost of the deck for each type of material:

Treated wood: 36 × 8.28 = 298.08

Cedar: 24 × 12.18 = 292.32

Both of these answers are in dollars, so it is appropriate to leave them with two decimal places: $298.08 for treated wood and $292.32 for cedar. Although rounding to the nearest whole number was appropriate when determining the number of boards needed, it is not appropriate when determining the cost for each material. Thus, throughout the task, students need to consider their intermediate results in relation to the context of the problem (SMP 2) and attend to precision with the quantities as needed (SMP 6).

This discussion has outlined only one way in which this task may be solved. Students may have many different ways of approaching it, including very concrete representations or drawings. Materials that may be useful include graph paper, Cuisenaire rods, linking or snap cubes, and rulers. As students work, the ways in which they determine the necessary numbers of treated wood and cedar boards will be important to observe and record, since this translation from linear dimensions to the deck space to be covered is likely to be the most challenging aspect of the problem.

STRATEGIES

- Students may iterate a 12-foot board of decking material across a diagram or graph paper drawing of the deck. For example, in considering treated wood, they may draw one 12-foot board, starting from the top left corner of the deck, and then draw a 5-foot section of another board. They may continue this strategy until they have completely covered the deck with boards of this length.
- Students may represent decking material by using popsicle sticks or paper strips, and use the dimensions (either to scale or not to scale) to calculate the surface to be covered.
- Students may represent decking material by using snap cubes or another manipulative, considering the scale of the manipulative's dimensions, and build the deck from this material.
- Using the dimensions of each material, students may construct the deck to its dimensions by using graph paper or rectangles in a diagram.
- Students may use fractions to reason about the area covered by the boards. For example, they may recognize that one board of treated wood covers 1/3 of a 1-foot by 12-foot rectangle, or 1/3 of 12 square feet. Similarly, cedar covers 1/2 of a 1-foot by 12-foot rectangle, or 1/2 of 12 square feet.
- Students may calculate the number of square feet covered by an individual board of each material, as discussed above.
- Students may use the area covered by an individual board of a particular material and determine how many boards are required by dividing the total area of the deck (or sections of the total area) by the area of an individual board.
- Once students have determined the number of boards required for each of the decking materials, they may calculate the total cost by multiplying the number of boards by the cost per board. (Note that these calculations may be performed in a variety of ways.)

Misconceptions/Student Difficulties

- Students may struggle to visualize or conceptualize how the boards are laid out to create the area of the deck.
- Students may struggle with composing or decomposing measurements when they iterate boards in working with a diagram, graph paper, or a manipulative.
- Students may calculate the perimeter of the deck and divide this value by 12 feet (the length of a board) to determine how many boards are required.
- Students may not realize that they need to buy a whole number of boards or may make a calculation that results in fewer boards than needed because of a rounding misconception or error.
- Students may inappropriately round the cost to the nearest whole dollar.
- Students may miscalculate how many boards fit widthwise across a linear foot.
- Students may incorrectly calculate the area of the deck.

Launch

Begin this task by asking the students if they have a deck or porch on their house. Ask them to describe the material that the deck is made of and the activities that they like to do on their decks. Finally, ask them if their families have ever had to replace their deck or build a new one. Talk about the materials that are typically used. If possible, bring in samples of wood that might be used for decking so that they can make sense of the dimensions of the wood in the problem.

Explain to the students that they will be exploring a challenging problem that asks them to determine how much the wood would cost for the McCools' new deck. Read the problem aloud to the class while using the diagram to provide a visual display. Ask the students to turn to a neighbor and try to restate the problem in their own words. After this, ask the students to share what they know about the problem, what they are being asked to do, and any preliminary ideas that they have about how to get started. At this point, it might be helpful to emphasize that this is a challenging problem, so it will be important for them to take their time in reasoning about it and potentially try multiple strategies.

Explore

Provide multiple materials to each group of three or four students. Ask them to spend the first few minutes talking in their groups about their different ideas for figuring out how much treated wood and how much cedar will be needed for the deck. Avoid redirecting students from a process that may not work; instead, let students' reasoning play out and allow them the opportunity to discover mistakes in their reasoning.

As students explore, ask them questions to check for understanding:

- How are you using these materials to help you solve the problem?
- Can you explain what you have sketched on this diagram?
- Can you explain how the 4-inch measure (or the 6-inch measure) fits in the deck measurements? How can you show me?

- How are you determining how many boards of each material would be needed to build the deck?
- Once you've determined how many boards of each material you need, how will you determine the total cost?
- Have you rounded any numbers? Which ones, and why?

Because there are multiple ways (some of them probably unanticipated) for solving this problem, it is especially important during this portion of the lesson to simply listen to students' thinking. Questions that check for understanding should respond to their descriptions of their reasoning, helping them clarify and justify their strategies and calculations.

Finally, ask each group to make two separate posters, one that explains their reasoning for the cost of treated wood and one that explains their reasoning for the cost of cedar. Hang posters for the cost of treated wood for the class discussion, grouping together those that have answers or strategies that are the same or similar.

SUMMARIZE

Bring the class together, and identify the different numerical answers that the groups have provided for the cost of the deck constructed with treated wood. Ask, "Which students would like to be the first to explain their reasoning about their answer?" Have the students in this group discuss how they solved the problem. Ask questions as needed (and encourage classmates to do so) to clarify the students' thinking. Ask other students to revoice some of the strategies or computations and the reasoning behind them. If needed, offer a summary of the reasoning, or ask other students to do so. Be sure that the group's work is clearly visible to the rest of the class, and allow some time at the end for any clarifying questions.

After each group shares, ask, "Is there another group that would like to defend the same answer or present a different answer?" In this fashion, give all groups interested in presenting their reasoning the opportunity to do so. If there are competing answers, errors in students' reasoning may be sorted out through this discussion. If there are lingering disagreements, consider asking students to go back to their groups to try another method for solving the problem. Have them examine other groups' thinking to determine whether they agree with the answer or can find some step in the process that they think is an error. Reconvene the class, and continue the discussion with groups arguing for or against other groups' reasoning.

Once a consensus has been reached, ask students to rejoin their groups to reexamine their reasoning about the cost of the deck constructed with cedar boards. Groups may want to change their strategy in light of the previous discussion of the deck constructed with treated wood. Circulate throughout the room as this happens, noting groups that are effectively incorporating strategies or concepts from that discussion. For those groups that are satisfied with their answers, provide information about a third decking material and ask them to apply their reasoning to the new material (see Differentiation).

Bring the class together again to discuss the problem related to the cedar decking material. Have groups that are interested present and defend their reasoning, allowing questions and clarification from peers throughout. Again, if there are competing answers, provide opportunities for students to critique others' reasoning and work toward a consensus through respectful disagreement.

DIFFERENTIATION

- For students who struggle with the shape of the deck, consider creating a deck that is composed of a single rectangle.

- Consider changing the length dimension to a multiple of 12 feet, so that students can iterate a board unit without decomposing the board.

- For students who struggle to conceptualize how a four-inch width fits into a foot, ask them to solve the problem for the cedar boards only. The treated wood can be a challenge.

- To extend this task, challenge students to research other types of materials that might be used for decks. Composite materials tend to be more expensive but require less maintenance, and the material lasts longer. Ask students to research factors that might influence the decision and make a recommendation to the McCool family.

- To extend this task, challenge students to find dimensions of rectangles that could be made by exhausting an assigned quantity of treated wood or cedar boards.

ROLLER COASTERS

Three friends rode three different roller coasters at the amusement park. Mya's ride lasted 3 3/4 minutes. Abigail's ride lasted 2/3 as long as Mya's ride. The length of time of Kaelie's ride was halfway between the times of Mya's and Abigail's rides. How long did Kaelie's ride last? Use equations and drawings to support your answer.

CCSSM STANDARDS FOR MATHEMATICAL PRACTICE

Practice 8: Look for and express regularity in repeated reasoning.

CCSSM CONTENT STANDARDS

5.NF.B.4a: Interpret the product $(^a/_b) \times q$ as a parts of a partition of q into b equal parts; equivalently, as the result of a sequence of operations $a \times q \div b$. *For example, use a visual fraction model to show $(2/3) \times 4 = {}^8/_3$, and create a story context for this equation. Do the same with $(2/3) \times (4/5) = {}^8/_{15}$. (In general, $(^a/_b) \times (^c/_d) = {}^{ac}/_{bd}$.)*

5.NF.B.6: Solve real world problems involving multiplication of fractions and mixed numbers, e.g., by using visual fraction models or equations to represent the problem.

PROBLEM DISCUSSION

In this task, students determine the duration of a roller coaster ride by using visual models and equations to multiply fractions and mixed numbers (5.NF.B.6). To determine how long Kaelie's ride lasted, they must first determine how long Abigail's ride lasted. Students may use a variety of visual models, such as fraction strips, area models, or number lines, as well as equations, to determine the duration of Abigail's ride. Students will be encouraged to connect their visual models with the standard algorithm for finding the product of two fractions (5.NF.B.4a). For example, students may see the product of 2/3 × 3 3/4 as 3 3/4 partitioned into three equal parts with two of those parts representing the duration of Abigail's ride. Students may use a number line as shown on the next page and partition the distance from 0 to 3 3/4 (the whole) into fifteen 1/4 units and then partition these fifteen units into three equal-sized lengths of five 1/4 units (i.e., 1/4 of a minute) each. They will then select two of these lengths to see that the duration of Abigail's ride was ten 1/4 units (10/4 = 5/2 = 2 1/2 minutes).

Using multiple models such as the number line and others discussed in the Summarize section, students may begin to notice the connections among these models, allowing them to interpret the product of 2/3 × 3 3/4 as two of three equal parts of a whole that is 3 3/4 minutes (5.NF.B.4a; SMP8).

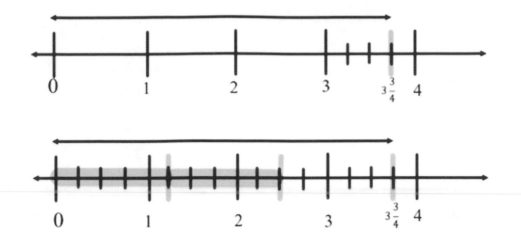

Once students have determined the duration of Abigail's ride, they will use this information to find the midpoint between two mixed numbers, which will give them the duration of Kaelie's ride. Students may explore this portion of the task by using diagrams or operations on fractions. For example, students may use a number line model to find the midpoint between 2 1/2 and 3 3/4 by starting at each end point and moving toward the midpoint by 1/2 of a minute to get to 3 minutes and 3 1/4 minutes (see the diagram below). Next, students may recognize that they need to partition the 1/4 unit into two parts to get the midpoint of 3 1/8 minutes. Notice that this representation requires students to apply their knowledge of *half as much* to recognize that half of a fourth of a unit is an eighth of the unit (SMP 8). Students may also use their knowledge of *average* to add the fractions to get 6 1/4 and then take half of this to arrive at a duration of 3 1/8 minutes.

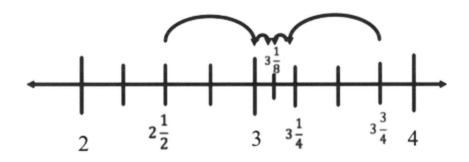

A possible extension of the Roller Coaster task would be to ask students to determine how many times longer Kaelie's ride was than Abigail's ride. To answer this question, students might use a missing factor approach (such as 2 1/2 × ___ = 3 1/8) or an area model. This work would allow students to conjecture that when a fraction is multiplied by a number greater than 1, the result is larger than the starting number. Students could then generate multiple examples to verify this conjecture (SMP 8).

STRATEGIES

- To find the duration of Abigail's ride, students may convert $3\,3/4$ minutes into 3 minutes and 45 seconds and then take $2/3$ of each.
- For the length of Abigail's ride, students may use a visual representation to find $2/3$ of $3\,3/4$ (e.g., fraction strips, area model, number line).
- For the length of Abigail's ride, students may use the distributive property to find $2/3$ of $3\,3/4$ (i.e., $(2/3 \times 3) + (2/3 \times 3/4) = 2 + 1/2 = 2\,1/2$).
- For the length of Abigail's ride, students may convert $3\,3/4$ to $15/4$ and apply the standard algorithm for multiplying two fractions.
- To find the duration of Kaelie's ride, students may use a visual model such as a number line to locate the durations of Abigail's and Mya's rides and then move toward the midpoint of these points by using equal-spaced units along the number line until they arrive at 3 and $3\,1/4$. Students then find half of $1/4$ to find the midpoint.
- For the length of Kaelie's ride, students may add the lengths of Abigail's and Mya's rides, arrive at $6\,1/4$ minutes, and then use an equal groups idea to find the midpoint. For example, a student may reason that half of 6 is 3, and half of $1/4$ is $1/8$, so $3\,1/8$ is halfway between the two times.

MISCONCEPTIONS/STUDENT DIFFICULTIES

- Students may interpret "$2/3$ as long" as either adding $2/3$ to or subtracting it from $3\,3/4$.
- Students may have difficulty partitioning their visual fraction models into equal parts.
- Students may think that multiplying two numbers always results in a product that is greater than the factors.
- Students may not know how to interpret "halfway between" in the context of this problem.
- Students may not know how to find the point halfway between 3 and $3\,1/4$.

LAUNCH

Ask students whether they have ever ridden on a roller coaster. If possible, show students a video of a roller coaster ride. Ask them to estimate how long the ride lasted, and record a few of the times on the board. If you are unable to show a video, ask students to estimate how long a typical roller coaster ride lasts, and record a few of these times on the board. Tell students that rides on some of the longest roller coasters in the world last anywhere from two minutes and twenty seconds to five and a half minutes. Ask students to convert these minutes into fractions of minutes ($2\,1/3$ and $5\,1/2$, respectively). Next, ask students to create a number line to display the fractional durations that they shared as well as these two given durations. Ask questions to check for understanding:

- Is there another way to write that fraction? How do you know it is the same fraction?
- How did you find $2\,1/3$?

- How did you know where to place 2 1/3 on the number line?
- Why did you decide to partition your number line in this way?

Tell students that they will be working on a task involving the times of three different roller coaster rides.

EXPLORE

Hand out the task and have students read it silently. Ask students to share two things they know about the situation and one thing they need to find. Have them share their ideas with a partner and then work with this partner to solve the problem. As students work on the first part of the problem—the duration of Abigail's ride—ask questions to check for understanding:

- Is Abigail's ride shorter or longer than Mya's ride? How do you know?
- How does your model show 3 3/4 minutes?
- Why did you decide to partition your model in this way?
- How does your model show the duration of Abigail's ride?
- On your number line, why did you choose to partition each whole into fourths?
- What operation do you think your model represents?
- How do you know 3 3/4 is the same as 15/4? Can you draw a picture to show this?
- Why did you decide to multiply 2/3 and 3 3/4?
- Why does your rule for multiplying fractions work? Can you draw a picture to show why this works?

As students use their work on the first part of the problem to solve the second part—the duration of Kaelie's ride—ask questions to check for understanding:

- What does it mean to be halfway between your house and the school? What do you know about the distance from your house to the halfway point and the distance from the school and the halfway point?
- Do you think the halfway point would be more than or less than 3 minutes? Why?
- Could you use a number line to help you find the halfway point? Can you estimate the location of the halfway point on your number line. How could you partition your number line to verify your estimate?

Next, tell students they will be sharing their solution strategies and diagrams with another pair of students, so they will need to take time to organize their work for this sharing process. Allow students time to reconstruct their drawings if necessary. As students organize their work, identify pairs of students who used different strategies to form sharing groups for the summary portion of the activity.

SUMMARIZE

Assign sharing groups according to the strategies that students used to solve the task. Ask students to share their diagrams and solutions and verify that each solution and model makes sense in the context of the problem. Next, as a whole class, select different strategies and make connections among them. If all the strategies below are not shared, students could be encouraged to use one (or more) of the models and connect it with the one they used. Begin by selecting students who created a visual fraction model, followed by students who used a general formula. Below are several examples of possible models of the multiplication of 2/3 by 3 3/4, paired with examples showing how students might explain their model. Note that in these models students may either (1) partition the 3 3/4 minutes (the whole) into three equal parts and select two of these equal parts or (2) partition 3 minutes into three equal parts and partition 3/4 minutes into three equal parts. In the second representation, students are applying the distributive property by taking 2/3 of 3 plus 2/3 of 3/4 (i.e., $2/3(3\,3/4) = 2/3(3 + 3/4) = 2/3(3) + 2/3(3/4)$).

Number Line Models

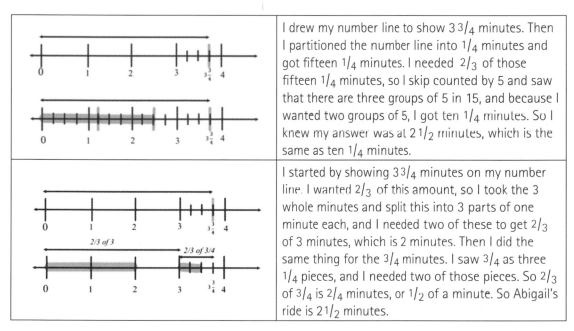

| | I drew my number line to show 3 3/4 minutes. Then I partitioned the number line into 1/4 minutes and got fifteen 1/4 minutes. I needed 2/3 of those fifteen 1/4 minutes, so I skip counted by 5 and saw that there are three groups of 5 in 15, and because I wanted two groups of 5, I got ten 1/4 minutes. So I knew my answer was at 2 1/2 minutes, which is the same as ten 1/4 minutes. |
| | I started by showing 3 3/4 minutes on my number line. I wanted 2/3 of this amount, so I took the 3 whole minutes and split this into 3 parts of one minute each, and I needed two of these to get 2/3 of 3 minutes, which is 2 minutes. Then I did the same thing for the 3/4 minutes. I saw 3/4 as three 1/4 pieces, and I needed two of those pieces. So 2/3 of 3/4 is 2/4 minutes, or 1/2 of a minute. So Abigail's ride is 2 1/2 minutes. |

Fraction Strip Models

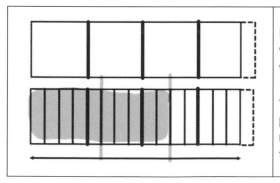

| | I drew 3 3/4 minutes as 3 wholes and 3/4 of another whole. I saw that I could partition each of the wholes into four 1/4 pieces, which gave me fifteen 1/4 pieces. I distributed these fifteen pieces into three equal piles because I wanted 2/3 of the fifteen pieces. This gave me five pieces in each pile, and I needed two piles. So I was left with ten pieces, or ten 1/4 minutes. This is 2 1/2 minutes. |

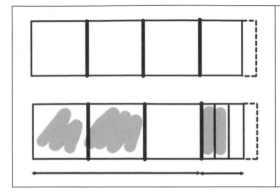

I drew 3 3/4 minutes as 3 wholes and 3/4 of another whole. I saw that I could shade 2 of the three wholes and shade 2 of the three 1/4 pieces. This gave me 2 wholes and 2/4 of another whole, which is 2 1/2 minutes.

Area Model

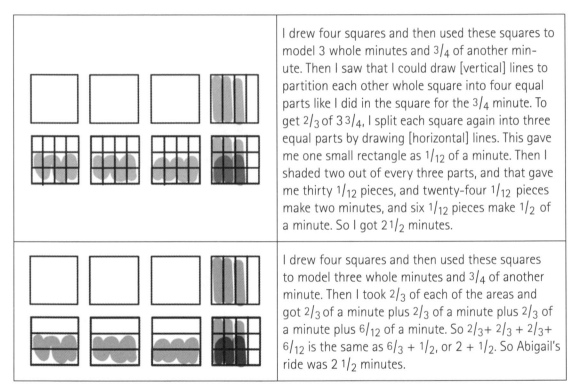

I drew four squares and then used these squares to model 3 whole minutes and 3/4 of another minute. Then I saw that I could draw [vertical] lines to partition each other whole square into four equal parts like I did in the square for the 3/4 minute. To get 2/3 of 3 3/4, I split each square again into three equal parts by drawing [horizontal] lines. This gave me one small rectangle as 1/12 of a minute. Then I shaded two out of every three parts, and that gave me thirty 1/12 pieces, and twenty-four 1/12 pieces make two minutes, and six 1/12 pieces make 1/2 of a minute. So I got 2 1/2 minutes.

I drew four squares and then used these squares to model three whole minutes and 3/4 of another minute. Then I took 2/3 of each of the areas and got 2/3 of a minute plus 2/3 of a minute plus 2/3 of a minute plus 6/12 of a minute. So 2/3 + 2/3 + 2/3 + 6/12 is the same as 6/3 + 1/2, or 2 + 1/2. So Abigail's ride was 2 1/2 minutes.

Select a group that used a visual fraction model, and ask the students to share their work on the board. Pose questions to connect the number line and fraction strip models to the meaning of taking 2/3 of a whole:

- Which model shows 3 3/4 is the same as 15/4 ?
- What does it mean to take 2/3 of 15/4 ?
- How does your model show that you partitioned 15/4 into three equal parts?
- Why did you select two of those equal parts?

Next, ask a group that used fraction multiplication to share their work on the board. Ask questions to connect the area model with the standard algorithm for fraction multiplication—in this case,

$$\frac{2}{3} \times 3\frac{3}{4} = \frac{2}{3} \times \frac{15}{4} = \frac{2 \times 15}{3 \times 4} = \frac{30}{12} = 2\frac{1}{2}$$

- How does the area model show $30/12$? How does the area model show $2\,1/2$?
- How does the area model show the duration of Mya's ride?

Finally, ask a group that used fraction multiplication with the distributive property to share their work on the board. Ask questions to connect the number line, fraction strips, and area models from above with the general formula for fraction multiplication:

- How does each model show $2/3 \times 3$?
- How does each model show $2/3 \times 3/4$?

To summarize strategies for finding the duration of Kaelie's ride, select a student who used a number line model and ask that student to share. Then ask if any student used a different strategy to find the halfway point between $2\,1/2$ and $3\,3/4$. Continue this process until all strategies have been shared. Below are possible models for how students may find the duration of Kaelie's ride.

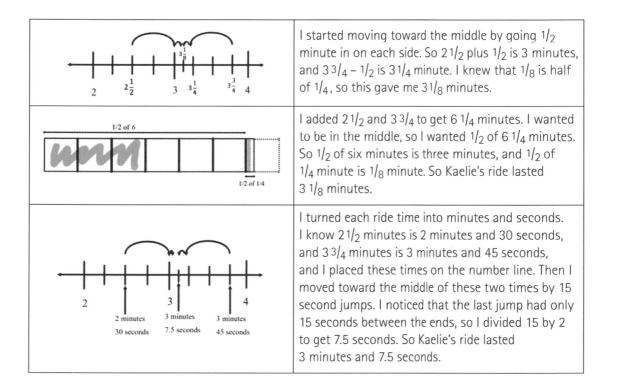

	I started moving toward the middle by going $1/2$ minute in on each side. So $2\,1/2$ plus $1/2$ is 3 minutes, and $3\,3/4 - 1/2$ is $3\,1/4$ minute. I knew that $1/8$ is half of $1/4$, so this gave me $3\,1/8$ minutes.
	I added $2\,1/2$ and $3\,3/4$ to get $6\,1/4$ minutes. I wanted to be in the middle, so I wanted $1/2$ of $6\,1/4$ minutes. So $1/2$ of six minutes is three minutes, and $1/2$ of $1/4$ minute is $1/8$ minute. So Kaelie's ride lasted $3\,1/8$ minutes.
	I turned each ride time into minutes and seconds. I know $2\,1/2$ minutes is 2 minutes and 30 seconds, and $3\,3/4$ minutes is 3 minutes and 45 seconds, and I placed these times on the number line. Then I moved toward the middle of these two times by 15 second jumps. I noticed that the last jump had only 15 seconds between the ends, so I divided 15 by 2 to get 7.5 seconds. So Kaelie's ride lasted 3 minutes and 7.5 seconds.

To conclude the task, ask students the following questions:

- How much longer does Abigail's ride need to be to last as long as Kaelie's ride?
- How much shorter does Mya's ride need to be to last as long as Kaelie's ride?

Students should realize that the answers to these two questions should be the same, since the halfway point is equidistant from the end points.

DIFFERENTIATION

- To support struggling students, change Mya's time to a whole number, such as 4 minutes.
- To support students who struggle to partition, allow them to use fraction tiles or premade number lines.
- To support students who struggle to partition a number line, allow them to use a ruler to make their model.
- To extend the task, ask students to find the duration of a single roller coaster ride if the durations of Mya's, Abigail's, and Kaelie's rides were redistributed equally among the three rides.
- To extend the task, ask student to determine the answers to the following questions:
  - How many times longer was Kaelie's ride than Abigail's ride?
  - How many times longer was Mya's ride than Kaelie's ride?

THE LARGEST ANIMAL ON EARTH

Bryce and Shea go on a whale-watching expedition in Massachusetts on their summer vacation. While they are taking pictures of a humpback whale feeding, a naturalist is sharing information:

> "Adult humpback whales range from 39 to 52 feet long. The shortest length, 39 feet, is about $2/5$ of the length of an adult blue whale, which is the largest animal on earth."

Approximately how long is an adult blue whale? Show your work, and explain your reasoning.

CCSSM STANDARDS FOR MATHEMATICAL PRACTICE

Practice 1: Make sense of problems and persevere in solving them.

Practice 5: Use appropriate tools strategically.

CCSSM CONTENT STANDARDS

5.NF.B.7c: Solve real world problems involving division of unit fractions by non-zero whole numbers and division of whole numbers by unit fractions, e.g., by using visual fraction models and equations to represent the problem. *For example, how much chocolate will each person get if 3 people share $1/2$ lb of chocolate equally? How many $1/3$-cup servings are in 2 cups of raisins?*

PROBLEM DISCUSSION

By the end of fifth grade, students should be able to reason about word problems involving division of whole numbers by unit fractions (e.g., $5 \div 1/8$) (5.NF.B.7c). This problem will push their thinking forward and connect that learning with what they will learn in sixth grade—dividing fractions by fractions (6.NS.A.1)—by asking them to reason about a problem that could be solved through division of a whole number by a non-unit fraction.

The Largest Animal on Earth provides a whole number (39 feet) that represents a fraction of a different whole—the length of a blue whale. This is a partition division problem, which gives a value related to a particular fraction (39 feet is $2/5$ of the whole), and asks for the value of the whole. (This problem is qualitatively different from a measurement division problem, which would ask how many $2/5$'s could be made from 39.) The problem can be solved by calculating $39 \div 2/5 = 97 1/2$. Computation is not the goal of this task, however. In fact, students rarely recognize this as a division problem. Instead, the task offers an opportunity to consider ways that students might make sense of this problem and use this sense making to solve it (SMP 1).

Consider first how students might reason about this problem if 39 feet were $1/5$ of the whole length of the blue whale. The whole length would be five fifths, arranged end to end. Therefore, if $1/5$ represented 39 feet, then five fifths would be equivalent to five lengths of 39 feet ($5 \times 39 = 195$).

39 feet	39 feet	39 feet	39 feet	39 feet

Instead, the length of the humpback whale (39 feet) is actually 2/5 of the length of the blue whale. The shaded region below (2/5 of the whole) represents the entire length of the humpback whale (39 feet).

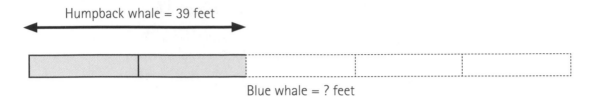

Humpback whale = 39 feet

Blue whale = ? feet

To determine the length that would be 1/5 of the blue whale, we can divide 39 feet by 2 (39 ÷ 2 = 19.5). Therefore, each 1/5 in the diagram below is equivalent to 19.5 feet. To determine the length of the whole—the length of the blue whale—we can determine 5 lengths of 19.5 feet (5 × 19.5 = 97.5). This is a good approximation of the length of a blue whale.

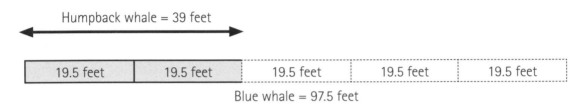

Humpback whale = 39 feet

| 19.5 feet | 19.5 feet | 19.5 feet | 19.5 feet | 19.5 feet |

Blue whale = 97.5 feet

Students may reason through the "invert and multiply" algorithm in a way that makes sense with the problem and to them: The divisor is 2/5; they have divided by the numerator of this divisor (2) and multiplied by its denominator (5). Unless students have been taught this algorithm (and even if they have), they are likely to need to work with some sort of manipulative or drawing to make sense of the problem and use that tool to reason successfully about a solution (SMP 5).

STRATEGIES

- Students may use a manipulative to represent the length of the humpback whale (e.g., 39 linking cubes or paperclips). They may use this length to determine 1/5 of the length of the blue whale by dividing this length into two equal parts, 19.5 units (abstract reasoning is required). Then they may determine the length of the blue whale by considering five times this length.

- Students may use a more abstract representation for the length of the humpback whale (e.g., a sketch of a humpback whale or simply a line or strip to represent its length). Then they may follow similar steps for the strategy above.

- Students may represent the length of the blue whale first and partition this length into five equal sections. Then they may consider two of those parts as equivalent to 39 feet, divide 39 by 2 to find 1/5 of the blue whale, and multiply this quotient by 5 to find its entire length.

- Students may apply an area (e.g., fraction circles) or set model to identify 19.5 feet as 1/5 of the length of the blue whale.
- Students may reason abstractly about the value of 1/5 of the length of the blue whale by dividing 39 by 2. Then they may multiply this value by 5 to determine the whole length of the blue whale.
- Students may multiply 39 by 5, reasoning abstractly that this would then be the length of two blue whales, end to end. Then, to determine the length of one blue whale, they would divide this product by 2.
- Students may recognize this as a division problem and divide 39 by 2/5, using a previously learned algorithm.
- Students may recognize this as a proportional reasoning problem if they have been previously introduced to such problems and use ratio tables, strip diagrams, or an equation to solve it.

Misconceptions/Student Difficulties

- Students may struggle with conceptualizing how the 39 feet is equivalent to 2/5 of another whole.
- Students may incorrectly apply a previously learned algorithm (e.g., multiply the whole number by the denominator or the invert-and-multiply algorithm) to this problem.
- Students may struggle with a non–whole number value for 1/5 of the whole (see the Differentiation section).
- Students may guess about the operation to perform with the values provided in the problem.
- Students may make computational errors with any of the four operations.

Launch

Ask students what they know about whales. Depending on students' geographical location, this knowledge may be limited or extensive, but provide some time for students to voice what they already know about these animals. This opportunity to share may also provide an opportunity to discuss the size of whales; it is likely that at least a few students will already know that the blue whale is the largest animal on earth. Follow this discussion by asking students if anyone has ever been on a whale-watching trip. Some students may have taken advantage of the yearly migration of whales to see them in their summer feeding grounds. As needed, discuss or explore whale-watching excursions and what might be expected on one.

Have a student read the problem aloud to the rest of the class while displaying it for the whole class to see. Ask students to turn to an elbow partner to discuss what they know from the problem about the size of a humpback whale in comparison with a blue whale. Ask, "Which whale is bigger? How do you know?" Also ask, "What does this fraction 2/5 refer to?" Have students share their thoughts; assist them with proper terminology for the comparisons as needed.

Next, ask students what tools might be helpful to them in solving this problem. Display their ideas in a list, offering other suggestions (fraction models, linking cubes, pen and paper) as needed. Explain to students that they will be working in small groups to solve the problem. Indicate that their final product will be a poster that illustrates and explains their reasoning.

Explore

Assign students to groups of three or four to work on this problem. Provide any requested materials so that students can explore different ways to make sense of the problem. Although some materials may not model the context well (e.g., fraction circles), allow students to use whichever model they wish. If they reason successfully about the problem, ask them to consider how they might use a fraction strip or a line to model the context more directly.

If students struggle to get started, ask them questions to prompt their reasoning:

- What ideas did you have for tools that you might use to make sense of the problem?
- How can you represent the length of the humpback whale?
- What do you know about the length of the humpback whale in relation to the length of the blue whale?
- How can you represent the length of the blue whale?
- If this is the length of the blue whale, about how long might you expect the humpback whale to be? (Consider this question in relation to a length of string.)

Help students get started with a manipulative or drawing as a tool to represent the length of the humpback whale or the blue whale. This initial assistance may help them think about how the quantity of 39 feet relates to the tool, providing an appropriate entry into the problem.

As students work, ask them questions to check for understanding:

- Can you tell me how you're using this manipulative to help you make sense of the problem?
- Can you explain your drawing to me?
- How did you know $1/5$ was the same as 19.5 feet?
- Why are you dividing 39 by 2?
- Why are you dividing this length into 5 equal parts?
- How does knowing what $1/5$ of the length of the blue whale is help you determine its whole length?
- Does your answer make sense to you? Where else might you check to see whether your answer is reasonable?

If students are struggling with the problem, allow them to get an incorrect answer, and then ask them to consider whether or not their answer makes sense. If the answer that a group generates is incorrect, say, "So if this is the length of the blue whale, then $2/5$ of this should be the length of the humpback whale. Can you use this fact to check your work?"

If students have successfully made a poster to demonstrate their reasoning, you can extend their thinking in multiple interesting ways (for possibilities, see Differentiation). Consider creating a list of additional questions to explore so that students can choose an idea that interests them.

SUMMARIZE

If possible, provide an opportunity for each group of students to share and explain their reasoning. Encourage students in other groups to ask questions that help them make sense of the presenting groups' strategies, as well as to make connections with their own or other strategies. Take note during the Explore phase of groups that have similar strategies and groups that have represented the situation by using manipulatives or drawings. Ask those groups to share first. Then call on other groups that have distinct similarities in their strategies.

As students present, ask questions to tie their strategies together or assess their understanding:

- Why was dividing 39 by 2 so important to some groups? What does this tell you?
- Once you knew what 1/5 of the length of the blue whale was, how did you find the whole length of the blue whale? What other groups did that same calculation? Why does it work?
- How is this problem different from other problems that we have solved with unit fractions? Why couldn't you just multiply 39 by 5 to get the length of the blue whale?
- How was it different for groups that started by representing the length of the humpback whale and groups that started by representing the length of the blue whale? What benefits does each strategy have?

Be sure that students can follow the trail of computations and why these computations make sense in the context of the problem. Consider summarizing computations visually by displaying $39 \div 2 \times 5 = 97.5$. Connecting this with the invert-and-multiply algorithm is not necessary at this time.

If students have had an opportunity to explore other questions related to this context, consider taking the time to share what they investigated and discovered. This process could extend over several days if time allows.

DIFFERENTIATION

- For students who may struggle with operations involving non–whole numbers, consider changing the 39 feet in the problem to 40 feet. This will result in an answer of 100 feet, which is still a good approximation for the length of a blue whale.
- For students who struggle with conceptualizing the problem, consider a similar entry problem involving division by a unit fraction. Possibilities include the following:
  ○ An orca, or killer whale, may be approximately 1/3 the length of a right whale. If an orca is 20 feet long, how long might a right whale be?

- ○ Minke whales are approximately 1/4 the length of a fin whale. If a minke whale is 23 feet, how long would a fin whale be?
- ○ A 6-foot person is approximately 1/15 the length of a fin whale. How long is a fin whale?
- Ask students to investigate other length comparisons between whales, whales and dinosaurs, or 6-foot humans and whales. Have them use these comparisons to identify other comparative statements that the naturalist might make and pose these new situations to other students.
- Ask students to investigate other measurement comparisons, such as comparisons involving weight or volume. For example, they might investigate the weight of a blue whale in comparison with the weight of a particular kind of car. They may also make comparisons involving parts of whales. For example, the blue whale's heart is the size of a small car. Have students write comparisons, using fractions whenever possible.

POLAR BEAR EXHIBIT

The zoo is building a new polar bear exhibit with a pool in the shape of a right rectangular prism. The volume of the polar bear pool needs to be 640 cubic meters. Help the zoo decide the dimensions and shape of the new polar bear pool. Include the dimensions for two pools, a drawing of each, and an explanation of why you think each pool would be a good choice for the polar bear exhibit.

CCSSM STANDARDS FOR MATHEMATICAL PRACTICE

Practice 3: Construct viable arguments and critique the reasoning of others.

Practice 7: Look for and make use of structure.

CCSSM CONTENT STANDARDS

5.MD.C.5: Relate volume to the operations of multiplication and addition and solve real world and mathematical problems involving volume.

5.MD.C.5a: Find the volume of a right rectangular prism with whole-number side lengths by packing it with unit cubes, and show that the volume is the same as would be found by multiplying the edge lengths, equivalently by multiplying the height by the area of the base. Represent threefold whole-number products as volumes, e.g., to represent the associative property of multiplication.

5.MD.C.5b: Apply the formulas $V = l \times w \times h$ and $V = b \times h$ for rectangular prisms to find volumes of right rectangular prisms with whole-number edge lengths in the context of solving real world and mathematical problems.

5.MD.C.5c: Recognize volume as additive. Find volumes of solid figures composed of two non-overlapping right rectangular prisms by adding the volumes of the non-overlapping parts, applying this technique to solve real world problems.

PROBLEM DISCUSSION

In Polar Bear Exhibit, students investigate concepts related to volume. In grade 3 (3.MD.C.5 and 3.MD.C.6) students work with area and the spatial structuring of two dimensions. The emphasis in grade 5 is on finding volume of right rectangular prisms. Adding this third dimension creates a challenge for students when packing unit cubes into a rectangular prism (5.MD.C.3). For example, when structuring the rows and columns of square units to find the area of a two-dimensional figure, students have the advantage that all the unit squares are visible. When packing a three-dimensional right rectangular prism with unit cubes, they face the challenge that some unit cubes are not visible. In the Launch of this task, students will use manipulatives to find possible dimensions of a rectangular prism, given a number of cubic units as the volume of the figure (5.MD.C.5a). At this time, students will engage in a discussion regarding the spatial structuring of the cubic units (SMP 7). For example, students will be asked to fill the bottom layer of their right rectangular prims with cubic units. Next, students will be asked to discuss how they could use this single layer to find the total volume of the prism. Students may also use this reasoning to apply the commutative and associative properties of multiplication to find different dimensions that would result in a volume of 640 cubic meters (SMP 7). For example, once students have a pool with dimensions of $1 \times 2 \times 320$, they may see that dividing 320 by 2 would require multiplying one of the other two dimensions by 2 to keep the total volume the same ($2 \times 2 \times 160$ or $1 \times 4 \times 160$).

As students work to create two different polar bear pools having the same volume (5.MD.C.5), they will apply formulas for finding the volume of right rectangular prisms (5.MD.C.5b) to determine reasonable dimensions for the two polar bear pools. Students will need to justify why each pool's dimensions are realistic in the context of the problem (SMP 3). Students could be encouraged to create a pool by combining two right rectangular prisms in an L or a T shape, for example. Again, students may be asked to use their knowledge of the spatial structuring of volume units to compose two right rectangular prisms and find the volume by adding the volumes of each right rectangular prism (5.MD.C.5c; SMP 7). This task also asks students to make a drawing of their two pools. Drawing three-dimensional figures that include the cubic volume units is often challenging, and students may have difficulty creating equal-sized units, straight lines, and figures with a reasonable scale.

Strategies

- Students may use a guess-and-check method for finding three numbers that multiply to 640 and use these as the dimensions of the pool.
- Students may first consider the length and width of the pool and then check to see that the resulting height is adequate for the context of the problem.
- Students may apply the commutative and associative properties of multiplication to find different dimensions that would result in a volume of 640 cubic meters. For example, once students have a pool with dimensions of $4 \times 2 \times 80$, they may see that dividing 80 by 4 would require multiplying one of the other two dimensions by 4 ($16 \times 2 \times 20$ or $4 \times 8 \times 20$) or both dimensions by 2 ($8 \times 4 \times 20$) to keep the total volume the same.
- Students may decompose 640 into two factors, such as 10 and 64, and then decompose one of these factors into two factors (e.g., $2 \times 5 \times 64$ or $10 \times 4 \times 16$).
- Students may create a right rectangular prism and then decompose the prism into two smaller prisms and move one piece so that the pool is in the shape of an L or a T.

Misconceptions/Student Difficulties

- Students may not consider the reasonableness of the dimensions of the pool in the context of the problem.
- Students may have difficulty relating the packing of unit cubes to the abstract nature of the general formula for volume.
- Students may struggle to use the commutative and associative properties to manipulate the factors of 640 to find new dimensions.

- Students may struggle to draw their pools with equal-sized units, straight lines, and figures with a reasonable scale.

LAUNCH

Ask students whether they have ever been to a zoo, and if so, encourage them to share their favorite exhibits. Tell students that they will be working to design a new pool in the shape of a right rectangular prism for the polar bear exhibit. Ask students to look around the room and find a right rectangular prism. Next, give students 24 cube manipulatives. Ask students to use these cubes to create a right rectangular prism. Have students share the dimensions of their prisms. Possible dimensions include $1 \times 1 \times 24$, $2 \times 3 \times 4$, and $2 \times 2 \times 6$. If students do not create different right rectangular prisms, ask them to find another way to build their prism with different dimensions. Once students find the dimensions of their prism, ask them to determine its volume. Students should explain how they know the volume is 24 cubic units. These explanations should include both using the formula $V = l \times w \times h$ and counting unit cubes. Next, ask students to investigate one layer of their right rectangular prim and how they could use this one layer to find the volume of the entire prism. This discussion should lead to the formula $V = b \times h$, where b is the area of the base of the right rectangular prism. Ask students to discuss with an elbow partner whether a prism with the dimensions $3 \times 2 \times 4$ is the same shape as a prism with the dimensions of $4 \times 3 \times 2$. Students may realize that the context of the problem may affect which of these two sets of dimensions is the better choice. For example, in the context of the polar bear pool, the height of the rectangular prism—that is, the depth of the pool—matters, since a polar bear can grow to a standing height of approximately 3 meters.

Next, challenge students to create two right rectangular prisms that have a combined volume of 24 cubic units. Have students share these shapes and explain how they know the total volume is 24 cubic units. Students should be encouraged to find the volume of each prism to show that volume is additive.

EXPLORE

Ask a student to read the task aloud, and have students to work in pairs to solve the problem. Before the student pairs investigate this task, ask them to describe what a cubic meter would look like. A meterstick can help students understand the size of the unit of measurement involved in this task. As students work on the task, ask questions to check for understanding:

- How did you decide which dimensions to use?
- Are there other dimensions that would work? How do you know?
- How many cubic meters are in one layer of the pool? How do you know? How could you use this information to demonstrate that the total volume is 640 cubic meters?
- How could you decompose this pool into two smaller right rectangular prisms to make an L- or a T-shaped pool? Does this new pool have the same volume?
- Will you show me a cubic unit in your drawing?
- Which pool do you think is the best choice for the zoo? Why?

SUMMARIZE

To summarize the task, ask students to share their pools' designs and dimensions with another student pair. Have students verify that the other pair's dimensions result in a volume of 640 cubic meters. Students should then decide which of their pools is the best one for the bears. Allow students time to make this decision and justify their choice.

Next, ask each pair of students to share their choice for the best pool with the class. Record these dimensions for all to see. As students share their justification for their choice, encourage them to use two strategies for verifying that the volume of their pool is 640 cubic units. Because of the large number of cubes required to build a model of this pool, these two strategies are likely to involve the formulas $V = l \times w \times h$ and $V = b \times h$. Focus the discussion on the strategies that students used for finding dimensions giving 640 cubic units (see Strategies for possibilities).

Once the dimensions for each group's top choice are recorded on the board, ask students to pick any one set of dimensions displayed on the board and use it to create a new set of dimensions not shown on the board. Ask students to share how they used the given dimensions to find new dimensions, focusing the discussion on the use of the commutative and associative properties of multiplication. For example, a group may use given dimensions of $10 \times 8 \times 8$ to find new dimensions of $40 \times 8 \times 2$, explaining that they divided the height by 4, so they multiplied the length by 4. These steps might be shown as below:

$$10 \times 8 \times 8$$
$$10 \times 8 \times (4 \times 2)$$
$$10 \times (8 \times 4) \times 2$$
$$10 \times (4 \times 8) \times 2$$
$$(10 \times 4) \times 8 \times 2$$
$$40 \times 8 \times 2$$

At this point, students have explored many different sets of dimensions for pools, resulting in new thoughts about the best pool for the exhibit. Allow a few minutes for partners to work together to decide which pool they now believe is the best for the polar bear exhibit. To conclude the task, ask groups to share their thinking with the entire class.

DIFFERENTIATION

- To support struggling students, change the context to a fish tank, reduce the volume to 64 cubic feet, and provide 64 unit cube manipulatives.
- To support struggling students, provide one reasonable dimension for a polar bear pool.
- If students finish early, ask them to create polar bear pools in the shape of a T or an L.

- To extend this task, tell students that 1 cubic meter holds approximately 264 gallons of water. Ask them to use this information to determine how many gallons of water their polar bear pool would hold.
- To extend this task, ask students how many classrooms the size of theirs would fit into the polar bear pool.

REFERENCES

Battista, Michael T. "The Development of Geometric and Spatial Thinking." In *Second Handbook of Research on Mathematics Teaching and Learning*, edited by Frank K. Lester Jr., pp. 843–908. Charlotte, N.C.: Information Age; Reston, Va.: National Council of Teachers of Mathematics, 2007.

Battista, Michael T. *Cognition-Based Assessment & Teaching of Fractions: Building on Students' Reasoning.* Portsmouth, N.H.: Heinemann, 2012.

Chval, Kathryn, John Lannin, and Dusty Jones. *Putting Essential Understanding of Fractions into Practice in Grades 3–5.* Reston, Va.: National Council of Teachers of Mathematics, 2013.

Clements, Douglas H., and Julie Sarama. *Learning and Teaching Early Math: The Learning Trajectories Approach.* New York: Routledge, 2009.

Common Core State Standards Writing Team. "K, Counting and Cardinality; K–5, Operations and Algebraic Thinking." *Progressions for the Common Core State Standards* (draft). Tucson, Ariz.: University of Arizona, 2011. http://math.arizona.edu/~ime/progressions/#about

———. "Grades K–6, Geometry." *Progressions for the Common Core State Standards* (draft). Tucson, Ariz.: University of Arizona, 2013. http://math.arizona.edu/~imc/progressions/#about

———. "Number and Operations in Base Ten, K–5." In *Progressions for the Common Core State Standards* (draft). Tucson, Ariz.: University of Arizona, 2015. http://math.arizona.edu/~ime/progressions/#about

Eves, Howard. *A Survey of Geometry.* Vol. 1. Boston: Allyn and Bacon, 1963.

Hiebert, James. "Signposts for Teaching Mathematics through Problem Solving." In *Teaching Mathematics through Problem Solving: Prekindergarten–Grade 6*, edited by Frank K. Lester Jr., pp. 53–61. Reston, Va.: National Council of Teachers of Mathematics, 2003.

Lappan, Glenda, Elizabeth Defanis Phillips, James T. Fey, and Susan N. Friel. *Connected Mathematics Project.* 3rd ed. Boston: Pearson Prentice Hall, 2014.

National Council of Teachers of Mathematics (NCTM). *Principles and Standards for School Mathematics.* Reston, Va.: NCTM, 2000.

———. *Focus in Grade 3: Teaching with Curriculum Focal Points.* Reston, Va.: NCTM, 2009a.

———. *Focus in Grade 4: Teaching with Curriculum Focal Points.* Reston, Va.: NCTM, 2009b.

National Governors Association Center for Best Practices and Council of Chief State School Officers (NGA Center and CCSSO). *Common Core State Standards for Mathematics. Common Core State Standards (College- and Career-Readiness Standards and K–12 Standards in English Language Arts and Math).* Washington, D.C.: NGA Center and CCSSO, 2010. http://www.corestandards.org.

Van de Walle, John A. "Designing and Selecting Problem-Based Tasks. In *Teaching Mathematics through Problem Solving: Prekindergarten–Grade 6*, edited by Frank K. Lester Jr., pp. 67–80. Reston, Va.: National Council of Teachers of Mathematics, 2003.

Van de Walle, John A., Karen S. Karp, and Jennifer M. Bay-Williams. *Elementary and Middle School Mathematics: Teaching Developmentally.* 8th ed. Boston: Pearson, 2013.

Zietz, Paul. *The Art and Craft of Problem Solving.* New York: Wiley, 1999.